HARMONY, PEACE & JOY

MARY HUTCHINGS REED

AMP&RSAND, INC.

Chicago · New Orleans

ISBN 978-09722529-1-1
Kindle eISBN 978-09722529-2-8
Nook eISBN 978-09722529-3-5

Design
David Robson, Robson Design, Inc.

Published by
AMPERSAND, INC.
515 Madison Street, New Orleans, Louisiana 70116
www.ampersandworks.com

Printed in USA

*For my friend and editor David W. Bloom,
whose insightful and encouraging comments
vastly improve my work and my enjoyment
of the writing process*

*And for the expertise of one of the premier
pioneers of independent publishing, Suzie Isaacs
of Ampersand, Inc. and her team, especially
David Robson, Robson Design, Inc. for his award-
winning, insightful and evocative covers
for my five most recent books*

1

Even monkeys fall from trees.

Stone Hunnicutt stood on a polished mahogany platform in his Egyptian cotton Brooks Brothers boxers and crew neck under-shirt, about to buy the most expensive suit of his life, and pondered what Master Tailor Noge Katsu meant. The balding Katsu seemed to Stone a practical man — he charged three-quarters of typical Gold Coast prices and didn't bother with fancy furnishings: the walls of the dressing room were painted a dull eggshell color and the carpet-ing a clean but worn gray.

"Even the Pro Bono Lawyer of the Year needs to look successful," his wife Sydney had said a month ago, trying to convince him to make the trip from Madison to Chicago. She'd been chopping vegetables for one of her nutritious stir-frys.

"They all know I'm successful," Stone said. A few months earlier he'd been named Best Business Lawyer in Wisconsin by a state-wide magazine; the Bar Association would bestow this new pro bono honor. "That's the only reason I was nominated. To bring in the cash."

"Don't be so cynical," she'd said. "You do good works."

"Not like you," he said. Sydney was a real pro bono lawyer, work-ing for Legal Aid.

She threw a chopped breast of chicken in the wok, where it sizzled. "The Award is for a lawyer who *volunteers*. I get paid."

"I told Jackson you didn't get paid *enough*," Stone said. Jackson Wood was president of the Bar Association.

"I can afford it," she said evenly. "I'm married to a rich lawyer." She added chopped celery and onion, bean sprouts and twenty raw cashews to the stir-fry.

"What if I weren't?" he asked.

"Then we'd make do," she said. He wanted to believe her. It was the girls — Meredith in medical school in Chicago and Caroline, a drama major in college in New York — who'd talked her into upgrading the old Formica kitchen countertops last year and even then, she'd waited for a sale on the granite the girls recommended. It occurred to Stone that even if they lived in a trailer, Sydney could be happy.

"Truth is, you couldn't pay me to do what you do. That year in Boston nearly did me in," he said. After getting his law degree, he'd worked for a landlord-tenant Legal Aid clinic near Harvard, waiting for Sydney to graduate.

"You've never said that before," she said.

"I was afraid I'd lose you if I told you, but I hated it. I hated representing tenants who were months in arrears on their rent and deserved to be evicted, but then demanded damages for emotional harm if the landlord failed to obey every technicality of the law, a law they knew far better than I did." In truth, he'd felt powerless to help the clients who came to the Legal Aid office. They'd needed so much more than what he or the law could offer. "I hated it when they cried."

"And when they smelled," Sydney added knowingly as she put a plate in front of him.

"So you agree, I don't deserve it," he said. He stabbed a piece of chicken with his fork. Usually the Bar Association chose one honoree who could hit up his or her friends for contributions, but this year for some reason, three persons had been nominated, all to be honored at the dinner, with one to be announced as the winner. "I don't need a new suit."

Sydney sighed. "You do, and you do. Who do you know who deserves it more?"

He busied himself with his rice — a dirty brown — and added extra soy sauce to the chicken. She stared at the bottle but didn't say anything.

"Michael Mitchell?" she teased, naming the previous winner. "You know I hate false humility." Secretly, Stone had been shocked that Mitchell had won; Stone was older and had a longer and more diverse record of public service.

"It's not false," he said. "I'm just saying I didn't do the work myself." He'd been instrumental in doubling his firm's commitment to pro bono work and had encouraged the young lawyers to get involved with work on behalf of single mothers, veterans and disabled persons. But he hadn't done the work himself. He had in fact been jealous when the younger man had been chosen, not because he was more deserving, but presumably for the sole purpose of inspiring more participation at the junior level.

"And your billings are what enable your associates to do the work for free and better yet, utilize the firm's considerable clout. So you deserve it as much as any of the corporate pigs." He heard the tease in her voice. He and his best friend, Lou Desmond, were the two biggest rainmakers at Gordon & Newman, a large Madison firm. The duo pretty much ran the place.

"They shouldn't have changed the format," Stone complained. "I have to stand up there and be declared a loser! Reminds me of when Ted didn't win that *First Novel Award.*" Ted was his younger brother and an acknowledged genius whose first novel had won two national awards and been named a *New York Times Notable Book of the Year.* At the much less prestigious *Midwest America* prize ceremony, each of the three nominees was asked to read for ten minutes after the broasted chicken dinner. Then they had to wait on the dais for the winner to be announced. Pia something. Not Ted. Although he applauded politely, Ted didn't look genuinely happy for the winner — how could he be? In her overwrought acceptance speech, Pia thanked everyone who'd ever encouraged her, including her fifth-grade spelling bee coach. She'd sounded to Stone narcissistic and pain-fully insincere.

Adding insult to the already public injury suffered by the "los-ers," Pia disingenuously confessed that her book had started as a common writing exercise, a slavish imitation of her favorite novel, *Little Women,* and that virtually every sentence in her winning entry mimicked its style and content. Ted's jaw dropped, and Stone had had to put his hand on their father's shoulder to restrain him from jumping out of his chair. Within earshot of the judges and the buoyant winner, their father said loudly that all such regional prizes were rigged and had more to do with sexual politics than ability. Stone took his father by the arm and steered him away from the literati, feigning intoxication as an excuse for the old man's rude and obnoxious behavior. If their father were alive today, he'd still be complaining about how "that bitch" stole the Award from his son. "Give 'em a test," he'd spewed. "We'll see who's smarter." No amount of cogent argument could get him off that point; only someone as smart as Ted could judge Ted's work, and their father had yet to meet such a person.

At the time, Stone had thought that it must take talent to pull off such a "creative" exercise. Afterward, Ted corrected him. "Without authentic emotion of her own, her work will never sing," he'd said. "She doesn't care about her characters at all, or she would have given them their own sentences, not mere imitations."

Consoling himself, Ted told Stone, "It's such an honor to be on so many short lists," which Stone thought was the kind of thing you could say glibly if you were, like Ted, on a lot of short lists, but not if you were Stone. Being on a Pro Bono short list and not yet the winner didn't fit his competitive sense of honor.

Now, he turned his face to Katsu's mirror and practiced a closed-lipped, "I deserve this" smile. Truth be told, he was fairly proud of the Pro Bono Award nomination, even if it felt undeserved. In the mirror, he was startled to see a slightly younger version of his father: a high, lined forehead; aquiline nose; bushy brown eyebrows; sharp, well-defined jaw. He wished his father could see him now; wished he could have seen his full-length picture on the glossy magazine cover for the business law honor.

But honors like Stone's Best Business Lawyer or Pro Bono Lawyer of the Year awards — which could be bought through fundraising or popularity — wouldn't have been good enough for his father. What *could* Stone have done that would be good enough for a man whose motto was "*Citius. Altius. Fortius, Scitius*"? Faster. Higher. Stronger. Smarter. That was Ted. Not Stone.

Their father had always had a certain blindness when it came to Ted. Stone wondered if the old man had even read Ted's *Pater Noster*, a coming-of-age story about a young man coping with the loss of his new wife while his demanding and unforgiving father slips into dementia. Their father had not acknowledged the extent to which Ted drew from his own experience in writing the book. Perhaps vanity hadn't allowed him to see himself through another's eyes.

"How did you dare to paint such an accurate picture of dad?" he'd once asked Ted.

"I knew he'd never recognize himself," Ted laughed. "It's what makes fiction more fun than memoir."

The whole book-prize evening was embarrassing to think about, and, staring into the mirror, Stone raised his chin and braced himself for the darts likely to be thrown his way at the Pro Bono dinner by people like his dad, people who thought he was undeserving. Thank goodness Sydney would be by his side, loaning him her impeccable public service credentials and her effervescent smile.

He hated the idea of not winning, especially since he, Gordon Newman, and his best client, Jay Shore, all had doubled their contributions. They'd raised a record amount for the cause, but that sort of took the nobility out of winning. Proved his father's case: Stone was not *altius*.

Still, Stone liked to be thought of as generous, as someone who would help in a pinch or just for the pure pleasure of feeling productive and useful. But he knew that deep down there were limits and that he was not nearly as generous as others thought him to be. When he'd been a young teen, he'd been taken with the notion of self-sufficiency, which meant freedom from having to make a case to his father for an annual increase in his allowance. He answered an ad for a newspaper boy and earned what he thought was pretty good money by getting up three mornings a week at four o'clock to throw papers at suburban lawns from the back of a truck. He'd been working for about six months, saving for the car he was determined to buy when he turned sixteen, when his father suddenly stopped going to work every day. His mother said he was taking a break from his job as Director of Research at an agricultural chemical company and there was nothing to worry about. But Stone noticed more casseroles on the dinner table. One day he was with his mother when she returned a lacey dress she'd purchased for a cousin's wedding.

"Why are you taking it back?" he'd asked. "Can't we afford it?"

Looking stricken, his mother had said of course they could afford it. "Your father says it just doesn't look that good on me," she'd said.

He didn't believe her. His mother was beautiful and anything she wore was just as stunning. By Stone's account, it was the money.

That Friday, when Stone came home with his paper route pay, he left his envelope of cash on the kitchen table while he ran to the bathroom. When he came out, his mother was holding the bills in her hands. He stopped in his tracks. His mother's lips were trembling and her eyes were wet. She rushed over to him. "I am so touched, Stone. You are such a good boy. Thank you! But, honey, really, we're OK. Your father's new job starts a week from Monday." Stone realized that his mother was giving him credit for an act of unselfish generosity that he in no way intended. "That dress, honey, really didn't fit. Come upstairs and let me show you the one I bought yesterday." He followed her to her room, where she took a beaded powder blue dress from the closet and swirled it so its full skirt looked to be dancing. She was so obviously delighted with her new purchase and the good son she'd raised, he decided there was no need to disabuse her, especially since she was returning his money. He hoped, however, that she wouldn't tell his father. He'd probably call Stone stupid for thinking his paltry paper route earnings could cover such an elegant dress.

Now, glancing in tailor Katsu's dressing room mirror, he saw his legs sticking out bright white from his dark socks and felt like a grand-champion pig headed for slaughter. Four more weeks of worried anticipation. Writing a speech that might not make it out of his suit pocket. Feeling like a fraud one minute and a cheated loser the next.

Choosing a suit at the tailor's had turned out to be more complicated than simply pointing to one of the finished suits. Seated at a library table in a windowless but brightly lit room lined with clothes racks, Katsu guided Sydney and Stone through a huge book of fabric swatches, much like an album of floor coverings at a home improvement store. Prodded by Sydney, Stone selected a medium gray cashmere and a somewhat darker silk lining. Then he had to answer dozens of questions about details he'd not noticed before: not just the size and shape of the lapel, but also of the collar, the jacket vent, the cuffs, the pockets. He'd had to choose buttonholes and thread colors. Stone pointed to the navy blazer he had on and Katsu nodded as if to say he understood that Stone dressed far from the cutting edge of fashion — that the less the suit drew attention to itself, the better. "Traditional," Katsu said.

"My wife says you were named the *Best Master Tailor in Chicago* by one of the local magazines," Stone said while Katsu stretched a yellow tape measure across his shoulders.

Katsu bowed slightly. "If one man praises you, a thousand will repeat the praise," he said.

"If that one man is very influential," Stone said. "There are many tailors in Chicago. The recognition must've been good for business."

"Only one customer," Katsu said, without much interest.

"Hard to believe," Stone said.

"One customer, one suit," Katsu said.

"But surely you got more than one new customer from the article. Me, for instance?"

"Not everyone wants the best," Katsu smiled. "Not everyone can pay."

"Still, it's nice to know that others praise you," Stone said. He had himself relished his *Best Business Lawyer* title. Of course it was subjective, but the recognition mattered to him.

"It's nice to know the suit fits," Katsu said. He lifted Stone's arm out straight from the shoulder.

"You are too modest, Mr. Noge," Stone said.

"Even monkeys fall from trees," Katsu said, but did not explain himself. "You have a special occasion, yes?" He dropped Stone's arm.

"No," Stone said, then realized he was about to buy the most expensive suit of his life and he should tell the truth. "Actually, yes. I'm being given an honor by my professional association back at home," he said. He feared "back home" sounded small-town and hick-ish, and so added, "in Madison."

"What did you do for the honor?"

It was the question he'd thrashed through with Sydney, but it still plagued him. On the surface of things, he probably deserved it, but inside, he wasn't so sure. Regardless, he wanted it.

"Not enough," he tried to laugh, and then he realized he hadn't won the Award yet. "I'm one of three nominees. The winner will be announced at a dinner."

"You write a book?" Katsu asked, running his tape around Stone's chest.

"No, I'm a lawyer. My brother writes books." He was relieved to shift the conversation away from himself.

"What kind of books? Have I heard of them?" Katsu asked.

"He's a literary writer," Stone said. As soon as he said it, he realized it sounded snotty and condescending. "He's not famous. One book. Not on the best-seller list or anything."

"Lists don't matter," Katsu said. "Did he write the best book he could?" He motioned for Stone to separate his feet so he could measure Stone's inseam. "I have very few customers, but my customers are very particular. They know the best when they see it. And they pay more for it," he chuckled. Stone could appreciate that. His clients paid more for him; he paid more for Katsu's suits. It seemed fair and just.

Katsu stood up and bowed slightly. "All done," he said. "Come back in two weeks. And don't worry. *Makeru ga kachi.*"

"I don't speak …" Stone started, but Katsu smiled, "Sometimes, to lose is to win."

2

Sorting the mail as he unburdened himself of his briefcase, linen jacket and rep tie, Stone didn't recognize the return address on the one personal piece of mail he'd received on the Monday before the pro bono dinner. He was impressed by the starched white envelope, but the letter inside felt bumpy, like paragraphs of Braille. Every so often a dot over an "i" or the crossbar of a "t" punctured the stationery, as if the typist had been banging on a war drum. "PEACE & JOY" was typed in capital letters at the top of the page, but the "J" was faint; at first he read it as "PEACE & OY."

While Ted lived in a rural community of some kind near Hurley, Wisconsin, called HARMONY'S PEACE & JOY, he didn't tend to waste his literary talents on letters to his family. Stone skipped to the bottom of the second page and saw that it was signed by Harmony herself. He'd never met the woman and Ted rarely talked about her. Her opening was casual: "Dear Stone." What could she possibly want? Was she promoting Ted's second novel? It was time for another one. How else to answer Katsu's question: was the first the best he could do?

Stone often did his pleasure reading — the mail, the paper and an occasional legal thriller — in his study, in the comfort of his leather La-Z-Boy. Because Sydney would be home soon, he wanted to be with her while she cooked dinner, so he settled at the kitchen table with the letter. There was an open bottle of red wine from last night's *coq au vin* on the table and he poured himself a stemmed glassful. Spotting a jar of dry-roasted peanuts on the counter, he got up and shook a small handful into a bowl. Sydney would've made him count out thirty nuts — one serving, per the label — to reinforce her intention that he not consume half the jar. One serving, she'd say, was enough to help process cholesterol and support his nervous system, which increasingly needed support. The pro bono dinner was Friday night, and even though he was tight with Jackson Wood at the Bar Association, he'd heard no rumors. He still feared public embarrassment if he lost. He knew it was childish of him to care so much. Sydney would say it was a mid-life crisis, and if he denied it, she'd diagnose a deficiency of some obscure and newly "discovered" vitamin. Who knew what she'd start feeding him?

He turned his attention to the letter, eager for good news. The first sentence was disappointing: "*We at Harmony's Peace & Joy are so grateful for your annual contribution.*"

She wanted money.

Stone didn't remember making an annual contribution to Harmony's Peace & Joy in the past. Had Sydney? Possibly, but not likely. Probably a form letter. Neither of them had been to Hurley, even though Ted had moved north some years ago. Once, when Ted first settled at Harmony's, he'd invited Stone and Sydney for a "Harmonization Retreat," but luckily Stone had a mega-deal in progress for his largest client, real estate developer Jay Shore. Jay viewed places like Peace & Joy as potential sites for lavish subdivisions of Executive Homes or resort complexes. Stone and Sydney hadn't rescheduled. Stone did, however, send Ted checks for $100 for Christmas and his birthday, and Ted's signature always appeared on the back, with an account number Stone assumed to be Ted's. Since Ted never expressed a need for any specific thing and never asked for money, Stone told himself that sending more than his usual amount would be lording his growing wealth over his smarter but less successful sibling.

As you know, all the money given to our members goes into our common fund to support our eleven full-time members and our mission.

No, he didn't know that. All the money he'd given Ted over the years had gone into a pool? Even though he knew his brother was a charter member of a meditation group led by this Harmony person, he'd always pictured Harmony's Peace & Joy as just a small, hapless ashram of aging hippies led by a frizzy-haired, much-too-buxom mother-figure sixties-style flower child. He'd assumed that either Harmony financed the place or one of her followers did — probably a disaffected heiress whose family was happy to keep her out of their hair.

Before he was far into the letter, Sydney rushed in, apologizing for being late because of a last-minute staff meeting on the new housing discrimination case her office was handling. Stone admired the work Sydney did — it was, he thought, truly important. But thankless. Plaintiffs never got enough, and fewer and fewer people believed in paying to preserve constitutional principles when their personal rights and entitlements weren't at stake.

She kissed the top of his head — he was happy he still had all his hair — and, spying the letter, asked, "Who writes letters anymore?"

"Fundraisers."

Looking over his shoulder, she said, "No pictures of starving children." She took a wine glass from the cupboard. "Who wants what?"

"I just started it. Looks like Ted needs money."

She stopped mid-pour. "He wrote you a letter? Asking for money?" She sounded incredulous.

"Not exactly," Stone said. "Here, I'll read it to you." She filled her glass and held up the jar of peanuts. He handed her the empty bowl from the table, hoping for more.

"Oh, you've already had some."

He waved his hand. "Come on," he said, and she obliged him, counting out fifteen more. "I was going to make apple salad with cashews," she said. "But now, no cashews for you." She chuckled and sat down opposite him.

He reread the first sentences of the letter aloud and continued: "*Dedicating ourselves to spreading peace and true joy, we have few material needs. Our truck garden has sustained us and our pumpkin patch continues to be the best in the county.*"

"Ted never was the material sort," Sydney said.

"Good thing, since he hasn't had a job since he got fired from the university," Stone said. "He's too smart to have to work *for* someone else and too solitary to work *with* a team."

"Not fired. He was denied tenure," Sydney said.

"Right. He didn't even have the ambition to be his own boss."

"Well, it seems they get by," Sydney said.

"On a pumpkin patch!" Stone said, not bothering to hide his sarcasm. In junior high, Ted had carved a pumpkin with an electric drill, forming a face with precise half-inch holes, creating a unique effect that added "creative genius" to their father's praises. But now his multi-talented brother with the lauded IQ was satisfied with the proceeds of a pumpkin patch? Again Stone heard the echo of Katsu's question: was he doing the best he could do?

Stone read on: *"Your brother is such an important member of our community, the glue that holds us together. I don't know what I'd do without him."*

His stomach roiled. "Without him? Does that mean he's sick?" he asked Sydney.

"I don't know," she said. "If he were, I think he'd be the one to tell you, not her."

"Then why 'without him'?" Stone repeated. Was Ted in some kind of trouble? "Oh geez, listen to this: *He always speaks so highly of you and is so proud of all the awards and accolades you've won for your legal work and not-for-profit work. We of course admire the enterprise of your clients, although we encourage them, in our prayer and meditation, to seek worker equality and economic justice for all."* The dots over the "i's" in "enterprise" and "clients" left pinpricks in the paper.

"Switching from pro forma to personal?" Sydney said. "Suspicious!" He couldn't tell if she was being serious or sarcastic.

"I bet Ted never even noticed my receiving an award, let alone remembering it, or telling her," Stone said.

"You didn't invite him to the pro bono the dinner?" Sydney asked.

"No, of course not. It would mean nothing to him."

"He would know you were doing good works," Sydney said. "He would be proud."

"I doubt it. He has no idea what it takes to be a successful lawyer — being at the beck and call of a client; making sure each one feels like he or she is the only one." Of course Ted couldn't know how Stone felt having to convince a haughty CEO that he and his local firm could do a complex securities offering just as well as a much higher-priced Wall Street firm. Or how sleazy it felt to promote his legal skills like a carnival barker in order to make the client happy to pay a premium fee for the privilege of retaining Stone Hunnicutt, *Wisconsin's Best Business Lawyer.*

"I guess he wouldn't have much to say to the clients who will be at the dinner," Sydney mused. "I can just hear him getting into it with Jay Shore about economic justice, to say nothing of the environmental and aesthetic blight his McMansions are."

Stone laughed and finished the last of his allotted peanuts. "There's talk, and then there's action. Ted told me last Christmas that this Harmony person drives an alternate fuel Mercedes."

"I call that subsistence, don't you?" Sydney chuckled. Stone scratched his five o'clock shadow to hide a sneer. *He* didn't drive a Mercedes, and *he* wasn't asking anyone for money. He thought owning a luxury car was boastful, and he prided himself on remaining humble, at least to some degree.

He continued reading. "*Our own mission promotes joy through self-expression, self-sufficiency and sharing with others. Teddy exemplifies our ideals and is an inspiration to us all, and we hope he can continue to live with us for many years to come.*"

Stone let out a hoot. "Teddy?!" He looked at Sydney but she didn't seem to see the humor in it. Of course, when Sydney and Ted had dated as undergrads at Wisconsin — before Stone met her at Harvard — she may have whispered, "Teddy" in his ear. Stone shook off the thought. It wasn't the kind of thing he could imagine ever asking her. His brother's full name was Theodore Franklin, after his father's idols, the Roosevelts. These days, "Teddy" connoted a stuffed brown bear, or a snippet of lingerie in the window at Victoria's Secret, but surely not the son of Thaddeus Newton Hunnicutt.

"Worthy goals," Sydney mused.

Stone sighed. "I suppose." Self-expression was, in his view, often vastly overrated. Certainly, under-compensated. Ted — a bona fide genius — had eschewed their father's expectations by majoring in creative writing at Madison. Although Ted's first novel had been critically acclaimed (and deservedly so, Stone thought), Stone knew from their father's muted enthusiasm that he had been disappointed Ted wasn't on a path to a Nobel in Medicine or Chief Justice at the Supreme Court. He was further disappointed when more novels didn't follow. Apparently, so was the university — they'd let him go. When asked when his next novel would be published, Ted would reply simply, "When it's done."

To say their father was a dreamer would be a polite understatement.

His aspirations for his children were as unrealistic as they were lofty, bordering on hallucinatory. Oh, possibly within the realm of the possible. But really! The steady push to be number one — at anything and everything — had tainted Stone's satisfaction with his own success to date. At fifty-three, head of his law firm's corporate department and one of their top rainmakers, he *should* feel satisfied with his accomplishments. But Madison wasn't Wall Street. It wasn't even Chicago. Still, there was no question that he and Sydney enjoyed a level of wealth far beyond both Ted's current financial position and their own youthful dreams. As well-to-do members of the community, they'd given generously to organized charities, both large and small, on their own as well as at the prompting of partners, colleagues and neighbors' kids. They'd worked hard for their money and had forgone luxuries their friends enjoyed so they could pay their children's college tuitions in cash. In fact, they didn't live as high on the hog as they could afford to.

"OK Here it is," Stone said. He read: "*At the center of our community is Harmony house, an E. Townsend Mix masterpiece built in 1885 by one of the original mining families of Hurley who is said to have found the town too spiritually confining. They moved several miles west. It is our goal to restore the house to its original splendor and secure its place on the National Registry of Historic Places. This slow and exacting work will occupy and help feed the talented artists, craftspeople and scholars of our community for many years to come. So it is with much humility and, of course, hope, that I write to ask you to share again by making a $10,000 contribution to the Harmony house Preservation and Restoration Fund. Please come see for yourself this special historic place. We are confident that you, too, will fall in love with it.*

We are so grateful that we can count on your continued love and support.

Peace and Joy,
Harmony"

Neither of them said anything right away. "Spiritually confining," he scoffed, just as Sydney said, "craftspeople," and he gave her a sidelong look.

"Seriously?" he asked and she smiled. He was a feminist, but he hated the neutering of the language, and it was one of the few things on which they agreed to disagree.

"What a phony," he said, tossing the letter down on the kitchen table. "Who the hell is E. Townsend Mix?"

"Ted doesn't care about this," Sydney said, reaching for it.

"How do you know?"

"He'd call. He'd ask you himself." Stone must've looked doubtful because she added, "I know him. He'd call me. Us." Stone's heart skipped a beat. In fact, Ted *hadn't* asked Stone. But Sydney? She thought Ted would call *her*? After all these years?

"He gave Harmony our address, don't you think?"

"Finding you isn't rocket science," she said.

"Maybe he's embarrassed to ask for that much," Stone said.

"If Ted wanted ten grand from you, he'd act like that was nothing to you. He'd make it sound like he was asking for ten bucks. He'd appeal to your ego."

"Because he thinks money grows on trees," Stone said. "Like I don't earn it by the sweat of my brow."

"You don't work in a pumpkin patch," she said, interrupting the rant he was about to launch. Ted always said lawyers were vastly overpaid. Especially considering how little they contributed to the public welfare.

She shook her head. "Why don't you call him?" She always got to the bottom line. A logical, doable next step.

"Well yes, of course," he said, as if he'd thought of it first. "Still, don't you think I should go see him?" His younger brother had turned fifty a few months ago, and how they'd grown so far apart was a mystery to Stone. He supposed it had a lot to do with their father's death, the girls' busy teenage years, and Ted's move north, although it wasn't, in fact, that far away. What was really going on with Ted? Stone hoped Ted had actually found peace and joy in the woods of Wisconsin, but he had his doubts.

"I've always thought you guys should be closer," Sydney said. Stone remained silent. If he and Ted were closer, that would make Sydney and Ted closer, and … He wasn't jealous, exactly, but he was never one to tempt fate. He would hate to lose Syd to a rekindled flame with his brother.

Ordinarily, siblings would be close, he thought. An image of Meredith and Caroline dressed in identical Christmas dresses and matching Halloween costumes made him smile. "Remember how you dressed the girls alike?" he asked.

"Come on, they were cute," she said. "You liked it."

He had.

"My father would've been appalled if *our* mother had done that with us, or anything remotely like it," Stone said.

"No, no. Your father thought the girls were cute. He even bought them matching dresses that one Easter, remember? Lavender and blue?"

What he remembered was that it snowed that Easter and the girls had worn their wool coats over the dresses. "The Hunnicutt boys were never cute."

Her eyes twinkled. "Oh yes they were," she said.

"Past tense?"

"They were. They are," she said.

"*They?*" Stone challenged. "Which one is cuter?"

She laughed. "Sibling rivalry never ceases to amaze me. Do all brothers think comparatively?"

"Doesn't everyone?" Stone asked. "How can I know if I'm smart or cute or rich or whatever, except in relative terms?"

"That tends to make people unhappy with who they are and what they have," Sydney said.

Stone rolled his eyes. "You didn't answer my question."

"I thought Ted was plenty cute the few months I dated him," she said, pausing dramatically. She'd been a junior when the brothers were seniors — Ted having skipped first grade and then his senior year of high school. She may have been Ted's first. He'd never asked either of them. "And I thought you were cute when I married you. OK?" She looked at him the way she looked at the girls when they pouted, partly disappointed, partly amused. "But we were talking about Hurley. I'd love to visit."

He thought for a minute. It *would* be better with Sydney there. She was no doubt the reason their past sailing vacations had always gone so well. She hurried Ted along when he dawdled on shore and urged Stone to breathe when she wanted him to slow down and spend more time at anchor. Ted could tell her things and Stone could tell her things and after a day or so, they could talk to each other, at least when Sydney was there and the three of them were downing gin and tonics.

Although Stone and Ted spoke on the phone only a few times a year, in the past he had joined Stone and his family on several Caribbean vacations. On Stone and Sydney's first trip to the islands, when the kids were young teenagers, they'd invited Ted along because they had four staterooms in a chartered catamaran. Ted had declined because of the expense of the airfare to Tortola, but Stone had air miles to burn and told him to come along anyway.

Then one year, without a big European deal on his calendar, Stone didn't have as many free miles "in the bank," and he delayed inviting Ted, who subsequently called in December suggesting that Stone's family drive up to northeast Wisconsin for some cross-country skiing. Stone abhorred winter as much as Ted did and Ted knew it. What could he do? Stone blurted out the invitation to join the family in the Virgin Islands in January and then had to pay for Ted's trip in real dollars. He could easily afford it, but still …

A week in the Caribbean wasn't a "material need," but it was a luxury Ted had come to enjoy and expect. The vacation always reminded Stone of how much he actually liked his brother and how little he understood him. The girls loved Uncle Ted, the "coolest" adult they knew — a brilliant and witty hippie who eschewed wealth, achievement and normal work. He brought them brownies wrapped in tinfoil and freezer-lock bags along with homemade berry jam and freshly-ground peanut butter. On the first trip, he'd thought to bring a guidebook and identified the reef fish by name. He was always the first in the water while Stone was still adjusting his mask. The girls thought he was so smart, and particularly courageous when he pointed out the nurse sharks, not knowing they were fairly harmless. They begged him for stories of what Stone had been like as a kid — assuming, of course, that Stone had been an unpopular dork and wondering how Ted could possibly have been Secretary of the Chess Club and a gangly runner on the "boring" cross-country team. That Stone had been elected Senior Class Vice president and a member of the Homecoming Court amazed them as much as Ted's confession that he hadn't had a single date in high school. When the girls reached college age, they weren't so interested in taking vacations with their parents, even if Uncle Ted were included, and so the annual trips faded to shared memory.

But then again maybe *she* was the reason Ted and he weren't so close. Not just their dating history, but their reliance on Sydney to run interference, to keep old sibling rivalries from boiling over. They hadn't figured out how to be adult brothers.

"You don't think I should go alone?" Stone asked. He didn't know what the right answer was, but he trusted that Sydney would know.

"Yes. You probably should. This time. I guess I could go shopping in Chicago," she said. "While the brothers are bonding, maybe Meredith will want to bond with her mother."

He couldn't tell if she was miffed or not. "Of course she will," he smiled. "You've got the no-limit credit card."

"I remember when we didn't have to bribe them," she said. "How can I be the mother of a twenty-four-year-old? Makes me crazy!" Meredith, the med student at University of Chicago was easier to visit than Caroline, the drama senior at NYU.

"My dad used to say that time speeds up exponentially as you grow older," he said. I used to think it was just because it took longer to put your socks on in the morning, but now ... I mean, Ted's been up north — just four hours away — for the past few years and I've never been there. Seems wrong somehow."

"Ten," Sydney said.

"What?"

"He's been there ten years."

"And you know this how?" Stone asked, embarrassed to be so ignorant of the details of his brother's life.

"He was so devastated, remember, after Madison cut him? I felt sorry for him. He wasn't used to failing." That she thought Ted had failed at something oddly satisfied Stone, but he was also annoyed that Ted had confided his secret disappointments to Sydney.

"I thought he was relieved, actually," Stone said, "not to waste his time teaching. At least that's what he told me." Stone hadn't registered Ted's not getting tenure as a real failure. Like his father, he rationalized that Ted had the talent and smarts but hadn't played politics. That refusal to do the expected thing — whatever it was — was what annoyed Stone the most.

"He loved nurturing new talent," Sydney said.

"Did he have any talented students?" Stone asked with more edge to his voice than he intended. "I imagine he had many with blind ambition, but none with genius talent."

"Genius is *your* thing," she said.

"A Hunnicutt thing," he corrected her.

"Ted's always been able to meet people on their own level," she said, obvious affection in her voice.

"Since when?" Stone demanded.

"Ever since I've known him," she said.

"Not the Ted I know," Stone said.

"Back in college, he spent hours showing me how to solve Rubik's Cube," Sydney said.

Stone felt his cheeks brighten. In high school, Ted held the school record for solving the puzzle, yet repeatedly refused to teach Stone the solution. It wouldn't have hurt Ted — he'd still be the winner, the record holder, the one who'd figured it out rather than having to be shown — so Stone had always held a bit of a grudge, though he knew it was childish of him to do so.

"You should go see your brother," she said.

"I'll call this weekend."

She made a point of looking at the small leather-banded watch he'd given her several years ago. "That will get us past the pro bono dinner and give you time to figure out what to say," she said.

"Oh. You're right. Maybe I should call him before I lose." Stone said.

"What difference does that make?" Sydney said. "You said yourself he doesn't care about such things."

"Well, *I* do," Stone said, feeling sheepish.

"I know how much you want it," she said. "I wish I could guarantee it. *I* think you deserve it, but I'm not in charge."

"It's not that big a deal," he said, contradicting himself. "I'm sure the others are more deserving."

She ignored his plea for reassurance. "Listen. Why don't you just send them $100 tomorrow and be done with it?" They really can't expect more than that from you for a house you've never seen, and with no proof that it is historic or that they can even pull it off. Just send the token and wait for him to make the ask for more. If he ever does."

Stone was surprised. Sydney routinely gave $100 to almost any cause that came her way — the homeless, the hungry, the vets, the war refugees, the falsely imprisoned, the storefront theater she liked so much and the animal shelter where she volunteered — but he would have guessed that restoration of an old house in obscure semi-mountains that most people didn't even know existed, would not have merited even that token.

"I should find out, first, if he really cares about this. $100 might be insulting. Or maybe it's worth more. I don't know. I should see the house for myself. And meet Harmony."

She nodded, then got up from the table and filled his bowl with another handful of peanuts, not even bothering to count them out. "The person you need to see is your brother."

3

Stone spent most of the Friday morning of the pro bono dinner and much of the lunch hour nibbling on fruit and bagels and listening to his partners whine about their annual draws before they voted themselves — and him — hefty bonuses. The irony was not lost on him. By the firm's standards, he deserved it. He generated the clients whose business generated the firm's income. Then, before the inevitable litany of dissatisfactions could begin, he went home to get ready for the dinner that night. He took a leisurely, steamy shower, splashed on some of the Ralph Lauren after-shave Caroline had given him for Christmas and put on the new custom suit Sydney had insisted he buy. He was reminded that even monkeys fell from trees, and desperately wanted the event to be over. Impulsively, he dialed Ted's number.

He'd planned to wait until after the dinner, when he hoped he could tell Ted about his do-gooder award, so he hadn't figured out exactly what to say when Ted answered. It had been a while since they'd spoken, but they were, after all, brothers. How hard could it be? He figured they'd fall into their old patterns. "Been well?" Stone asked.

"Fit as a Stradivarius," Ted answered, his usual highbrow humor.

"And just about as old," Stone said. "How's fifty treating you?"

"Just a number," Ted said. "But thanks for the card." Stone was glad he'd picked a simple, "Happy Birthday" card, finding the "over the hill" variety puerile in a way neither of them had ever been. He himself had downplayed turning fifty a couple of years ago, refusing any major bash and begging Sydney not to surprise him. But for Ted he'd added $50 to his usual $100 gift.

"Doing anything next weekend?" He jumped right to the point. "Sydney's going to Chicago to see Meredith. I was thinking I'd drive up and check out your new digs."

Ted laughed. "I've got ten years of dust on my new digs."

Ted probably didn't mean to sound unfriendly, but Stone heard a mild rebuke. He'd expected that his brother would offer some litany of excuses, apologies and regrets. At least, Stone assumed that's how the more socially adept would cover for a long absence. Nor did Ted immediately insist that Stone come see the historic mansion; it occurred to him that Ted might not know of Harmony's letter.

"Time flies," he said. He didn't mean it quite as cavalierly as it must have sounded to Ted.

"You OK? Why come now?"

"No, not sick," Stone said, trying to hide his frustration. Why couldn't Ted — supposedly such a hippie — just go with the flow? "I guess when one's brother turns fifty ..."

"I'm fine, too," Ted said. After an awkward pause, he added, "Are you sure you don't want to wait until Sydney can come, too? I think she'd like it up here."

Of course she would. Who didn't have a soft spot for an old college lover? "I'm sure," Stone said. "I'll scope it out for her. Make sure it's safe enough." He forced a laugh and suggested that he drive up the next Friday night.

"The grizzlies are pretty well fed this time of year and are mostly tame," Ted chuckled. "But you'll never find us on GPS. This place is pretty remote."

So much for Harmony's hope for tourists. "Southwest of Upson, right?" He'd looked at a map prior to calling so that he could visualize the location when Ted insisted on giving his usual, insanely detailed directions: the old blue and white Pure Oil sign shaped like a seal of approval, the red barn across from the cemetery with the iron gate (not the one with the chain link fence), the fresh egg stand just after the mushroom farm.

The recitation reminded Stone of Ted's prodigious memory. Photographic. So photographic that reading was equivalent to knowledge for him, no study or drill required to commit to memory the facts of history, geography, English literature, science — any subject, really. As a kid, Stone had resented the ease with which Ted breezed through school, although once he'd taken some silent solace when Ted's memory had backfired. Without the benefit of a computer program, Ted's sophomore English teacher — just out of school herself — suggested that Ted's essay on "The Spirituality of Running" sounded familiar, but her own memory wasn't good enough to cite the source of the suspected plagiarism. Their father had been appalled at her insinuation and had tried to have her fired, but the principal had pointed out that the teacher could be right — Ted could be both innocent and wrong: subconscious similarities were not unusual when someone was as smart and well-read as Ted. Stone concluded that if the principal was right, all so-called original thought was suspect. It made him feel better about himself as an agile borrower of other people's ideas.

The visit arranged, they hung up. Stone looked at his watch and realized with a start that "the hour was near," as if he were headed to an execution. He was to meet Sydney at 5:30 at the hotel where the dinner was being held. The traffic was inexplicably light and the valet took his car right away. Since it was pleasant outside and he was early, he decided to wait near the entrance to the hotel. As he stood there, he inadvertently caught the eye of a young man in an ill-fitting bright blue suit.

"Buy a newspaper to help the homeless?" the man asked.

Stone and Sydney gave thousands to the local Coalition for the Homeless and the Food Bank, but Stone rarely responded to the random individual requests that peppered every city block.

The man whistled. "Nice suit, dude," and Stone reached for his wallet. He took a bill — a ten, he realized too late — and shoved it at the man, waving off the free newspaper and moving quickly inside the hotel.

Thankfully, Sydney was already there, elegantly dressed in her understated black knit suit with the Swarovski crystal buttons. She'd pulled her shoulder-length hair back in an upsweep, revealing a few light gray hairs among her natural brown ones. Her one-carat diamond studs sparkled.

She spotted him immediately. "Thought I recognized you," she said, giving him a kiss on his cheek. She touched his hair. "Looks good," she smiled, then stopped and traced his jaw with her index finger, studying his face. "What's wrong?" she asked. "You've prepared some thank-yous, haven't you?"

"I've thought of some things," he managed, not admitting to the speech he'd typed on a single sheet carefully folded in his inside jacket pocket.

"Hey, no one's listening. The old folks are deaf or green with envy, the middle-aged are drunk and self-possessed, and the young'uns are back at the office making you guys richer."

"Syd, it's not the speech," he pleaded.

"Then what?" she asked. When he didn't answer, she said, "False modesty? Bored contempt?"

"Just false," he said. "I'm not a pro bono lawyer."

"We've had this conversation already," she said.

"But my motives have always been …" He still needed reassurance.

"Highly suspect," she said for him. "You've always needed me to keep you from straying too far from the pro bono path."

"And that's OK?" he asked.

She shrugged. "You just like to win too much!" she said. Of course, Stone thought. That had been the family motto: winning.

She reached up and straightened his bowtie. "We all do what we can do, Stone, and you do it better than anyone." He took a deep breath and let it end there.

Hand-in-hand, they entered the anteroom of the hotel's grand ballroom where bars were set up against all four walls. Hands were thrust at him from left and right, colleagues and mere acquaintances eager to congratulate him on his success, as if he'd already won. His stomach churned as he shook hands and tried to appear both humble and worthy. The Dinner Chair — herself a likely nominee someday — gushed that they'd set a record for fundraising. Stone congratulated her, although deep down he thought it had been Lou who'd put the finger on Gordon & Newman's clients and Stone's friends. Still, the personal congratulations felt sincere. Surprised by how many people he knew, he was caught up in the spirit of the evening. Maybe Sydney was right: as much as anyone, he did deserve this honor, and was entitled to relish the moment. In choosing him, the Bar Association had imposed on him a certain noblesse oblige. They wanted him to be universally admired — inspiring, brilliant, cordial, humble, even if he didn't feel it.

A waiter strolled through the anteroom with a small xylophone, calling the crowd to dinner in the ballroom. Stone and Sydney found their assigned seats — at the Bar president's table at the front of the room. Lou Desmond and his wife, Jay Shore and his, and Christina Falcon, the senior associate who'd worked so hard on the vets' project and her fiancé, rounded out the table of ten. While it wasn't official, it sure seemed likely that he would indeed be given the Award, although his heart sank a little when he noticed that the other two nominees were also seated with Bar Association officers. He tried not to get ahead of himself. Gordon & Newman had two other tables to his right. Other large firms, like Albright & Gill; McGrady, O'Reilly & Reid, and Bornstein Rosen, were given front row tables in honor of their large gifts to the Bar's pro bono efforts.

President Wood came to the podium to welcome the guests and outline the evening's activities: dinner, introductions, stories by two clients helped by the Bar Association, the Award presentation, and dancing to the music of the Bar Association's big band, "The Bar-risters." Stone caught Jackson Wood's eye when he returned to the table, but there was still no sign.

The others made lively small talk during dinner, Christina telling heart-rending stories about the veterans' project and Lou and Jackson exchanging court room war stories and unflattering anecdotes about sitting judges. Every so often, Jay would slap Stone on the back and interject that he was the one paying for Stone's Award — "nomination," Stone corrected — and the firm's good work, and Stone heartily agreed, as he did whenever Jay preened. Preening was not an uncommon occurrence when Jay was surrounded by folks who had the college degree he lacked. "I wish I had your smarts," Stone would quip, "then I wouldn't have to work so hard for a living."

Stone was finishing his salmon when Jackson kicked off the pro-gram. Two clients gave short and emotional talks about how their lives had been turned around by pro bono lawyers who saved a family home and won disability benefits for a hard-working single mother. Then the Chief Judge of the Federal District Court, announced — finally! — that the Award was being presented to Stone Hunnicutt. At the sound of his name, Stone sat momentarily stunned, then strode confidently to the podium and smiled for the camera while the Judge handed him a small crystal memento. He realized immediately that he couldn't possibly pull out his prepared speech. Like a robot, he stepped to the microphone. He adjusted it, smiled at Sydney as he surveyed the room and took a breath. Thank goodness he'd taken the time to memorize his remarks. He was stalling a bit, but he'd learned from Lou that an extra second or two of silence builds suspense and adds a certain gravitas to what is to follow. Sydney was probably right: how he sounded would be remembered long after whatever he might say was forgotten. He shook his head as if to clear it and took another breath.

"I am flattered, Your Honor, by your kind remarks and humbled by this Award. While pro bono is part of a lawyer's ethical responsibility as a member of this profession, I know there are many in this room tonight who deserve this honor far more than I do, both my fellow nominees whom I greatly admire, and especially my wife, Sydney, a life-long attorney at Legal Aid and their Chief of Advocacy. Seeing her daily dedication to clients inspires me every day." As anticipated, the crowd applauded that line as Stone joined in. He gestured for her to stand, and reluctantly, she bobbed up and quickly sat down.

"There's been a lot in the news recently about skyrocketing legal fees," he continued.

"Highway robbery," he heard Jay say, much too loudly, and saw Lou reach over and pour Jay some more wine. Stone continued, "And it's no secret that in economic times such as these, most individuals are of 'limited means' when it comes to their ability to pay for the best legal services." There'd been a recent story in one of the legal papers about the estimated profits-per-partner of the top ten firms in Madison, and Gordon & Newman had been at the top of the list. Wearing the most expensive suit of his life — "nice suit, dude!" — he'd decided to address that anomaly head-on.

"And while it has been reported that Gordon & Newman had a record year …"

"At my expense," Jay said, again too loudly, causing a stir at the front row of tables.

"… I am proud to say that we also had a record year in terms of the number of hours devoted to pro bono. I stand here today representing my partners and associates who devoted their time to some nineteen different pro bono projects—from veterans' benefits to students' First Amendment rights to battered women, housing and immigration. Our per-lawyer average far exceeded the fifty hours per year recommended by the state Bar."

Again there was applause. He almost quipped, "Nobody starved," but thankfully thought better of it. He glanced at his table and was pleased to see that Lou had his hand on Jay's shoulder.

"We at Gordon & Newman" — he couldn't say the firm's name too many times — "work for clients who share our core values and generously partner with us in supporting these projects. Because of them, we can do well while we do good. We are grateful for this recognition and pledge our continued commitment and support." He looked directly at Jay, who nodded with a grin as Lou removed his hand from Jay's shoulder.

He returned to his seat during the standing ovation. He knew better than to take it personally. People needed a stretch after all the eating and sitting and they were congratulating themselves as much as him. Still, it was heady stuff to have a roomful cheering for you, and he briefly experienced the intoxicating high of celebrity and applause.

Sydney gave him a thumbs-up as he approached the table. "Mercifully brief," she smiled.

"Attaboy," Jay said, a bit thickly. "Give 'em hell." Stone smiled at Jay and nodded his thanks to Lou.

"OK?" he whispered to Sydney. He couldn't help himself; more than any applause, he needed her reassurance.

"Of course," she said. "The suit fits well, too."

4

The next week flew by, Stone riding a pink cloud of contentment, but Friday night, driving north, Ted's directions put him on edge. The GPS was working just fine, but Ted's description felt anything but innocent — more like a challenge, as if there might be a quiz at the end. Did you see the egg farm? How did you know it was the mushroom farm and not the organic nursery? How much was the price of gas at Pure Oil?

Stone consoled himself that Ted's details were fine for a novel, but of little use in the real-world: the Pure Oil sign hovered over a convenience mart, not a gas station, and was obscured from the south by trees. Surely Ted knew that, just as he'd known as a kid how to hide Stone's sneakers in plain sight, right where they should've been: on the shoe tree in his closet.

Tired from his day at work and the drive through unfamiliar territory, Stone made it to the dirt road that led to Ted's at 9:30 p.m. He turned into the first drive on his right, through open wrought iron gates and toward a grand Victorian house, three stories high and topped by a tower, like an elegant fire look-out station. It reminded him of a fixer-upper Sydney and he had considered buying when they were first married — the idea of creating their future by repairing the past had appealed to both of them. It had boasted high ceilings, walnut staircases, ornate crown molding and arched doorways. Ultimately, they'd decided it was too much house and too much work for two people starting their legal careers. Sometimes, when he looked back, he regretted not having taken on the challenge.

In the twilight, Stone could see that the mansion's distinguished age had been ignored. The house had been painted lavender, with maroon, sky-blue, lime and yellow accents, as if to mitigate the ostentation of the home's sheer size with the playfulness of Caribbean colors. It was hard to believe this was Ted's. Stone double-checked his directions. When Ted had said, "The first place on the right," Stone had envisioned a bungalow, possibly a faux log cabin. Was this the house Harmony wanted to restore? He smoothed his shirt and lifted the large brass lion-faced knocker.

The door opened and a long-haired, middle-aged woman in a flowing green and gold caftan greeted him. "Stone," she said. "I'm so glad you've come to see us."

Stone hesitated.

"I'm Harmony," she said. "Welcome to Peace & Joy." Her green, wide-set eyes glittered between perfectly arched brown eyebrows and high cheekbones.

"I've heard so much about you," Stone said. He hadn't known they lived together. But then again it was a commune, so they probably all lived there. It seemed to be a large place. Still, if Ted owned half of this, he was better off than Stone had imagined. Plus, Harmony was a striking woman. Ted wasn't doing badly for himself, after all.

"Come in, come in," Harmony said, bowing slightly and clasping her hands as if in prayer. "Oh, no. Silly me. Of course, you came for Teddy. Let me take you to his place."

Teddy. Hearing it was even worse than seeing it in print. Two cats, a tabby and a blue-eyed Siamese, rubbed against his pant legs. Stone set his smile.

Tossing back a mane of light brown waves that curled down her back and made her look like a teenager, Harmony stepped past him in the doorway and stooped down to shoo the cats back inside. He couldn't help but notice the tabby's orange hair now clumped on his right leg. "Hurry now," she said to him, "or they'll all get away. You know what they say."

Stone fumbled in his pocket for his car keys, not sure how he'd gotten "Teddy's" address wrong.

"We can walk," Harmony said. They turned to her right, across the front lawn to a continuation of the driveway. The battered asphalt continued under the *porte cochère* on the side of the house and then back a few hundred yards toward eight small cottages set in a semicircle around a cement reproduction of Venus de Milo in the middle of a reflecting pool. The cottages looked like wagons surrounding a campfire.

"Quite the place you have here," Stone said, a prickle of resentment teasing the hairs on his arms. It was getting too dark to see whether the grounds were well-maintained, but still, the place was substantial. The mosquitos swarmed in droves. Someone should drain Venus's pool. He waved his hand around his head, but Harmony seemed unfazed, as if bathed in DEET.

"We feel very blessed," Harmony said. Half a step ahead of him, her robe trailed regally behind her, reminding Stone of the cover of a romance novel he'd seen in the Miami airport on a business trip a month ago. She appeared accustomed to being followed. Stone was a bit unnerved.

It dawned on Stone that Peace & Joy could be a motel and campgrounds. Perhaps his brother had a business interest in the operation, which would explain how he was supporting himself. Funny he'd never mentioned it.

At the far end of the semicircle, beyond the last cottage, Harmony pointed at a 1960s aluminum Airstream trailer. A dozen silver bracelets on Harmony's outstretched arm jangled. "Isn't she a beauty?" she asked.

"A classic," Stone answered, surprised when she headed straight to the trailer, calling, "Teddy? Teddy, your brother's here!" Stone winced.

Almost immediately, Ted opened the door and bounded toward them. He wrapped his arms about Stone, who wasn't used to being bear-hugged and freed himself as soon as he felt it polite to do so. "Hey, bro," Stone said, sounding to himself like a parody of the young men at his health club.

"Hey," Ted answered, and there was an awkward beat. "Hey, yourself." Harmony slithered next to Ted, her hip touching his. He put his arm around her shoulders and pulled her to his side.

His tan face and neck suggested that Ted spent a fair amount of time outside. In clean khakis, he was still slender like the runner he used to be, but whether from poverty or healthy living, Stone couldn't immediately tell. Unlike himself, Ted had never had to count calories, let alone peanuts. He just had all-around better genes.

"I'll leave you two to catch up," Harmony said.

"Thanks, Harmony," Ted said, kissing her on the cheek. The back of Ted's neck was neatly trimmed; his light brown hair didn't seem to have thinned at all. He wore an unbuttoned, long-sleeved plaid shirt over a plum tee shirt. Turning from Harmony, he draped his arm over Stone's shoulder and pointed toward his trailer. "So, you found us."

"Hate to disappoint you, little brother, but 230 miles from Madison isn't exactly remote." Not even a touch of gray at the temples.

"But that's as the crow flies," Ted corrected. "It's 276, driving," he said, opening the door to his trailer, "to this little bit of heaven. All 175 square feet of it."

"Cozy," Stone said gamely.

"No, I don't," Ted said.

"Don't what?" Stone asked. Ted always thought he knew what Stone was going to say even before he spoke.

"Get claustrophobic," Ted answered. It was even more annoying since most of the time he was right. "We go up to the main house for meditations and on Saturday nights for group dinners." What about nights with Harmony? It was too soon to ask.

Ted motioned to Stone to take a seat at the dining table which was built into the end of the trailer. The galley kitchen was on the right, near the door, and the bed was at the opposite end, twenty-some feet away. The entire space was devoted to the basics of sleeping and eating, not unlike the cabin of the sailboats they chartered in the Caribbean, but without teak trim and granite counters. Ted closed an old laptop on the table, which apparently doubled as a desk. Stone looked around for a TV but found only an iPod station with two small speakers. He reached for his smartphone and again Ted answered his own question before he could ask it.

"Spotty cell service and internet. No cable. At least not here. Basic, at the main house." Stone felt a mild rebuke. He wasn't addicted to TV, but there were certain crime shows he enjoyed, if only for their altogether unrealistic portrayal of the law. "No one in a law firm has time for that much sex," he'd assured Sydney when they were young lawyers,

"Really?" Sydney had said. "The public interest types are like rabbits." He was taking himself so seriously then, in those pre-partner years, that it had taken him a few beats to understand the joke. He was probably *still* taking himself too seriously. Ted brought that out in him.

"I told Sydney I'd text her when I arrived," Stone said, by way of mild apology.

"Give her my love," Ted said.

"Of course," he said routinely.

"Only if you have extra space," Ted said, chuckling to himself. "A hundred and forty characters can be a challenge. Actually a pretty good exercise, brevity being the soul of wit and all that," he said. "It can take a whole day to get one right."

"It's not a tweet, Teddy. Besides, you could always send a second tweet, if that's what you were doing, and you'd still have twelve hours left over to do something else."

Ted's brow furrowed. Stone surmised that a twelve-hour workday was beyond his brother's experience. "I just mean it might be more efficient to settle for something less than perfect, just to get it done," Stone said. Ted seemed to flinch at "done," but Stone had been sincere. One of the secrets of his success as a lawyer was knowing when good enough was good enough.

"Wordsmithing entertains me," Ted said.

Stone wanted to say, "But does it feed you?" but that would start something, and it was too early in his visit to begin that particular dialogue. They were different people; hard to believe that they'd had the same parents, privileges and opportunities, but had ended up in such different places.

"Glass of wine?" Ted offered.

"Oh, I brought you some. It's in the car," Stone said, starting to get up.

"Thank you!" Ted said. "But let's save the good wine until last." He took a bottle from a cabinet over the sink. "It's homemade," Ted said. "Trailer-aged for at least a year."

Stone tried not to look alarmed. He wasn't a terrible wine snob, but he knew the difference between good and not-so-good. Cheap wine was bad for his stomach. Why wouldn't Ted let him go get the decent bottle from his car? Even if the campgrounds were successful, it was apparent that, compared to Stone, Ted was just eking it out. Stone didn't need to be force-fed Ted's homemade wine to be sympathetic to his brother's relative poverty.

Ted poured a small amount into a surprisingly fine balloon goblet, like the new ones Sydney and Stone had bought at Tiffany's to celebrate their twentieth wedding anniversary. Ted held the fragile glass to the light and extended it to Stone. When he didn't reach for it, Ted said, "I guess you're right," although Stone hadn't said anything. "I should make sure it's not poison." Ted swallowed, considered, and poured Stone a full glass, midway up the belly of the balloon. "Appreciate your coming," Ted said.

Stone nodded, took a tiny sip, and looked up. "Not bad!" he said. "Three stars!"

"I'm hurt!" Ted protested. "Only three?"

"You've never cared about stars," Stone chuckled.

"Right," Ted said. "Who needs stars on a night like this?"

Stone's high school French saved him." *Une nuit sans vin est comme uné nuit sans étoiles.*"

"Impressive," Ted said. Raising his glass to meet Ted's toast, Stone agreed. They were off to a good start. He was glad he'd come.

5

Groggy but not hung over, Stone woke to a banging on the window behind his head. It had been nice of Ted to insist on taking the spare "bed," the cushions cleverly arranged on top of the dining table, which was lowered to the bench level. Stone sat up and saw that Ted was gone. Then another tapping startled him as he caught a glimpse of something moving away from the window. In just a few seconds, it was back — a cardinal fighting with his own reflection in the window. Stone reached up and knocked against the glass to chase the crazed bird away.

He hadn't slept particularly well — he preferred more support than was provided by the modest layer of foam rubber that constituted Ted's "good" bed. He stepped toward the galley, hoping the commune didn't have a rule against caffeine.

Next to the two-burner stove, there was what looked like a brown sock hung in a simple wooden stand with a coffee mug underneath. Freshly-ground coffee beans sat in the bottom of the sock. Stone quickly understood that he should boil water in the tea kettle and fill the sock.

Ted had deconstructed his bed and left a loaf of brown bread, a crock of butter and a jar of hand-labeled clover honey on the converted dining table. When the coffee had dripped through the sock, he took it to the table and found a note from Ted: "Shhhh! I'm at the house, in meditation, until 8." It was signed with a smiley-face, two half-circles representing closed eyes. Apparently meant to convey serenity, it looked flirtatious. It was 7:15 a.m., later than Stone's usual 6:45 rising time. The internet was working and he checked his email messages on his phone — one gave him *The New York Times* headlines, the rest were spam. Not much of interest. The lack of major news was a good thing, unless you considered that violent skirmishes in some parts of the world had become so routine they were buried in the "world round-up" on page five. He feared he was becoming jaded. Even as "Pro Bono Lawyer of the Year," he'd had to admit that many times he was more interested in the status of his retirement funds than the welfare of the world.

The bread was dense, mealy, most likely organic. Delicious. He wondered if Ted had made it and if his kitchen were stocked with anything other than the homemade, home-canned and home-grown. Whether because of financial necessity or politics, something about the self-sufficiency of it all was attractive in its extreme purity and simplicity. Still, Stone was relieved when he opened a few cabinets and found packaged wheat flour, oatmeal, tea bags and some canned fruit among the cut-glass jelly jars and baggies of bulk-bought dried fruits and nuts. In a bottom cabinet, there was no food, only a stack of dark cardboard boxes. Each had a white label on the end, numbered two through five. Number two was on top. With a glance at his watch and the assurance that Ted wouldn't be back for half an hour, Stone sat cross-legged on the floor and opened the box.

As far as he knew, Ted hadn't written anything since his time in Madison. At least, he hadn't published anything. When his first book came out, he'd been named to a national list of the ten best new talents under forty. Since then, nothing.

And no apology to his fans. No explanation of why another book wasn't "done." Sloth? Arrogance? Poor health? Terminal writer's block?

Inside the box was a stack of white paper with a cover sheet that read, "ABSOLUTUS AMOR by Theodore Franklin Hunnicutt." There was also a thumb drive.

Lifting the title page, Stone quickly read the first page of text, then the next and the next. From the first few pages, he wasn't sure what the novel was going to be about, but he was already curious enough about the characters: a professor of astronomy and his ambitious, anthropologist girlfriend. He wanted to keep reading — Ted's prose was as wry and humorous as ever — but Ted would be back soon. He could ask him for a copy when Ted returned, but since Ted had hidden the manuscripts away, he'd probably put Stone off with some excuse about their not being ready. He fingered the thumb drive, struggled to his knees and lifted his laptop from his overnight bag. In seconds, he downloaded the novel and replaced the drive and the box and pulled out another box. It was ten to eight by the time he'd downloaded three of the four thumb drives he'd found. He added more coffee to the sock and stood over the kettle, urging it to whistle. After a minute it hadn't boiled, but he poured another cup anyway. He was at the dining table, reading the paper, drinking lukewarm coffee and feeling mildly guilty for his theft — to say nothing of his invasion of Ted's privacy — when the trailer door swung open. Stone wasn't sure what transformation he'd expected, but Ted looked just as he had the night before — no more or less serene.

"Been out?" Ted asked, pouring himself a glass of juice.

"Just barely awake," Stone said.

"You look a little flushed," Ted said. "Not allergic to the wine, I hope?"

"Not at all," Stone said. "Caffeine revs me up. You sock-drip sure makes a good strong cup."

"Doesn't it?' Ted agreed. "Richard, the artist, brought it to me from Costa Rica."

"What was he doing there?" Stone asked. It had been on Sydney's bucket list for a few years, but they'd not yet acted on it.

"A fellowship of some kind," Ted said. "An exchange program, I think, for young artists."

"Do they have such things for authors?" Stone asked.

"Old ones?" Ted smirked. "Probably." He bent down to study the insides of his refrigerator, a quarter the size of the Sub-Zero Stone and Sydney had at home.

"Have you applied?"

"Oh, no," Ted said.

"Why not?" Stone asked. "A full ride to some exotic locale in the dead of winter? Sounds like a good deal to me."

"I'd never leave Harmony," Ted said.

"Oh!" Stone said. "So, this is permanent?"

Ted sat across from him at the dinette, a ceramic bowl of yogurt in his hand. He looked to the right and then to the left. "Is anything?"

"Well, is it?" Stone asked. "Come on, man. I'm your big brother."

"Right. I should get relationship advice from the brother who married my college sweetheart."

For a moment, Stone wondered if this time Ted wasn't just teasing. They'd joked about this for years, especially in the beginning, when Stone's marriage to Sydney was an awkward reality. "One last time, for the record, I didn't steal her from you. As I understand it, by mutual consent, you two had already broken up."

"Yeah," Ted said. "I was too young for her."

"She was too old for you," Stone said, staring at Ted's eyes. Ted looked away first.

"You're avoiding my question," Stone said.

"I am," Ted said. "As is my right." He held out his arms in a circle and closed his eyes. "Ohmmmmm," he chanted and broke into a wide grin.

Stone smiled. He wasn't going to get anything more from Ted on the subject of Harmony. The fact that Harmony lived in the mansion and he in a twenty-five-foot Airstream said a lot. Stone wasn't sure what, exactly, but there was no doubt in Stone's mind who called the shots around here.

Ted had always been too nice a guy, too eager to please adults, too easy a catch for most girls. Activities that adults thought important — school, athletics, avoiding booze and drugs — had come effortlessly to Ted. Girls, on the other hand, were thrilled by his perfectly metered sonnets, but put off by his failure to insist on a kiss. Although Ted passed for normal in most situations, positive relationships with women seemed to be a struggle. If Harmony and he were sexual partners, and even if Ted was here for the long haul, there was nevertheless *something* unsettling to Stone about their arrangement.

"I didn't come here to watch you meditate," Stone said.

Ted snapped to attention. "No. No, you didn't. At ten, we have to be in town to work our shift at the farmers' market. Quick tour now and then we'll head out. OK?"

Stone hesitated. Part of him wanted to see if the meditation exercises were really brainwashing. He'd also considered driving up to Lake Superior, perhaps over to Ironwood or one of the tourist villages that Sydney had mentioned to him. Plus, he wondered why someone else couldn't cover for them at the market.

"Just go with the flow, bro," Ted said, chuckling. "Everyone should work retail at least once. Experience the art of the deal, from the ground up. See what an exciting life I lead here in the North Woods."

"When do I get to see the house?" Stone asked.

"I thought that might impress you," Ted said. "Harmony will have to invite you, so be nice. Here, I can show you the grounds." He grabbed a beige Tilley hat from a peg near the door and offered Stone some mosquito spray. "There's only so much nature one can take."

Stone looked at the bottle. So the secret *was* DEET. "This is like napalm for gnats," Ted said. "You'll be glad you have it. Some of the hard cores go with geranium and coconut oils, or even Citronella, but it's like Alaska up here. Skeeters the size of birds."

They ventured out, back around the semicircle of cabins, Venus de Milo and what Stone thought of as the mosquito pool. A single white waterlily bloomed, but the pool itself was grungy with weeds flourishing around its banks.

They turned away from the house, down a grass service road and past the stand of fir trees behind the cabins. After perhaps a few hundred yards, the trees gave way to a huge field. To one side was a staked-out truck garden with rows of corn at the far end, marigolds and tomatoes in close, and neat rows of everything imaginable in between. In the distance, Stone could see a dozen or so squat white boxes.

"You keep bees?" Stone asked. He remembered one day at camp when Ted, standing on the swimming pier, had taken a sip from an orange soda can, not aware of the bee crouched just under the can's pull-tab. It crawled out and attacked Ted's lip, causing him to drop the can and scream so loudly that the lifeguard and two counselors came running.

"Are you allergic?" one kept asking, but Ted didn't respond, and Stone didn't know the answer. "Eppy just in case?" one of the counselors said to the other and fumbled in his fanny pack for a pen with a needle on the end. The sight of it elicited a horrified screech from Ted, who, nine at the time, was crying his eyes out and calling for his mother. The rest of the afternoon Ted suffered not just from his swollen lip but from Stone's relentless teasing about being a crybaby.

"God, no," Ted said, touching his lip. "They belong to Mark and David. You had their honey."

"It was delicious," Stone said. "So was the bread."

"Mark and David do most of this," Ted said, sweeping his arm across the field. "We all help with the harvest on Friday for the Saturday market. They took it in this morning. You and I will sell from ten to twelve with Mark. Cody will help them close. I usually do, but he'll help out because you are here."

Stone resisted the desire to probe the economics of the truck garden: the costs of production and distribution and the return on investment. He slapped a phantom mosquito on his forearm.

"Got it?" Ted asked.

Stone lifted his palm. "Looks like I missed," he said, holding Ted's gaze in the bluff. Of course, these people didn't care. All they needed was enough for the short term. It occurred to him that whatever they had was probably deemed to be enough and, if not, Harmony would seek donations from people who *did* care about mundane things like money.

"We have a couple of sheds on the other side," Ted said and led him to two ramshackle outbuildings and two newer, corrugated metal buildings behind the stand of trees on the shaded side of the house. The older buildings housed farm equipment: a faded green and yellow John Deere garden tractor, a wide-gauge lawn mower (a hand-me-down from a golf course), a rototiller and a newish two-seater utility vehicle with a carry-wagon on the back. A snow blade rested against one wall, along with a variety of hand rakes, hoes and shovels. The other old building was a working garden shed, half filled with dried herbs and flowers hanging on hemp ropes that drifted down from the ceiling. The other half of the space was filled with rough wooden tables, peat pots, grow lights and trays for starting plants in the spring.

"No," Ted said, again ahead of Stone's thoughts. "All legal."

One of the newer buildings had huge windows and a skylight. One-half was filled with canvases, some on easels; the other half with a potter's wheel and kiln. The second new building housed a heap of rusted junk on one side, with what might have been sculptures-in-progress on the other.

"Alan and Alexis make trash into art," Ted said. "You'll enjoy meeting them. Great imaginations, both. Transformative thinking at its most creative, if not always practical."

They took Stone's car the twelve or so miles into town. On the border of the Upper Peninsula of Michigan, the sign welcoming motorists to Hurley, Wisconsin, proclaimed the population to be just over 1,500. Soon, it seemed like all 1,500 were out on the streets.

"Tourists," Ted explained. They drove along the main street, Ted pointing out the hotspots: the Full Moon Saloon, Shooters, the Silver Dollar, the Branding Iron Pub, The Beer Barrel, Mar's Bar, and about a dozen more. "Fishin', huntin', drinkin'," Ted said, deliberately. "It's the life."

Stone studied Ted's profile and saw the corners of his mouth strain against a smile. No, Ted wasn't a vegan yet, but he probably hadn't skinned a bear or hooked a muskie, either.

Ted turned up a small hill and parked near the county historical museum, a substantial brick building about the size of Harmony's house, crowned by a six-story clock tower. "Culture," Ted deadpanned. The museum was on the National Register of Historic Places and the town, founded in 1888, was old, by Midwest standards. "It was named for a lawyer," Ted added, somewhat amused. "He won a case for the iron company and took no fee on the condition that they name the town for him. You guys sure have egos."

"I prefer cash," Stone said. "Can't spend ego."

"Can't take either one with you," Ted said.

"Fleeting," Stone said, thinking that between taxes, mortgages, tuitions and charitable requests, even big fees didn't go that far anymore.

There were a dozen tents set up in the VFW park across from the museum, but Peace & Joy's display was by far the largest — two eight by ten foot pop-ups — and the most impressive. Their tables were dressed in red-and-white checkered cotton cloths and colorful chalkboard sandwich signs advertised the day's specials. Buckets of pink stargazer lilies perfumed the air. One table displayed honey, jams, jellies and breads; another, cherry tomatoes, basil and dill, and a third, small to medium-sized clay vases, mugs and bowls, hand-thrown by Dylan, the potter, and country aprons hand-appliquéd by two women they all called "the Girls." There were also several trash sculptures and collages, the kind of thing a tourist might bring home for his or her office: a bonsai made of recycled Green Bay Packer tee shirts, a miniature city the size of a post card built out of discarded circuit boards and a set of unicorn bookends fashioned out of bottle caps. Stone was most intrigued with remarkably accurate portraits of the Queen of England, Nelson Mandela and Elvis Presley, all made from buttons and odd pieces of costume jewelry. He silently rethought his notion that the art was meant for tourists; according to the price tags, only serious collectors could afford it and at least half of it was worthy of collection. For a moment he imagined a bottle cap portrait of Abraham Lincoln hanging in his office. It was tempting. But if he had money to spare for tony bottle cap art, Harmony would clearly expect he also had money for the reconstruction of Peace & Joy. So far, he'd seen no reason to satisfy her request, and he didn't have the energy to bargain with Alan or Alexis for a price more agreeable than the outlandish ones displayed.

Ted took his place near Mark behind the produce table. The two of them busied themselves selling and chatting up customers and bagging, weighing and caressing zucchini, tomatoes and green peppers. Knowing neither the merchandise nor the clientele, Stone studied the art, fingered the produce, and took Ted's and Mark's pictures with the vegetables. He felt at first like a tourist, then after a while like a shill, and finally just plain useless. He told Ted he was going to walk around. "Good idea," Ted said. "Watch out for bears."

• • •

"So what's for dinner?" Stone asked during the drive home.

"Don't know yet," Ted said.

"You're cooking for twelve and you don't know? Have you shopped?"

"Here's how it works," Ted explained. "After the Market closed, Cody bartered with the other sellers, and left his booty on the counter.

The cook's challenge is to figure out what to do with whatever Cody brings home."

"Sounds like a reality TV show," Stone said.

"More of a spiritual exercise," Ted said lightly, his lips poised in a self-deprecating smile.

"I didn't know you were a cook," Stone said. "Remember the time when we were in high school and the folks went away for what, three days? Mom left baggies with casseroles in the freezer, but we ate hot dogs the whole time."

"I don't think we even changed the water," Ted said.

"Because you, the Wisconsin Young Scientist of the Year, said boiling water would kill any germs."

"We lived large, didn't we?" Ted laughed. "Besides, I was third in that contest."

"The old man always said you were first."

"No doubt," Ted sighed. Stone waited for Ted's complaint about how their father always pushed them both too hard. It didn't come.

They entered the mansion through the back door and found a heap of vegetables near the sink: tomatoes, dark green peppers, zucchini, oversized onions and a pile of something that looked like a cross between a baby jade plant and a scraggly weed. Ted went to the sink as Stone sat on a stool at the kitchen workstation. "What's this?" he asked.

"I thought you'd become a foodie," Ted said.

Stone shrugged. Some of his partners had formed a gourmet dinner club, once a month visiting the best restaurants that Madison and Milwaukee had to offer and once a year pulling a double-header on Friday and Saturday nights, splurging in Chicago. Stone didn't fully appreciate the food-as-art/food-as-architecture ethic. He didn't appreciate why two morel mushrooms should cost more than a T-bone and thought the multi-course meals astronomically overpriced per ounce of nutrition. But Sydney and he went along with his partners' dining rituals. As the lead rainmaker at his firm, his presence was expected; his absence could telegraph unfounded rumors of slim days ahead for the firm.

"Got roped into it," Stone said. He raised the weed to his nose.

"Purslane," Ted said. Stone had never heard of it. "Kind of like watercress?" Ted added. "Or spinach. Very nutritious. Good for arthritis, high blood pressure, cholesterol, you name it. Go ahead, taste it."

"I'll wait," Stone said. A mild gurgle in his stomach reminded him that he was glad Sydney always stored a few nutrition bars in the car's glove compartment — "for emergencies," she said, "like when we're caught in a snowstorm." He thought purslane should count. "What are you going to do with it?"

"It can go wherever spinach or lettuce or watercress would go, or in something with a Turkish flair. Or Mexican. We can be as adventurous as we want."

"Inflict your experiment on others?" Sydney never made a new dish for a dinner party; she always tried it out on Stone a week or two in advance.

"Well, I know my way around a kitchen pretty well at this point," Ted said. He started rinsing the vegetables. "I'm not afraid of being adventurous. But you're right. Some of our members don't have good culinary sense. Heather and Sunshine, for instance. Everyone calls them 'the Girls.' In June, they made a pie." Ted paused, as if for dramatic effect. "Now I love strawberries, and I love broccoli, but together?"

Still wary of the purslane, Stone forced a laugh.

"Heather said she thought red and green went well together, and she cut the florets to stand up like little trees but, of course, when they baked the pie, the broccoli wilted all to hell."

"What did the group say?"

"We believe in honest self-expression, but that doesn't mean we don't know when *not* to express ourselves," Ted said, raising his eyebrows over a crooked smile. "Here," he handed Stone two jumbo onions. "Chop these."

"OK," Stone said. He took off his blazer and hung it on a chair, then looked around for an apron.

Ted wiped his hands on his jeans, reached into a bottom drawer and gave Stone a pink and white flouncy apron, apparently made by the Girls. Stone sensed a taunt — sissy! — from some long-forgotten playground incident, but dutifully tied the apron around his Brooks Brothers chinos. Just because he could afford to replace them many times over didn't mean he didn't take good care of the things he had. "Better safe than sorry," he said, trying to sound cavalier. He prided himself on being way beyond any threat from pink.

"It's an *onion,*" Ted said.

Stone hesitated.

"A *candy* onion," Ted insisted.

Stone may have spent five hundred bucks on a meal in the big city, but he'd never heard of a candy onion. "So a *candy* onion won't make me cry?" he asked.

"I don't know what makes you cry," Ted said. Stone thought his brother's tone was not entirely sympathetic. He heard his father's voice telling him not to pout when Ted got the better of him in an argument or at chess. Their father always told Stone to "man-up" — he was the older brother, after all. But he'd be angry as hell with Stone if he inadvertently made his little brother cry.

"He's very sensitive," their father would say when tears came to Ted's eyes after innocent teasing by Stone. The kid would cry at the drop of a hat — deliberately, Stone thought — and inevitably Stone was sent to his room.

Ted cocked his head to the side. "It wouldn't kill you to cry," he said.

"Can't you just give me a piece of bread to chew on?" Stone asked. He thought he remembered Sydney putting a piece of white bread in her mouth when she chopped a lot of onions. "Or are you *trying* to make me cry?"

"It's a natural release," Ted said wearily. "Really, the onion is very mild. If it's too much for you, do this." He opened his mouth and let his tongue hang out.

Stone pulled the brown papery tunic off the onion and then the outermost layer. He sliced off the root end with a sawing motion. Immediately, his eyes watered, and stepping back a few feet, he opened his mouth and let his tongue droop.

Ted shook his head in mock dismay, then lit a small candle and placed it near the onion. Ted took the knife from Stone. "Use one quick swift motion," he said, demonstrating. "No crushing. Also, the root end is the worst. Point it away from you."

"Who knew chopping an onion could be so complicated?" Stone said, cutting off the top of the onion.

Ted smirked. "That's a start," he said. He sounded like he was encouraging a five-year old. "Now, smaller pieces."

"You *are* trying to kill me!" Stone said, sniffing back tears.

Ted took the onion and with a few rapid-fire strokes minced the onions and pushed them to one side of the chopping board. Stone reached in and started to gather up the green stalks to toss them in the garbage.

"No!" Ted said, alarmed.

"Oh, come on," Stone said.

"Waste not, want not," Ted sing-songed. "We can use the greens and the rest goes to the compost heap." He pointed his knife to a plastic garbage pail near the sink. Stone picked up his knife and pointed it toward his own gut, but Ted pointed toward the greens and again to the pail. Stone made a show of trimming off the very smallest slices at their ends and sprinkling them on top of the compost heap like a garnish.

"You still haven't told me what tonight's special is," Stone said.

"Well, you missed the Friday fish boil in town," Ted said. "And it *is* Saturday night. How about crab cakes?"

"Fabulous," Stone said. He loved crab, and when soft shells were in season, he and Sydney tried to make a trip to the Outer Banks, supposedly to see a high school friend of Sydney's, but as far as he was concerned, for the crab.

"Can't believe you can get fresh crab all the way up here," Stone said. "Sometimes I marvel at the distribution infrastructure in this country. Isn't it amazing?"

Without missing a beat, Ted said, "Even more amazing is that I can make the best crab cakes you've ever tasted … without crab." He smiled his best smile, but Stone sensed an implicit challenge. Ted took a tin grater from a cabinet and put half a dozen medium zucchini next to Stone. "But now you have to grate."

A few minutes later, certain that Ted was showing off, he watched with stingy respect as Ted expertly formed dozens of cakes from eggs, homemade breadcrumbs, chopped green onions and a few teaspoons of Old Bay seasoning,

He helped Ted lay out a buffet on the kitchen counter of corn-on-the-cob, sliced tomatoes with fresh basil and the "crab cakes." Stone's hands felt stiff from grating — didn't Sydney use a food processor? — but he was in reluctant awe of his brother's culinary skills. He'd come a long way from hot dogs on the stove.

Ted's housemates — Stone didn't know what else to call them, though no one lived in the house except Harmony — were also appreciative of Ted's special meal. They sat around a huge square table in the gigantic dining room, three to a side, and passed the dishes among them, family-style. Harmony was seated in the middle on one side, with Ted opposite her. Stone was placed in the middle of the adjoining side, between Heather and Sunshine. Harmony asked for a moment of silence before the meal.

At "amen," the conversation swelled, breaking into half a dozen pairings. At first Stone answered a myriad of questions from the Girls about living and working in Madison. They were the youngest members of the house, as far as Stone could tell. Sunshine — predictably blond, her fine hair pulled back in a ponytail — looked like she belonged in northern Minnesota. She would scorch in California or Florida. She was trim with solid shoulders and a flat chest, reminding Stone of a professional golfer. Heather, on the other hand, bordered on plump. Her startling red hair hogged all the attention. It was cut short like a man's, but was loose, and tousled like a boy's. The Girls talked about how much they had enjoyed Madison when they were students at the university, especially the used bookstores and the Goodwill fashion collection.

In a general lull in the conversations, the kind that Stone had read happens every seven minutes in any crowd of talkers, Harmony directed her attention to Stone.

"Tell us about your legal practice," she said, and everyone hushed.

Stone felt himself turning crimson. "Very boring, I'm afraid," he said weakly. "General business law, mostly mergers and acquisitions. My wife is the one with the interesting practice."

"Then you know about acquiring land," Harmony asserted.

"Actually, I don't," he said. "But there are others in my firm who do."

"They represent Jay Shore," Ted said, but the name didn't seem to register with his housemates. Stone stared at him quizzically. "It's public knowledge, Stone. On your website, With Jay's permission, I assume."

Harmony ignored their exchange. "What does he develop?" she asked. Stone licked his lips. Harmony and Ted would be horrified by the McMansions upon which Jay had built his bourgeois empire. Stone tried to remember if Jay had ever razed historic buildings to create his "communities." Stone didn't think so, although once Jay had to relocate a dozen graves in an old country cemetery when a survey found them to be on his property. Luckily, there were no remaining family members to object.

"Suburban communities, mostly," Stone said, as sanitized a description as he could muster.

"He's done a couple of family resorts, too, hasn't he?" Ted said.

Stone bit the inside of his cheek, appreciating the euphemism for "water park." "Yes," he mumbled.

"Do you need a real estate lawyer, honey? I could probably get you the friends and family discount at Gordon & Newman," Ted said.

"I'd have to ask my partners," Stone countered.

"I'm not sure what I need," Harmony said. "Just curious."

"Historic preservation and land use are very special areas," Stone said. "Many real estate deals and most land use issues are best handled by politically-connected local lawyers." Harmony nodded slowly, as if deep in thought. But Stone, who thought he was usually good at reading silences in negotiations, couldn't read her thoughts. Something about her put him on edge.

"This place will never qualify as historic," Mark said, and Harmony shot him a nasty glance. "In my opinion," he added tartly. "Besides, I think, Harmony, that you really don't want all that goes with the designation, all the restrictions. You lose a lot of control."

"Ever practical," Ted said.

"Historic preservation is not all it's cracked up to be," David said. "The rich misuse it all the time to keep the riffraff out of urban neighborhoods that otherwise might be the site of decent affordable housing."

"There are no minorities here," the red-haired "Girl" said. "And no urban anything, so that's not a problem. I love Harmony's idea. I think it would be neat to live in a real historic building." Stone saw Ted swallow his lips. Stone thought that if the house were in fact historic, she — he decided it was Heather — was living in the shadow of a "real" historic building. What made her think she'd get to live "in" it if it were restored?

"It's a very expensive process," Ted said. "I don't think we could afford it."

"Even if we could," Mark said, "I'm not sure there would be much of a return on the investment." So at least one person at Peace & Joy understood basic economics.

"How much?" Stone asked.

Ted and Harmony shook their heads. Apparently elementary business concepts such as ROI escaped the proponents of the project.

"Can't expect to do a project like that without a budget," Stone said.

"Cut to the chase," David chimed in. "The truth is that simply having the nonprofit with a stated goal of restoration has some tax benefits."

"Fair enough," Mark said. "Hey, if the ruse works, I say go for it."

Ruse? He was shocked the housemates would use the word in front of Harmony, but she seemed unfazed. A hundred issues about the bona fides of tax exemption and nonprofit corporations went through Stone's mind, but he had no reason to voice them. He wasn't going to give money to a sham nonprofit. No one had asked him directly for money since his arrival and it wasn't clear to him that anyone other than Harmony knew that he'd been solicited for a donation. Besides, Ted hadn't said he needed the money.

After dinner, Harmony invited Stone for Sunday breakfast — the one meal a week she cooked — and promised him a tour of the house. Although the invitation was expected — a routine courtesy to a member's relative, especially one being tapped for cash — she made it sound like a favor she'd fashioned just for him. It was unsettling the way she tried to keep him off guard. Stone thanked her as she disappeared up a gleaming staircase in the hallway outside the dining room. The others helped with clean-up and then only Ted and Stone were left.

"Cup of tea?" Ted offered.

"What, no home-distilled cognac?" For most of their adult lives, any serious one-on-one conversations between the two of them — and there had been very few — were over just such a civilizing influence. Without it, Stone doubted Ted would loosen up about those novels or that Stone would summon the courage to ask.

"Not at the moment," Ted said. "Sleepytime or orange pekoe?"

Stone said, "Sleepytime," thinking he would need all the help he could get to pass another night on the thin foam rubber in the trailer.

Standing near the stove, they were quiet while the tea steeped. Finally, Stone broke the silence. "So, how's your writing going up here in the North Woods?" he asked, thinking it worth at least a try.

Ted shrugged. He nodded toward a small wall needlepoint on the wall behind Stone. Stone turned and saw what might have been a framed warning to employees to wash their hands. He got up and walked close enough to read, "One cannot think well, love well, sleep well, if one has not dined well. — Virginia Woolf."

"We certainly dined well," Stone said. "So, are you writing well?"

"So-so," Ted finally said.

"Published anything recently?" he asked.

"Oh, no," Ted said.

"You must have stuff to send out," Stone said. "You've been up here a bunch of years."

"Ten," Ted smiled — sadly, Stone thought. "Great art takes time," he said.

"Who's got time for great?" Stone chuckled. "Excellent would do. Hell, even very good. Maybe just plain good."

Ted took a sponge and started scrubbing the sink, which had already been scrubbed.

"Have you been sending stuff out?" Stone pressed.

Ted shook his head.

"Why not?" Stone asked. Ted didn't say anything. "I mean, don't you need the money?"

"It's always money with you."

"No, it isn't. I do wonder, though, how you support yourself."

"None of your business, big brother," Ted said, an edge in his voice.

Stone bit his tongue to stop himself from mentioning Harmony's solicitation. He tried a different tack. "Hey, I'm just a brother looking for something to brag about," he said.

"*Lawyer of the Year*," Ted said. Stone was pleased he remembered that. Sydney must have mentioned it in passing on the phone. Yes, he could admit that he'd spent enough time and effort lawyering that he should be recognized for his work. "I can't imagine spending all your time writing but not finishing anything."

"I finish stuff," Ted said.

"What happens to it? Who reads it?" he asked.

"It gets read," Ted said.

"By whom?" Stone asked.

"Harmony reads it," Ted said. He sprayed water over the twice-cleaned sink. "I wouldn't send anything out unless she said it was ready."

"And when will that be?" Stone asked.

"She says we're not ready yet," Ted said. He sounded somewhat discouraged.

Stone lowered his mug noiselessly. "Oh," he said. Of course, Ted must be embarrassed. He'd written over the past few years, but apparently not well enough to please Harmony. Stone felt a wave of brotherly concern wash over him. But now was not the time to continue this conversation. He yawned, and Ted nodded. "Country air can wear a person out," Ted said as they walked in silence to the trailer.

On the way, the tree frogs chirped madly. In many ways Ted's simple lifestyle was bucolic and idealistic. But had it been wholly his choice? Ted, the genius, had ceded his autonomy to a self-styled guru. She could be charming, true, and she projected a certain personal authority — even an annoying moral superiority — but was she an authority on fiction? Stone could understand Ted's desire to escape the fickle academic world that had rejected him, but how much of Ted's current creative reclusion had been coerced by Harmony?

It was on odd relationship. At first, Stone had thought they adored each other. Then, at dinner, they'd sat opposite each other and directed all their attention to their housemates. They lived apart, like members of some religious sect. Too many nagging questions were on his mind as he showered in the toy-sized stall in the trailer and later pulled up the summer blanket against the evening chill. "I'll come back and get you for breakfast," Ted said.

"I get to see the house tomorrow," Stone said.

"If that's what you came for, I hope you're not disappointed," Ted said.

"Nonsense, I didn't even know about the house," he said, though of course he had. The house had piqued his curiosity about what his brother was up to. He wanted to see the house, but he also wanted to see Harmony in action, whether she would ask him directly for a donation or manipulate him into volunteering one.

"Is it really historic?" Stone ventured.

"We all have history," Ted said.

6

"Rise and Shine, oh babe of mine." Ted mimicked their mother's greeting when they were still boys, and Stone shielded his eyes from the morning light. "Breakfast is served," Ted announced. "In the house," Ted said. He tossed a pillow from the dinette, landing it squarely on Stone's face. "Up, up, up."

Stone swung his legs around and raised himself to a sitting position on the edge of the bed. While he hoped there would be a sock of coffee to get him started, apparently, he was not to dawdle. He ran his razor quickly over his morning stubble and splashed on some after-shave. Ted opened the door to the trailer as Stone took a fresh shirt from his duffle. Ted grabbed the cardboard and plastic wrapping before Stone could find a place to throw them out. "For Alan and Alexis," Ted said.

Stone put on his blazer and Ted shook his head in resignation. "It's breakfast, not brunch at the Ritz," he said. Stone started to take it off. "That's OK," Ted said. "I wouldn't want you to feel naked. C'mon."

Harmony was just lifting a pan from the oven and the housemates were milling about when Stone and Ted arrived at the house kitchen.

"We can knock 'em out with a hose and soapy water, but we've got to strike today," Mark said.

"I guess we're lucky it's this late in the season," David said. "Morning, Stone."

"Morning," Stone answered, taking a place behind Ted at the counter. "Pesky neighbors?"

David and Mark looked at each other, totally baffled. Then Mark blurted out, "aphids!"

"You can tell by the presence of ants nearby," David said.

Stone felt foolish. Although he was usually excellent in social situations such as bar associations, law conferences and neighborhood block parties, he found himself tongue-tied, with no way to explain how little he knew of the North Woods. He started to fill his plate from the spread on the counter: a platter of sliced pork butt, a bread bowl full of cut fruit, a skillet of scrambled eggs with zucchini, basil and tomato, and a tray of cinnamon buns, fresh from the oven. "This looks great. Do you always eat this well?"

Mark leaned across Ted and said, in a low voice, "Depends who's cooking. Plus, you have to like zucchini."

"Cinnamon buns!" Ted rubbed his hands together. "These are the best," he said, plopping one on Stone's plate.

After breakfast, Ted left to supervise the clean-up. Harmony gestured for him to follow her to the hallway. Stone pointed toward the kitchen, expecting Ted to come along.

"He's busy," Harmony said. "Besides, he knows the house inside-out."

Harmony stopped before the grand staircase, her hands clasped prayerfully at her chest, a gesture Stone was beginning to think of as her "spiritual guru stance." It seemed unnecessary and pretentious. "The house was built in 1885 for a wealthy banker in these parts, whose primary clients were in the mining industry. Quite the sensation at the time," she said, sounding like a well-rehearsed docent. It was awkward to be the only tourist. He soon realized that Ted had deliberately abandoned him. "Combining Queen Anne and elements of Eastlake Victorian architecture," she continued. Stone felt as though her eyes were drills, boring into his as if looking for his core, perhaps the wetness which would open his wallet. He arched his back, reminding himself to pay attention. "The wood throughout the house is mahogany, with some walnut finishing. We have sixteen large Oriental rugs and several runners like these." She pointed toward the front door and then along the side of the staircase leading to the back.

The Asian runner under Stone's feet was faded, a small white rose blotched by what looked like a coffee stain. She must've noticed his glance at the spot, because she added, "Some wear and tear is natural with old things. It speaks to our authenticity."

"Of course," he said.

"When we got the place — fifteen years ago now — it was in total disrepair. I can't tell you how many thousands of hours have gone into its restoration."

Stone did a quick calculation. "New construction would've been cheaper," he chuckled. He suddenly thought she might take this wide-open opportunity to ask for his financial support. "What's the overall budget for the restoration?" he asked, hoping to sound casual.

"Restoration of a historic treasure is a priceless endeavor," she said, without apology for evading the question.

"A bit circular, though, isn't it?" he asked. He hoped he sounded sympathetic with the expense and personal sacrifice of her effort. "It's merely old and run down until someone invests enough to make it a treasure."

"Being old is never enough for the National Registry," Harmony said. "The restoration must be top notch." The words "top notch" appealed, of course, to the Hunnicutt ego, but they seemed, in her mouth, to include a built-in excuse. Without money — Stone's money or someone else's — the restoration would fail to be "top notch." It would be amateurish. Good intentions, but little class.

"Exactly my point," he said. He wondered if the "get them nodding yes" technique would fool her into thinking they were on the same side, and she might now hit him up for the funds.

Stepping from the hallway into a large room, she said, "This is the East Parlor." Crammed with rosewood and ebony end tables, velvet plum chairs, Tiffany lamps, fringed pillows, and framed pictures and porcelain pots, the parlor was neither inviting nor lived in, despite a cozy fireplace dwarfed by a giant gilded mirror. Stone thought it strictly a showplace of faded Victorian glory. How did this accumulation of antique paraphernalia square with the "peace and joy in simplicity" theme exemplified by Mark's and David's truck garden, Alexis's and Alan's lost-and-found art, and Ted's trailer? He wondered if Harmony took this room seriously, or if it was indeed a ruse, perhaps to satisfy the local historians, the National Registry, the IRS or some other so-called public purpose.

"It's beautiful, yes?" Harmony asked, the affectation of "yes?" grating on him. In truth, he hated superficiality.

"It feels very authentic," he said. Then he noticed a glass cake-stand in the center of one of the side tables. Under the cover, there was a small, framed painting of a piece of cake. "Except for the Magritte imitation," he said. His nailing the artistic reference should impress her, he mused.

"It's not an imitation," Harmony said, her voice brittle with resentment.

Stone was fairly certain it was. "I should've said, 'parody.'" He bowed slightly. "My wife and I saw an exhibition in Chicago not too long ago. 'This is a Piece of Cheese,' was one of my favorites by Magritte."

Harmony scowled, as if he'd accused her not of plagiarism per se, but of not *knowing* of the nod in Magritte's direction. Was the whole house like that — a parody of itself, with clues in clear view for those in the know?

"Does the National Registry allow modern art in historic houses?" he asked. The question came out as more challenging than he'd intended. Harmony turned on her heel, ignoring the query as if the answer wasn't to be covered in the docent's briefing.

"Now, to the South Parlor," she said. She led Stone past the staircase to the back of the house, along a hallway lined with a gallery of framed portraits of people who might have been the first settlers in these parts, but who he thought were more likely a graveyard of random garage sale finds, the frames glaringly spray-painted gold. At the end of the hall, where it turned right, two portraits hung side by side, drawing Stone's attention. One looked like a finger painting, with fat, imprecise strokes in bright primary colors. He stopped in front of it as Harmony turned around to him.

"Einstein," she said.

Stone cocked his head. He supposed he could discern a halo of multicolored hair, a boxy face, thumb-print eyes, and a broad smear of a mustache. "Of course," he said. Next to Einstein, a portrait of a woman was pieced together from old jewelry, buttons, bottle caps and pieces and parts of anything one might throw away — ballpoint pens, pop tops, wrapping paper, ribbons, Cracker Jack toys. It was by far the more creative of the two. He was intrigued by the trompe l'oeil.

"I was much younger then," Harmony said.

He was amused by her audacity in pairing herself with Einstein, but again he noticed how patrician she looked, her skin taut across those high cheekbones, her forehead untroubled by wrinkles or worries. "You haven't changed a bit," he said, nodding his head toward the portrait.

"Well-intentioned dishonesty is still dishonesty," she said, looking up at him, her green eyes soft and amused, but somehow impenetrable. He was taken aback when she dipped her chin, almost flirtatiously, and said, "Yet still appreciated." She probably thought she had him now, but he thought he had her. First the flirt, then the "ask." Of course she'd crack first. She was up against the Best Business Lawyer in Wisconsin.

As she turned to enter the South Parlor he took his phone out of his pocket. When she stopped in the doorway to invite him in, he snapped her picture, her "come hither" look framed by the arch.

"No!" she shouted, dropping the feathery lightness of her docent voice. "Don't do that."

"It's lovely," he said, pointing the phone screen toward her.

"I didn't grant you permission to photograph me," she said, refusing to even glance at the phone, her nose angles in a regal taunt.

He was shocked. Friends and families took pictures of each other all the time. She was almost a sister-in-law; it had never occurred to him to ask permission. "No, no you didn't," he stammered. "I'm sorry. I assumed 3…"

He wished he hadn't left her that opening and hoped she wouldn't condescend to take it. But she did. "When you ass-ume, Mr. Hunnicutt," she said, but he held up his hand. *An ass of you and me.*

"Please forgive me," he offered with false humility. He held the screen up to her again and made a show of turning it off. Realizing that she hadn't asked him to *delete* the photo, he stashed the phone in his pocket. Sydney would want to see what Harmony looked like, and a picture would spare him the awkwardness of describing her — "pretty, but not as pretty as you, dear."

They entered the South Parlor, a slightly less ostentatious version of the East, this one done in rust and deep gray and dominated by a large walnut dining table with a jigsaw puzzle, a quarter of the way finished. It looked like it was going to become an impressionist painting ultimately. Oddly, someone was working on it from the inside-out, rather than from the frame in.

"You enjoy puzzles?" he asked, as if he were a fellow enthusiast.

"A useful exercise in doing nothing," she said.

"Made more difficult, I see, by not starting with the frame."

"The pieces fit, just the same," she said.

Stone nodded his disagreement. The woman was obstinate. Insistent on doing things the hard way. Clutter a historic mansion with weary antiques, decorate it with craft-show art, exile your boyfriend to a twenty-five-foot trailer, have the opportunity to corner someone and ask directly for ten grand, and not seize the opportunity. It was baffling.

"I've always found puzzles easier with two people working on them," he said. "My wife's very good at them. So was Ted, as a kid." It struck him that inside-out was Ted's specialty. When they did puzzles with their mother on rainy Sunday afternoons, Stone handled the borders and Ted the interior. Maybe Ted lived in the house and used the trailer only as a studio. And if he lived in the house, perhaps he had encouraged Harmony to make the ask. Stone was getting oddly impatient. He wasn't even sure how he wanted to respond.

"The house is quite special, Harmony. So large. I can understand your wanting to maintain it." The question he really wanted to ask was "Why live here alone?"

"In fact," he asked. "Have you thought about renting rooms to the others here in the house, and renting out the cottages? Wouldn't they want to live here, too?" "You'd have to ask them," she said, her tone frigid.

"They seem like such a lovely group. They've been so welcoming to me. But I've wondered," — he thought he still might get her to volunteer more information about the house and what she was really after — "don't creative people need to be, I don't know, more in the mainstream of life, say, in a more dynamic urban area? Don't you feel like you and the other members are missing out?"

"We're not here to escape or hide from the world," she scoffed.

"I didn't …" he started, although in fact he had suggested something of the sort.

"In reality, the isolation, intensity and simplicity of this way of life demand that we become more intimately involved with it," she said.

"We strive for a life not driven by personal concerns or material needs," she continued. She had recovered her breathless tone:

ethereal, fragile, sexy, self-satisfied and somehow, still commanding.

"The art? The antiques?" He took a breath. "The Mercedes?"

"Not needs, Mr. Hunnicutt. We can enjoy these things without being defined by them." She looked around, palms upward. "They are solely for our pleasure, not to boost our standing among our peers."

"Because of the isolation, you have no peers," he nodded, pretending to understand, but he was disconcerted. He stared at the built-in walnut bookcases on the south wall. In front of him, the complete short stories of F. Scott Fitzgerald nestled next to *The World According to Garp*, the two volumes flanked by gold-leaf editions of Maupassant on the right and Schiller on the left. He felt Harmony studying him as he ran his hand across the hard-bound spines. He guessed there was a message hidden in the organization, but he wasn't getting it. "You have wide-ranging tastes, I see," Stone said, taking a step down the row. He felt his heart rate rise; if this was a test, he was determined not to fail it.

She nodded, perhaps to encourage him. *The Basic Writings of C.G. Jung* sat next to Colum McCann's *Dancer,* which sidled next to *Dreams from My Father* and *The Buddha's Act of Healing.* "And you don't mind mixing things up," he said, then smiled to himself. "I get it. R-O-Y-G-B-I-V?" He had to look down the rows of shelves to get it right.

"You started at the beige," she said. "But when you got to red, you got it."

"How do you find anything?" he asked. He'd once read a story about all the ways one could arrange a library of books, but he'd never seen it done by color.

"Once you've read it, it's yours. How many times have you gone back to a book to find a fact or a quotation?" she asked. "These days, most people merely push a button on a keyboard."

"I come from a profession that used to organize its literature — case law — by concepts and topics. Now, of course, it's all by the actual words used in the case report." He felt a wave of nostalgia for his days as a young lawyer, long nights in the library searching for clues, for the perfect precedent that would carry the day.

"How confining!" she said. He agreed; the law's adherence to stare decisis straight-jacketed judges to the tiniest of incremental changes, small deviations and distinctions from what came before. It ensured the rule of law by principle, not personality. But the word "confining" reminded him of the phrase "spiritually confining" in her letter, describing how Hurley had become too conventional, just like Key West. "So color makes as much sense as Dewey?" he asked.

"I'm told the aesthetics are much improved," she said. She swept her arm from left to right. "There's even an argument to be made, counselor, that color arrangements promote cross-fertilization of ideas among books."

"So Shakespeare can talk to Malcolm X?" he said.

"I wouldn't rule it out as a possibility," she said playfully.

She turned abruptly. He followed her out, expecting to move down the hall from the library, but Harmony returned to the main foyer, where she took the first step up the grand staircase and then, looking down on him, clasped her hands in that annoying pose of hers. "Thank you for visiting Peace & Joy," she said. "Perhaps next time you will not be so pressed for time." If she'd allowed him, he would've said that his weekend had been very relaxing and that, in fact, he did have time to see the rest of the house, but she added, "Next time, Ted and I would enjoy sharing meditation with you."

He felt oddly let down. He realized he'd been itching for a confrontation. She'd not asked for money — not for Ted, not for the restoration of the house, not for the commune's mission — and he'd been denied the option of saying "no." He felt entitled to reject the solicitation in the letter, to explain himself, but there was no one to hear him out. Ted didn't seem to know about the ask, and Harmony wouldn't acknowledge it, so he left the house mumbling, "Thank you," when he was feeling nothing of the sort.

7

Ted walked Stone to his car, satisfied with his brother's visit, but relieved that he would soon return to his routine. Life at Harmony's Peace & Joy was simple. Houseguests, especially family members, complicated things. They knew things. They remembered you one way, the way the family approved or disapproved of. They had emotional weapons at the ready, even if they hadn't used them in years. Honestly, his trailer was small for two grown men.

"Whose idea was the hybrid?" Ted asked.

"Sydney's. She makes pretty good choices," Stone said, and Ted wondered momentarily if he meant more than car choices. He was glad that Stone and Sydney were happy.

"Give her my love," Ted said.

"She'll like the honey," Stone replied. "Thanks."

Ted watched Stone back out of the driveway, around the house and out of sight. He exhaled.

He'd had a pleasant enough time — after all, they *are* brothers — but it wasn't clear to him why Stone had shown up. They hadn't spent that much time together since their last sail in the Caribbean, a few years ago. Something seemed to be on his mind, but Stone never got around to saying what. Maybe the old guy was feeling sentimental. They were never going to be best buddies — they were too different — but Ted now felt a greater tenderness for Stone than he had in years.

Stone seemed to have mellowed. It was unlike him not to be full of questions about every last thing. He hadn't been snobby about the trailer or even the house, which anyone could see needed some TLC. He had liked Ted's wine, which, Ted thought, wasn't in fact his best. It was as if Stone had lost that judgmental edge that marked the difference between his brother's success and his own; he wouldn't invoke the word "failure," but "lack of success" might indeed be apt. Someday, he should look up a more forgiving word for what their father would've called his "not living up to potential."

But Stone's lack of judgment was also unnerving. It implied, in a way, that there wasn't any potential for "better." Lukewarm compliments hurt because they implied a lack of talent worth perfecting. Without saying a word, Stone had forced Ted to confront the disappointment of those in his past who'd had such high expectations for him — his father, his publisher, the chair of the Creative Writing Department.

Mark approached, rake in hand. "Your brother seems like a decent guy," he said. Ted didn't respond right away. He was surprised that someone as strait-laced as Stone would make a good impression on Mark, someone Ted thought was one of the more advanced spiritual types at Peace & Joy. "For a lawyer," Mark added.

"He's one of the good guys," Ted said. "Does a lot of pro bono stuff. Usually on the right side of things."

"Good. I wouldn't want to disagree with him," Mark said. "He's too smart."

"He is," Ted said. "Although sometimes he thinks he knows what's right for everyone."

"So he doesn't approve of the Airstream?"

"He didn't complain too much. Can't quite figure it out."

"People mellow as they get older," Mark said. "Closer to the grave, all the material stuff just doesn't seem as important anymore. You and I, we just figured that out earlier." He flung the rake over his shoulder and whistled his way off to the garden, an intentional parody of himself.

"I'm going to tidy up the homestead and then I'll come help," Ted called after him. There wasn't much to do in the trailer, but he was still puzzled by Stone's visit. What Mark had said about the grave made him worry that Stone might be sick, although he hadn't seemed sick. In fact, Stone had looked healthy, like a middle-aged guy who watched his diet (or had it watched for him), someone who worked out enough to look fit but not emaciated, and was, for all of that, maybe ten or fifteen pounds above the ideal. Not unlike himself.

But perhaps Stone had less of a bounce in his step and not quite the same familiar energy. On the boat in the islands, Stone was always in motion, retying a line, hanging out a towel or checking an engine fluid. This weekend, he seemed calm. Not lethargic, but revved down, and different somehow.

No, he probably wasn't sick. If he were, Sydney'd have him on some kind of health food binge. He'd be playing the dutiful disciple, trying to get everyone to see the benefits of acai or canola or seaweed or whatever the latest life-extending foodstuff was, but Stone didn't even know what purslane was.

Still, fifty could play with a man's head. Ted had himself just turned fifty, and while he felt healthy, never healthier, the number fifty — "more than half done," he'd joked with Harmony — the number made you think twice. Fifty, and living in a trailer. Fifty and "Best Lawyer in Wisconsin." Their father would've been surprised. So was Ted, in a way.

There'd been lots of times when he'd envied Stone's clear career path. Law school. Top-tier firm. Partnership. All very rewarding financially. At each milestone of his career, Stone had known what was required and what he had to do to get there. At first, Ted had thought teaching creative writing would be like that too. He'd write some books, teach some classes, earn tenure. He'd published his first book, *Pater Noster,* and there'd been a lot of genuine praise, but the success had been disappointing: he'd go to readings and book signings, and young people would look at him as if he were a modern-day Melville. They'd ask for a piece of profound advice, but he didn't have any to offer. They'd ask him about getting published, and he'd say it was a "crapshoot." They'd leave crestfallen. Some were even pissed off. He was just trying to be honest, which wasn't, apparently, appreciated in a fiction writer or novelist.

He hadn't known what to write next. Perhaps it was because he was bombarded daily with half-baked ideas clumsily presented in his student's stories and he feared unconsciously borrowing from them. Perhaps it was his own search for something so original that it couldn't possibly be written. In desperation, he'd repeated his first-love theme, this time with a comedic tone but a serious title (*Absolutus Amor*). Latin gave the work a certain gravitas, and he used it because it would appeal to his dad. But it wasn't the book he wanted to write. It wasn't big enough in scope or imagination.

He'd wanted his second novel to be an epic — a grand, generation-spanning tome of social importance. He'd made lists of subjects that interested him and was then paralyzed by their magnitude: madness; the story of Job; enlightenment; misfortune; if, how and why people change. But his life had been too easy. When he tried to write about rivalry, unfettered ambition or inner demons, he didn't have a well of disappointment or hardship from which to draw. Ultimately, his grandiose dilly-dallying cost him tenure.

He'd been astounded when his colleague, a short story writer who'd never turned out a novel, was awarded tenure. The man confessed that he got his wildest and most original ideas at NA meetings.

"Not fair!" Ted had protested, only half in jest.

"As fair as any other piece of luck," the newly tenured professor said. "Besides, they've kept me clean and sober for eight years."

No wine or weed. "A high price for a story," Ted had tried to joke, but the man had been dead serious.

"Best thing that ever happened to me as a writer was to get out of my own head and hear so many incredible but true stories," the new professor had said. "Really, what's an original idea anyway? Do yourself a favor. Start eavesdropping."

It hadn't been bad advice; when he lost his job, he took it. He traveled and eavesdropped in a dozen countries, and then, back in Madison, he overheard a conversation about Harmony's Peace & Joy. Harmony Miller was said to be a wealthy poet who'd founded a fledgling literary journal and was on a mission to discover and nurture new writers. He hadn't been aware of the journal and hadn't submitted to it, but he read the first two issues and was impressed with what he read. Humbled by his own inaction and the power of the stories he'd heard on the road, he presented himself at Harmony's Peace & Joy.

At first he'd spent his days in a borrowed trailer, waiting for inspiration. Then, Harmony suggested the formal mediation group and he started working in the garden with Mark and David to pass the time. One morning when he opened his journal after meditation to record what he'd heard the day before, he realized that he was fabricating most of what he was writing, mining what he'd been hearing from them and the others, at meals and during work. He was finally writing fiction again.

He found that from a single line he could imagine his way into a story. Harmony had advised him to keep it simple — the way his first book had been simple — so that the complex could slowly but surely emerge. He'd written his third novel, *Where We Started* in four parts (an homage to Eliot) and from two points of view, a mother's and her daughter's, both before and after the onset of the mother's Alzheimer's. Why a story so far afield from his own experience? Because Mark had returned from a visit to his mother's and had said, "She didn't know me. She had no idea who I was." Ted had banged out the first chapter in a week.

Before Mark gave voice to his devastating truth, Ted hadn't known how to write about his love for his own mother — too sentimental, too close to home — or even about his father, who seemed to Ted not to understand him at all. He could barely imagine Mark's agony, but his empathy was the energy that fueled the novel. It was in essence a simple, mother-daughter story, complicated by the dilemma posed by the daughter when she is offered a test to predict her likelihood of inheriting the disease.

Ted discovered that he wasn't as unique as his family myth would have it. Everybody had something in their present or their past hanging over their future. Until Stone's visit, Ted had almost forgotten the expectations that hung over his. Harmony was a strict editor, and she didn't care where an idea came from or if he thought it too banal. For her, originality was in the expression of the idea, rather than the idea itself. Sometime during his work on *Where We Started*, despite her ongoing critical comments and suggestions, he'd fallen in love with her. He'd used what was left of his inheritance to buy the Airstream and some land. During the ten years of their relationship, he kept writing. To keep the personal and professional separate, he never submitted to her journal, and she never solicited manuscripts from him.

The fourth novel followed when Richard let it slip that his sister had once been his brother. "I thought I was a pretty open guy," Richard had said, "until my brother underwent gender reassignment surgery without telling us. It took me longer that I thought to get over the shock." Ted shook off a fleeting image of Stone in a skirt. Richard confessed, "I still sometimes forget and call my sister Bob." Hence, the title, *My Sister, Bob.*

Since then, he'd realized anything could become a story, and enough intertwined stories, a novel. Every character had a story — not just a backstory, but an ongoing life, to be rendered on the page. Sunshine was studying to become a clairvoyant, which Ted frankly thought was hooey, but he'd leeched a narrative out of it: *Mrs. Satan,* his first historical effort, set in the mid-1800s, during the upsurge in spiritualism. Oddly enough, now that he wasn't worried about identifying a story, what he worried about was the writing itself. He was never sure that it was up to snuff, and Harmony never approved it for submission to a publisher. Still, she always encouraged him, and he labored to make it just that much better.

He hadn't thought so much about his body of work or about the tenured Professor Pothead in years. Another thing age could do — haunt you with memories you'd long since tried to forget. He was happy for Stone's success, but the comparison that gave Ted pause was not his own lack of material success, but his failure (if it could be called that) to give himself — and his work — a chance.

Harmony always admonished him that comparative thinking was not useful. She was constantly reminding the Girls not to compare themselves to each other or to the young literary phenomenon of the day. "Not your lot," she'd say.

Now, he changed into work jeans and a tee shirt, sprayed on the DEET, and headed out to join Mark in the garden. Mark handed him a metal bucket.

"You can pick some baby carrots for dinner, if you like," Mark said.

Gently, he placed his first pickings in the bucket. "My brother might be rich, but he doesn't get vegetables this fresh, ever," Ted said.

"With his money, I suppose he *could,* if he were so inclined," Mark said.

"The closest he comes, I think, is when his foodie partners insist on going down to Chicago to eat all weekend at their fancy schmancy restaurants," Ted said.

"Probably spends in a night what together we spend in a month," Mark said.

Ted studied a squat carrot with a bump on one side. An asymmetrical carrot would never be served at such a place. "I can't imagine any meal anywhere that could possibly be worth it," he said.

"I thought your family had money," Mark said.

"Not *that* kind of money," Ted said. "We were brought up middle-class. When there *was* a middle-class. Stone's richer now than our dad ever was."

"The Great American Dream come true," Mark said.

"It makes me wonder what it's like to be Stone. Whether any of it makes him truly happy," Ted said. He rubbed the dirty baby carrot between his fingers.

"He seemed happy enough."

"You don't think he sold out?" He broke the carrot in two, and held it to his nose, taking in its fresh woody smell.

"Not necessarily," Mark said. "Lucky for him, he doesn't have artistic talent," he laughed.

Ted shook his bucket. "Enough?" he asked.

"A couple more, and then you're good to go," Mark said. He leaned on his rake, looking down at Ted. "At the risk of pissing you off, art never pays unless you put it up for sale."

Ted tossed the last carrot into the bucket. "That does it," he said. He straightened, still on his knees. "I don't write for the money."

"Then you'll never know what it's like." Mark offered him a hand.

Standing up, Ted said, "Do *you* do it for the money?"

"My sculpture? Hell, no. But I wouldn't turn it down, either. More time for the art."

"Then who'd plant the carrots?" Ted asked.

"We'd eat a lot more zucchini," Mark said.

Ted snorted a laugh. "Well, there's an incentive for you." He decided to play along. "And who'd tend the bees?"

"I suppose they'd have to fend for themselves." Mark paused for a moment. "Like the lilies of the field."

Both of them had long ago decided that the intellectual arguments they had with organized religions were not resolvable, but in a pinch

Mark fell back on the stories he'd learned in Sunday school. "Do you remember the parable about the laborers in the field?" he asked.

After their mother died, Thaddeus Hunnicutt, not being a churchgoer, had forsaken the boys' religious indoctrination, but Ted remembered enough to ask, "Switching Gospels?"

"Like mixing metaphors," Mark grinned. "This is the one where one guy works eight hours for, like, fifty bucks, and at noon they bring on another guy, who gets fifty for four hours, and at the last minute they bring on a guy who does one hour and *he* gets fifty."

"Grossly unfair, unless we're talking about a labor pool that gets scarcer as the day wears on and there is growing time pressure to finish the job before the end of day," Ted said.

"Assume no such elaborate economic justification. Just Jesus saying, 'I love you all equally, no matter how late in the game you come to me.' It's kind of like that. We all get what we get. It's just the way the world works."

Ted stared at Mark, remembering with a smile the time he'd tried to cite Jesus to Thaddeus. In fourth or fifth grade he'd been bullied for being the teacher's pet. One kid had wanted to fight him to show off his Tae Kwon Do, but Ted had refused. He told his father, "Jesus said to turn the other cheek."

"Jesus is dead," his father had said. As he remembered that now, he was both amused by his father's audacity and appalled by his assumption that a son would appreciate the sarcasm of a jaded adult. Before Ted could deliver his retort, Mark said, "As the Buddha says, 'Be happy for your good fortune.'"

Mark had him there. Money or no, he loved Peace & Joy, the peace and quiet, the landscape, the night sky, the community meals, his fellow artists and especially, Harmony.

"I am," he said.

Harmony was at the kitchen table when Ted brought the carrots into the house, legal size papers spread out in front of her. It reminded him of how Stone used to write his high school term papers: a dozen books open on the dining room table, a half-dozen piles of photocopies, and three legal pads going at once. Even if students had not been expected to have an original thought (or even an original synthesis), they *had* been expected to have thoroughly researched the assigned topic. Stone had nearly drowned in facts and theories. Ted had found it easier to make up a theory — sometimes, even, to stumble upon an original one — and then forage for those facts that supported it. Stone's method was conventional and succeeded with his teachers. Ted's, of course, earned disproportionate praise as "truly exceptional," when, in fact, Ted understood he could just as easily have been accused of laziness.

If Stone's method marked him as a lawyer, always distinguishing this from that, right from wrong, case from case, Ted's had marked him as an imaginative writer of fiction. Now, Harmony's role was to demand from him the precision in language and detail that came naturally to him, a process that would be hard labor for Stone.

"What are you doing?" Ted asked. Usually, Harmony edited in the privacy of her upstairs quarters.

"Paperwork," Harmony answered. She draped her arms across the papers.

Ted opened the refrigerator. "Tea?"

"Green," she said. "Thank you." She added, "Whoever's cooking tonight will be happy to see those carrots. First of the season." Ted brought mugs of tea to the table.

"Stone left?" she asked. "Without saying goodbye?"

"My fault," Ted said, embarrassed. "I guess I rushed him. I didn't mean to, but ..."

"You probably did," she said. "Mean to, I mean. Sometimes distance works."

"Well, we were getting along well, so I decided we shouldn't push our luck. He appreciated the tour of the house. I'm sure he'll want to come back and see the rest of it."

"Good," she said. "I think brothers should be close. It takes work, of course."

Ted gestured between them. "Not us," he said.

"Time, then," she smiled, sending him a kiss. "Shared experiences, even if it's only a day or a walk or a meal."

"I'm glad you liked him," Ted said, aware that he was fishing and she'd know that he was, but he wanted her to say that while she liked

Stone, she liked him better. He'd be lying if he didn't admit that in between her well-intentioned but not inaccurate criticism of his work, he could use a little more appreciation and praise.

He put a mug of tea on the table and stood over her, curious about the papers strewn on the table. "For a stuffed shirt," she smirked, "he's not bad."

"I never said he was," Ted said.

"No, you didn't. But you know I have an inherent distrust of the rich and famous."

"Because your family …" Ted had heard this all before.

"Was rich and famous, once upon a time. Not being famous enough killed my father, and not being rich enough annoyed the hell out of my aunt and uncle, who never got over the shock of it, even after eating into half my trust funds." Resentment leached through her usual serenity. Only rarely did Ted detect a glimpse of jealousy in her, but now he noted an undercurrent of envy. Something to think about next time he tried to take exception to one of her comments.

Buoyed by Mark's remark about the Buddha, Ted said. "You're doing fine. We're doing fine. Just the way we are." He put his hand on her shoulder.

"We are," she said, taking her arms off the papers. "But we could be doing a little better." Ted pressed on her shoulder, as if to say there was no need to. Her voice became a whisper. "I've — we've — been given an offer on the river parcel."

"It's not for sale," he said, removing his hand and sitting down across from her. Harmony and Ted jointly owned a couple-hundred-acre tract on the Potato River. Harmony had inherited it — a largely useless parcel, though pretty enough. After they'd known each other a year, Ted had bought half of it with the last of his savings after the Airstream, allowing them to make his cash available for Peace & Joy while keeping the land "in the family."

"Not a sale. That's the beauty of it," she said. Her cheeks flushed pink.

"It would be a ten-year lease," she said.

"What can you do with a ten-year lease?" he asked. He couldn't imagine much. A golf range, maybe. Small game preserve perhaps, for hunting innocent quail and ducks. Terrible idea. A rifle range for disaffected paramilitary groups? Unthinkable.

"Mine copper." She bit her lip, then continued. "The company says they can open-pit mine it for ten years, take out a couple hundred thousand tons of fairly high-grade copper, maybe even some gold." Her voice rose with excitement, then leveled off. "And, they can restore the land to its original condition as soon as the mine is closed."

"I'll bet," he said, folding his arms across his chest.

"They promise to meet all federal and state rules and regulations," she said, reading from one of the papers.

"Good for them," Ted said. He finished his tea and took his glass to the sink. He decided to wash the carrots. The running water made it more difficult to have a conversation, but he didn't think there was much to discuss.

"Come here, dear, and talk to me," she commanded. "This is serious."

Reluctantly, Ted left the carrots in a colander, wiped his hands on a checkered dish cloth and slid onto the bench next to her. He saw "Good Earth Mining, Inc." in a bold, modern typeface at the top of the papers.

"Good God, how can they say that? By definition, they can't restore the land to its '*original* condition.'" Ted said.

"They have pictures to prove it," she said, reaching for an eight by ten glossy of a prairie surrounded by woods, looking as pristine as their own parcel.

"Why would you want me to even consider this?"

"It would be good for the community," she said. "It will create jobs." Her tone didn't invite questioning. How many jobs? What kind? Paying how much? For how long?

"We aren't required to be the economic engine of this town. You don't even know if these people want jobs, or these *kinds* of jobs," he said.

"Look around, dear." Two "dears" in one conversation betrayed her pique. "These people live in very modest homes, to say the least, and many of them spend the majority of their time hunting, fishing and recovering from hangovers."

"Aren't we judgmental today," he teased.

"I'm saying we could offer an alternative," she said, her voice firm.

"Not my mission," he said. "I happen to like my modest home. My simple life." He put his arm around her shoulder.

She shook him loose. "Of course you do," she said with an undisguised smirk.

"I contribute," he said stubbornly. "I work the market. The pumpkins. An odd job here and there, editing some grad student's manuscript. I make enough."

"Maybe once a year," she scoffed. He held his tongue; Harmony had a small trust fund, but otherwise she wasn't any more economically productive than he was.

"Whenever I can," he said. "Besides, I helped generate the income for this place when I bought half the parcel. You never said you wanted to develop it."

"I didn't, then. Now, I'm thinking that it could generate funds to restore the house and help make Peace & Joy independent. I could support *all* the artists who live here." He wanted to correct her, to say she should use the collective first-person pronoun. But then she would be all over him for his blatant egotism — challenging hers was off the larger point. He let her continue. "Free them of material concerns. So their priority can be creativity, self-expression, and art." She spoke slowly building a case with all the spiritual buzzwords that drew people to Peace & Joy.

"Not going to happen," he said, removing his arm and folding his hands on the table.

"You'd try to stop me?" she asked, her voice studied, as if truly curious.

All the morning meditations couldn't help him now. He felt his heart pounding. "I would," he said, his voice rising.

"You don't control me," she threatened, her chin rising as she glared at him.

"I would do whatever it takes," he said. He squeezed his hands together so hard he winced. "I'd sue you or them or whoever I had to in order to stop you from raping the land." He knew his language was incendiary, but so was her proposal.

"Your brother won't help you," she spat.

"Of course he would. He loves causes, especially ones with head-lines."

"Causes, not you," she said. She sounded nasty and determined. "I had to dangle the house in front of him just to get him up here."

Ted didn't understand what she was saying. "He came to see me," he said. "He had no idea about the house."

"He came because I asked him to."

He was stunned. He flexed his fists. "When?" he asked, as if he could coldly collect the facts like a lawyer and then respond. His whole body felt flushed with adrenaline.

"I sent a letter a few weeks ago, explaining what Peace & Joy is all about and how much you mean to us."

In a flash, Ted saw the whole picture. "You asked him for money?" He was incredulous.

"You don't control what I do or don't do," she smiled. He'd not known her ever to be so bitchy, so headstrong. This new role as a conniver was unnerving.

"How much did you ask for?"

"I don't remember," she said. It must've been a lot for her to lie to him like this. Of course she remembered. He didn't care whether Stone had said yes or no. What he cared about was her asking Stone in the first place. No wonder Stone had seemed so mellow, almost delicate. Stone had been embarrassed for him.

"Let me see the letter," he said.

"I didn't keep a copy," she said, her tone defensive. "I don't need your permission to ask rich people to support the arts."

"Common courtesy," he said. "Ordinary respect and decency."

He didn't think he could control his temper much longer. When she didn't respond, he said, "I'm going for a walk," and left the kitchen without looking at her. Once outside, he realized he didn't want to walk, he wanted to drive. Fast. Far.

How could she? His life partner going behind his back to ask for money, not for art's sake — such BS — but for him, for the artists, and for *herself.*

Harmony was kidding herself if she thought the writers came to Peace & Joy because of her. He was the only published writer among them and had a small but loyal following. The only reason he hadn't published more books was because of her. She didn't want him to compromise his standards. But they certainly didn't need his brother's money.

Without thinking about it, he grabbed a duffle from the bottom of his closet, threw in two tees, two shirts, another pair of jeans and some underwear and grabbed his keys. He suddenly realized that he was leaving. Going away. Just to drive, to be gone for a while so he could cool off. Not striking back, but not turning the other cheek, either.

It was mid-afternoon when he started his vintage Honda — two hundred thousand miles and still going strong. He turned onto the road away from Peace & Joy. He hit 65 mph on the two-lane road out of Upson. No traffic, let alone police. As soon as he came to a gas station, he stopped to fill his tank, clean his windshield, and buy a bottle of iced tea and a bag of popcorn. He sat behind the wheel for a minute and stared at the map. He recognized the name of a town that had been the site of picketing by UW students the first year he'd taught at Madison. Something about a mine and Native Americans. He hadn't paid much attention at the time: so many causes, so much rhetoric, so many demands on his time. His last year at Madison, another group of students picketed the mine again, after it had been supposedly reclaimed. Something then about Sacred Water and possible contamination. The town was only a couple of hours away. He decided to go see for himself.

How dare she.

8

He wanted to drive for hours into the dark night, but after he saw his first "no occupancy" sign, he began to worry. He wasn't fond of those roadside motels in the North Woods that were considered rustic or charming because they consisted of separate, micro-sized cottages, each half the size of his trailer. In the summer, he felt like he was living in nature in the Airstream He spent most of his time out of doors and kept the windows open at night. Despite what he'd told Stone, the Airstream in winter would feel cramped if he didn't have the house to go to. No use worrying about that now. Besides, if he was telling the truth — and why not, alone in a jalopy barreling down a two-lane state highway in North Central Wisconsin? — the house was painfully cluttered. For someone who claimed to crave serenity, calm and quiet, the *objets d'arte* scattered around the parlors bombarded his senses with their loud colors, twisted angles and wacko creativity. He got a kick out of some of the pieces Harmony chose for display, especially the parodies, like "This is a Piece of Cheese," but some, like the Mr. Potato Head Royal Family, were just plain silly, what he called "faux original," trying much too hard to be different, but without an aesthetic point. Sometimes, he wasn't sure how much of Harmony's collection reflected her desire to support the arts and how much was a material and loopy acquisitiveness that she simply couldn't shake. If her aunt and uncle hadn't raided her trust funds, she would've had plenty of money for her expensive tastes *and* her philanthropy.

She could be a story all by herself. Not that he would ever do such a thing. Too much an invasion not only of her privacy, but of his own. Besides, she was a mystery to him. Most people, in one way or another, were enigmas to themselves and others, but to try to commit such a character to the page would be to try to solve a mystery not meant to be solved. Part of their dynamic was that he knew he was, like all artists, a mystery to her as well. And to solve that mystery would ruin a relationship that somehow worked despite their separate secrets. Plus, he would have to exaggerate her flaws to make a successful novel out of her, and that would come with its own peril. He'd destroy their common trust and understanding of each person.

At 9:30 p.m. he stopped when he came to a Best Western two-story motel that he assumed would have normal-sized rooms, wi-fi and a decent TV. His guilty pleasure was watching reruns of the old *Law and Order* television shows; he only got to see them once or twice a week if, for some reason, Harmony was out of the house. He checked in and was given a first-floor room with two queen size beds, neither of which would've fit in his Airstream. He flipped through the channels and found an au pair claiming innocence for the poisoning of the infant in her care. He'd seen it before, but that never mattered — he was drawn to Detective Lennie Briscoe's wry sense of humor: "There's one British nanny who won't be singing Chim Cher-ee." He laughed, unbuckled his sandals and flopped on the bed furthest from the window. He hadn't had dinner, and realized he wasn't anywhere near a place that had a restaurant open past nine, so he went down the hall to the snack machines. They only had a few Snickers and Twizzlers. He bought one of each, and two of the better-stocked granola bars. Ted took his bounty to his room. He took out his laptop, logged on to the wi-fi and Googled the mine, surprised at the number of hits. He'd overshot the town by maybe fifty miles. No big deal. He'd be up early and enjoy the morning drive.

The mining company's official site was headlined, "Promises Made and Promises Kept." It touted the hiking, horse and nature trails on a reclaimed site, the millions of dollars in taxes paid to local communities and the guaranteed safety of local wells. They described their responsibility for the land as being "in perpetuity," a concept that baffled him. Whoever made that promise could not live long enough to keep it.

Photographs showed the park in bloom. There was a list of birds that could be observed, from the common (coots, crows, doves and robins) to the exotic (bobolinks, pie-billed grebes, green heron and scarlet tanagers). The writer in him especially appreciated the list of butterflies: "Sooty Skipper," "Tiger Swallow Tail," "Painted Lady" and "White Cabbage."

While putting a beautiful face on the reclaimed mine, the site didn't seem to oversell itself, if the pictures could be trusted. The official site also linked to the Wisconsin Department of Natural Resources, where the agency instructed consumers on how to access government documents and reports concerning the mine. There was even a link for citizens who wanted to have their own properties assayed for mineral content.

Of course, the most interesting sites were the ones developed by the local activists, easily identified by titles that included words like "Exposed," "The Truth" and "Myth." The sites described all the legal actions locals had taken to try to stop the mine in the first place and their demands for a moratorium on all metal mining in Wisconsin. He was flooded with technical information and claims of newly discovered ground water contamination that he had no way to evaluate.

Wearily, he clicked on one more site and read a long, impassioned essay by a Native American about "Sacred Water." It said, "We do not own the freshness of the air or the sparkle of the water." He paused at the word "sparkle." The first time he flew into the Virgin Islands and saw the translucent blue of the Caribbean, his eyes had watered. He'd turned away from Stone and faked a sneeze.

It was not right to facilitate the possibility of ground water pollution. Surely Harmony would see that!

As he logged off the computer his cellphone rang. It was Harmony. Feeling self-righteous, he let it ring until it kicked into voice mail. He immediately felt childish for not having answered. Of course she'd be worried about him, but she should've worried about his reaction before she'd hit up Stone for money. He was too tired to get into it again. He took off his jeans and crawled into bed, tossing three extra pillows to the floor and telling himself he'd call her in the morning.

The free breakfast at the motel was surprisingly good. They offered his usual fresh fruit, oatmeal and yogurt, but the sweet smell of fresh waffles tantalized him, so he followed the posted directions and poured batter into the waiting iron. He glanced at the morning

TV news but turned away at the sight of devastating tornadoes in Oklahoma, where a whole block of homes had been splintered to toothpicks, while neighboring homes remained perfectly intact. Random destruction. Reconstruction, not restoration. Of course there were causes more important, more appealing and more sympathetic than restoring an old mansion in the North Woods. Mark was right, in a way. If you choose art as a profession, you can't bank on comfort. Ted was fairly content with the choice he'd made. Harmony had made hers a long time ago. Why couldn't she still live with it?

He pocketed an apple for the drive to the mine. Before returning his key at the front desk, he checked the time and guessed that Harmony would still be in group meditation. He sat on the edge of the bed and dialed her number. He was relieved when it went to voicemail. "Hi, it's me," he managed. "I'm fine. Hope you are too. I'm sorry I ran out." He knew he'd get an earful when he got back, but better to get it in person than from a disembodied voice. "You know I hate conflict. I'll probably be back tonight or tomorrow, and you can yell at me then. OK. Love ya."

He imagined there wouldn't be much left to yell about regarding the mine. If Harmony asked anyone's advice at Peace & Joy, they'd probably give her a knee-jerk "no." After today, he would have to listen to her push-back, but he would have facts at hand and then Harmony would see the light. He was sure of it.

The bigger issue would be her breach of his trust. No matter how innocent or well-intentioned her letter, she'd humiliated him in front of his brother. That couldn't be undone, only forgiven. He would have to reach deep. In due course, he supposed he would.

It was a lovely summer day, clear and promising, in the low eighties. The drive was easy and peaceful. He followed the directions on his phone to the reclaimed mine, now labeled a park. There was a gravel lot for thirty cars. He parked his car next to a pickup and an old VW bus and read the welcome sign that duplicated the brief, one-sided history of the site he already knew. The map of the nature trails showed three loops: a half-mile, a mile and two and a half miles. He had plenty of time for the longer walk; his sandals were sturdy, designed for dirt trails and stints in the garden. Twenty yards in, the trail curled right, to a wetlands area with an informative sign and a weathered wooden box of some gaudy brochures listing the bird species Ted had read about. Without the aid of binoculars, he spotted only geese and ducks, much like home. He walked on, alert for tell-tale signs of reclamation. If it weren't for the information signs, visitors would have no idea that tons of rock had been ripped out below them and subsequently replaced. The prairie grass was high, laced with black-eyed Susans, coneflowers, milkweed and clover. The grassy part of the park, covering the area where the pit had been, stretched for acres to dense woods. At the furthest point in the loop there was a wooden bench. He sat down, thinking he would meditate for a while. He focused his eyes mid-point just past his nose, but was distracted by a glimpse of a white horse a few hundred yards away, quietly grazing. With a jerk, the animal reared its head, its nose in the air. Too small a head for a horse. Skinny legs. No mane. A short stub of a white tail. No rider in sight. Ears tuned like antennae toward possible danger. Ted held his breath, motionless. A white deer! In a state overrun with deer, here was a white one. *Totally white.* He'd heard about them but had never seen one. Rare. Other-worldly. He dropped to his knees. In that moment he felt the wonder of discovery. Completely in harmony with the universe.

The white deer looked just like a brown deer but wasn't. The reclaimed pit looked just like it had but wasn't. A gene had changed, a rock disturbed. He'd heard that misfortune came to those who harmed a white deer. A sign.

Slowly he reached in his pocket and took out his phone. He pointed it in the direction of the deer and took a picture, then trotted the rest of the loop out of the park and back to his car. He had to tell Harmony. Right away.

• • •

The white deer haunted Ted's drive to Upson like a persistent ghost. Stands of fir trees lined both sides of the road with the tell-tale human precision of a public works project. Nature, abhorring a vacuum, would've filled the empty space with perfect chaos. Humans had chosen one single species, measured the distance between seedlings precisely, and laid out three rows, paralleling the twists and turns of the road.

Ted drove with his left foot hovering over the brake. At any moment, a deer could leap across the road. More than twenty thousand deer were killed every year on Wisconsin roads; it was possible that he would encounter one. What he imagined, however, was rare: a white deer safely in front of him, leading the way to Harmony's Peace & Joy.

Ted entered the drive to Harmony's and parked beside his Airstream. The place felt abandoned, the shed doors closed, no one in the gardens, no music coming from the house. Heather wasn't at her usual place at the picnic table near the Girls' cabin, scribbling her notes on the heartache of self-imposed solitude. She was too young, he thought, to spend so much time brooding. When totally herself, she was effervescent, outgoing, ready to party. Having been told repeatedly by writing teachers that she needed to "go deeper," she'd adopted a "serious writer" persona that falsely promised depth. She needed more experience of the world, Ted thought, to mine her own depths.

He'd just experienced the poetry of a white deer; his writing was fueled by such experiences. It occurred to him that he now knew what "deeper" meant. Kids much younger than he were publishing, much like he'd done earlier in his life, and earning both literary praise and money for their efforts. He was confident his novels were at least as good as theirs, probably better, given his broader experience of the world. Maybe he could make up for denying the lease by publishing one or two of his books that were forever works-in-progress.

He took a deep breath and headed to the house. God, he hated conflict, but he was so excited about the white deer, he expected the issue of the mine to be quickly resolved.

There was remarkably little conflict in his relationship with Harmony. When Heather once asked if they ever fought, they'd replied "no" in unison. Nothing's that important. That was largely true. If he thought about it, there were very few areas of their lives where they even *faced* a potential conflict. They each decorated their own space, maintained their own cars and funds and managed their own relationships. They didn't have kids. If there were decisions to be made, they would be whether to entertain weekend guests together. In those cases, Ted almost always deferred to Harmony.

No wonder he was conflict adverse. He had so little experience, was so rarely criticized or corrected. When an editor suggested a change, he usually made it. He never understood how authors could be so sure that their editor was wrong. If a well-educated editor didn't understand his own authors' intentions, what hope was there for the average reader? Likewise, he'd believed that if Harmony, who clearly was better that the average reader, said he wasn't ready to publish a book, he wasn't ready.

But now, assuming he forgave her about her overture to Stone, there would be two conflicts: the lease and the publication of his book. It had occurred to him that he could make up for not signing the lease by selling *Absolutus Amor,* perhaps under a pen name if that would satisfy Harmony's concerns. Of all his manuscripts, that one — with its comedic romantic plot — had the most screenplay potential. He wouldn't earn much up front on either the book or the movie option, but it was a down payment, and maybe he'd get lucky. Or the notoriety might reboot his teaching career. And then there'd be the others, the books he cared the most about: *Where We Started; My Sister, Bob; Mrs. Satan.* All big and important tomes. Timely. The kind of thing he'd like to be known for, if he were going to be known at all.

The house door opened when he was halfway up the stairs. He paused. Harmony, in a rose and cream print sundress, sunglasses perched on top of her head, stepped out, then froze. She looked frightened. He hurried to her. He held out his arms, but she didn't move. "I'm sorry," he said, letting his arms fall to his side. "I'm sorry."

"You have no idea," she said, her voice cracking. Her eyes were puffy, but when she flipped down her sunglasses, she was beautiful.

"I," he began. To satisfy her, he knew his apology must be complete. "I panicked. I didn't want to fight with you. I should've stayed. Or at least told you where I was going." He thought to add, 'I should've answered the phone,' but he decided not to admit to it. He was in enough trouble as it was.

"Then you'll sign?" she asked. Tough. He'd not prepared himself for that. He thought they'd talk some more, that he would tell her about his trip, and she'd come around. She sounded as if signing was a condition for her forgiveness.

"I saw a white deer," he said. He nodded toward the fountain across the yard and sat on the edge of it. She followed, silent, unsmiling. "Look," he said, and showed her the picture. He was disappointed that in the camera's long perspective, the deer appeared as a white smudge against a curtain of green, not like the glowing, sacred symbol he'd seen.

Harmony didn't react. He'd experienced the full force of her "silent" soul only once before, three years ago, when she'd bought the alternate fuel Mercedes. As he recalled, he'd made an offhand remark about the extravagance in front of Mark and David, and she'd taken offense. He hadn't meant to criticize her, although he'd been surprised by her choice. In his view, alternate fuel did not cancel the blaring and inescapable ostentation of the Benz. Harmony didn't drive a car often enough for comfort or safety to be the motivating factors she claimed they had been. He didn't remember exactly how that issue had been resolved — she still owned the car — but he did recall that in about a week, they'd been back to "normal." In effect, they had agreed to disagree. Her funds, her choice, her responsibility, her conscience. His censure an admitted flaw, to be put aside in favor of community serenity.

This would be trickier — their investment joint, their responsibility for the land mutual.

"A white deer," he said again. "I went to see a reclaimed mine, and while I was there, a white deer appeared."

She turned to face him, curious. Ted explained how he'd first heard about the mine and the ongoing controversy and admitted that indeed the reclamation had been natural and compelling. He concluded, "So, you see, surface reclamation isn't the issue so much as the unavoidable potential disturbance of the Sacred Water."

The corners of her lips turned up. "Sacred?" she said, her tone accusatory, as if the word "sacred" was foreign to him.

"Sacred to our Native American brothers and sisters," he said, repeating what he'd read. "Wouldn't you agree the white deer is a symbol of that sacredness?" He knew it wasn't common knowledge, but still, he thought that she might know, since she was the local "guru."

"It was a white deer," she said. "It's only a symbol if you want it to be one."

"But it appeared for a reason, don't you think?" Of course she did. She was the one who preached synchronicity and being both "awake" and "aware" and in spiritual touch with the universe.

"Maybe it was a symbol of the purity of the reclamation," she said. He thought he might argue that the white deer was the mutant result of toxins on other lands, but he didn't know that for sure and he felt certain that Harmony would be most easily moved by the spiritual angle. "They say misfortune comes to those who harm the white deer," he answered.

"I think the Devil can cite scripture," she said.

He hadn't thought there was any other interpretation of the symbol and he'd never known her to be so unwilling to accept possible messages from the divine. "You're right about the Devil," he said tentatively. He saw a way toward a truce, to give her the time she apparently needed to consider the significance of the white deer. "I should meditate on this," he said. "We can talk about this tomorrow."

She looked at him, hopeful. He felt like Stone, attempting to negotiate an unnegotiable position. He would meditate, but there was little chance it would change his mind; his best hope was that it would change hers.

"You forgive me for running away?" he asked.

Harmony nodded and took his hand. "I was so frightened. I thought I'd lost you," she said. "I was afraid that once you got up the energy to leave, the momentum would keep you going."

"My budget got me as far as the Best Western," he said. "Where, by the way, I had five extra pillows." He kissed her on the forehead and in return, her lips brushed his cheek.

"Did you find a good organic restaurant out there?" she asked.

He rubbed his stomach. "Do granola bars count?" he asked.

"Come," she said, heading back to the house. "Follow me."

"Anywhere," he said.

9

When Stone had returned to the trailer after his tour, Ted was sitting at his table, a small black notebook open flat before him, a pencil between his teeth. He closed the book, fastening it with an elastic band, and let the pencil drop.

"Writing?" Stone asked, although the answer was obvious. "I don't want to interrupt."

"Musing," Ted said.

"About what?" Stone asked.

"About writing," Ted smiled.

"Musing about writing?" Stone repeated, not sure he'd heard right.

"Call it pre-writing," Ted said.

"So do you fill one of those books every week or so?" Stone gathered his tee shirt, jams and dop kit from his bed and put them in his duffel.

"Uh, maybe every year?" Ted said. "I don't have that many noteworthy thoughts." He grinned. "I'm not a lawyer."

"Not fair," Stone said.

"Just fooling with you," Ted said.

Ted — just like their father — knew how to push his buttons. "Do the musings sometimes become novels?" he asked, as if only idly curious.

"Sometimes," Ted said.

"What's the big secret?" Stone asked. He was used to talking about his own work with his friends, most of whom were lawyers, and with his wife.

"Only secret is how mundane my little musings are," Ted said.

"There's plenty here to stir the imagination," Stone ventured. "Harmony, for one."

"Yes," Ted said, although they hadn't agreed on exactly *how* she might stir the imagination. Stone was thinking she was quite good looking, but it would probably be politically incorrect to say so.

"Lucky man," Stone said. "I assume you ..."

"Yes," Ted said.

"So why don't you sleep up there?"

"I like it here," Ted answered, his tone clipped, cutting off any further inquiries and saving Stone from several unfortunate comments that crossed his mind. He could understand Ted not wanting to be perceived as a kept man, although he could do worse than to be kept by the likes of Harmony. He knew he wasn't going to get much more out of Ted on the subject of Harmony, and probably not on the subject of money, either. If Ted needed some support, Stone would, of course, provide it, but directly — not through his "keeper."

"You need anything?" Stone asked, sincerely concerned.

"Do I *look* like I need anything?" Ted shot back. He was dressed in what Stone understood to be his uniform: khakis and an open, long-sleeved flannel shirt over a matching-colored tee shirt. Today's color was green. Friday night it was purple. Stone had to admit, his brother didn't look like he needed anything. "No. No thank you." Ted tugged on his shirt. "As long as folks keep giving their old Brooks Brothers to the Goodwill, we'll be good."

Stone itched a spot near his collar bone. He couldn't imagine buying second-hand clothes, even for a costume party. A couple of years ago he had "needed" a flannel shirt for a barn-party fundraiser and he'd ordered one from L. L. Bean.

"It was good to see you, big brother," Ted said, getting up. He handed Stone a jar of honey with a handwritten label, "Peace & Joy Honey." "For Sydney," he said. "She should come with you next time." Wow, Stone thought, he's kicking me out.

"Thanks," Stone said. He'd been packing his things, but he'd thought they'd hang around for a while more, maybe get a look at the rest of the house. Yet, Ted was probably right; he should leave while all was good between them. Curiously, however, he felt somewhat let down. His brother really didn't need anything.

The drive home was so much easier than the way north — it was always that way when you know where you're going. Not having to pay strict attention to road signs and egg farms, Stone let his mind wander. Indeed, the folks at Harmony's seemed to be happy and easy-going, not particularly bothered by material concerns. There was lots of potential there — human as well as architectural, some of it explored, some of it not, but no one seemed dissatisfied with their apparent lack of productivity or their obvious under-achievement.

Four novels in a drawer! Stone knew he could be called compulsive: when he was given a new matter for a client or had the idea for a home project, like cleaning out the garage, it was torture until he got it done. "Getting it done" meant professional execution, measured by quantifiable standards: clients brought in, deals closed, hours and dollars billed. Or, a vastly improved, neat-appearing garage. If he'd had so much as an *idea* for a novel, he'd have a publisher — or at least an agent — lined up before he typed "Chapter One." Or at least he'd want it that way, not wasting his time trying to perfect hundreds of pages that ultimately would sit in a box in a drawer.

He came up on a bright green John Deere tractor chugging lazily ahead of him. A solid yellow line ran down the middle of the road. Glancing in his rearview mirror, he saw that he'd been holding up a parade of four or five cars. He must've been under the influence of Upson: it wasn't like him to be moseying at ten miles *below* the speed limit. Still, no one beeped. Didn't anyone up here have any place to go? Didn't anyone value their time?

What was wrong with Ted that he was so committed to *not* achieving his ordained success? Why had he given control to Harmony? Yes, she was an attractive woman and there was something mysterious about her that had great visceral appeal. But still!

Stone pictured Harmony floating across the lawn, posing on the grand staircase, leading her flock with a golden staff. He could see Ted was in love with Harmony, but that didn't make her the best person to judge his creative work. And who was she to proclaim that Ted's novels weren't ready? You'd think she would be frustrated that Ted wasn't producing publishable work. Maybe he was deliberately holding back. Maybe he just wasn't that talented. But if Ted the genius wasn't talented and successful, what did that make Stone? Never mind that. What bothered Stone the most was why he should care at all what his brother did with his talent or his life.

In a few minutes, the tractor turned off the road and Stone was soon back in familiar territory, five miles over the limit. Then a sign for McDonald's grabbed his attention and he turned off at the next exit. Cheeseburger, fries, vanilla milkshake. Sydney would be horrified, but Stone was tired of being "good," especially according to someone else's nutritional commandments.

When he got back in the car, he found a box of small breath mints in the glove compartment. What Sydney didn't know wouldn't hurt her.

Still, he hoped she would be home when he got there and pictured her kneeling on a cushion in her garden, gloved and dead heading the snapdragons and marigolds. Should he tell her about Ted's unpublished novels?

They had few secrets. He didn't tell her absolutely everything — now, for instance, he would downplay the sparkle in Harmony's citrine green eyes. He told her most things, unless there was a really good reason not to. There had been that time when, after too many drinks, the CEO and CFO of a small company in Missouri wanted to celebrate its merger with Stone's client by insisting they all go to a gentlemen's club. Much to the amusement of his clients and the Missourians, it had cost him a twenty, tucked carefully into her G-string, to get that blond off his lap. Had he confessed, he was certain he would hear about it for days, if not months. Sydney didn't need to know about Harmony's physical appeal.

As he got closer to home, his excitement about Ted's novels faded. If Harmony was right and they *were* unpublishable, Ted would be embarrassed. Stone had taken the thumb drives, impulsively, because he thought that he might save them from obscurity. Now he felt like he'd done something terribly wrong. But really, all he'd done was make a copy of some files, which he could easily delete at any time. He wasn't sure what had gotten into him, but if he deleted the files unread, then no harm, no foul. This was his go-to advice when his clients were in a technical legal jam, when the client was right but wrong — or wrong, but not so wrong that they'd done any tangible harm.

He beeped the horn when he pulled into the driveway. Sydney stood up to greet him, a hand trowel in one hand and in the other a cultivator that looked like a three-fingered claw. Her hair was drawn back in a ponytail. A visor shaded her face, and her gray tee shirt sprouted a variety of silk-screened herbs, but little actual dirt.

"Place looks nice," he said.

She pursed her lips for a routine kiss and he obliged.

"Tell me!" she said, banging the tools together. "How's Ted? What's going on up there?"

"He's good," Stone said.

"What about Harmony? Is she nuts or what?"

"Probably. But she's got Ted wrapped around her little finger, and for someone living in a trailer, he seems pretty happy."

"In a trailer park?" Whatever bucolic image she'd had of Harmony's Peace & Joy obviously had been shattered.

"No, an Airstream on Harmony's property. Pretty nice, actually."

"Well, good for him," she said. "He deserves it."

"I don't know exactly what he's done to deserve it," he said. "Seems to me he's been living off the fat of the land for some time." He bent down and picked a half-dead marigold bloom that she'd missed.

Suggesting he was being catty, she clawed the air with her cultivator, mouthing a sound like that of fingernails scratching against an invisible chalkboard. "So it's luxurious up there?" she asked with disarming sarcasm. "I always had the impression it was more primitive."

She was right, of course. He didn't know why he was being so testy. What was there at Harmony's to be envied or desired? Peace and quiet? Lack of pressure? Only if you lacked ambition and didn't want more than a simple life at the end of a dirt road. "You have to like zucchini," he said as he reached into the back seat of his car for his duffel and computer bag.

"So, is he writing?" she asked.

"I guess so," he said and slammed the car door shut.

"You didn't ask?" she said.

"He said nothing was quite ready yet." Stone hoped she'd drop the subject. Copying the files had been wrong, but he didn't intend to confess his crime. Either his genius brother was burying a Pulitzer-prize winning novel for no good reason or he'd failed to produce any publishable work at all. Either way, it really wasn't Stone's business.

"I can't believe that," she said. "He's been there ten years. You didn't push him?"

"I tried," he said.

He dropped his duffle in the kitchen as she washed up at the sink. "He gave me this for you," he said, holding out the jar of honey.

"How sweet," she said, studying the label. Then she looked up. "I could make you a sandwich," she offered.

"I had a little something on the road. How about some iced tea?"

She put a tall glass in front of him. "*I* should've been there. *I* would have held his feet to the fire. *I* would've gotten the truth. I'm probably the only one not cowed by the Hunnicutts."

"I'm not cowed," he said, but he remembered the first time she'd gone home with him, after they were married. She'd brought a fruit basket as a house gift, because Stone had said his father loved his morning grapefruit. Stone had warned her that his father could be persnickety.

When she prepared the Sunday morning fruit, Thaddeus said flat-out, "Stupid! That's not right at all." She'd cut around the rind to make the sections easier to remove, but the old man had tossed the fruit, uneaten, in the trash, saying she'd been careless. Stone should've stood up to his father right then, but he'd never been good at that. Without conceding the insult, Sydney calmly asked her father-in-law to show how he wanted the grapefruit prepared. The man spent ten silent minutes, using a paring knife, to cut each section individually, leaving the membrane intact. When he was finished, she inspected the grapefruit with exaggerated care and then said, so very sweetly, "You're right sir; any idiot could do that."

She'd made standing up to Thaddeus Newton look embarrassingly easy, but that was Sydney: not the type to be cowed at all.

"You and Harmony," Stone said.

"Me and Harmony what?"

"Show no surrender," he said, "*She's* the one who says his novels aren't ready."

"And we believe her why?" Sydney asked.

"I don't know," he said. He felt himself wavering. He wanted Sydney to know he wasn't intimidated by Harmony.

"We'll have to decide for ourselves." He got up and brought his computer bag to the table.

She stared.

"You of all people should know, I don't take 'no' for an answer." She still didn't seem to get it. "I found four manuscripts," he said. "I only had time to copy three."

Her eyes opened wide, cartoonish. "You *stole* them?"

"No. I said I *copied* them." He lifted his chin.

"Theft!" she declared. "Theft of intellectual property." She really sounded shocked.

"Not theft. He still has possession." She didn't look satisfied, and he squirmed. "Maybe a little like invasion of privacy," he said. He knew she was right and regretted that he'd told her what he'd done. Now he was forced to defend himself. "But there isn't any privacy between brothers."

"It's like reading someone's diary," she insisted.

"Siblings do it all the time," he said, waving her off.

"*I* wouldn't do such a thing," she said.

Of course, Sydney couldn't understand. "You didn't have a sister," he reminded her. Just because he'd shared a family, daily experiences and a room with his brother didn't mean he had a clue as to what Ted was thinking. If Ted didn't talk about important things, how was Stone to know?

She scowled. "What were you thinking?" she said, as if addressing a wayward child.

"I wasn't thinking," he said. "It was spontaneous."

"Spontaneous? When's the last time you did something spontaneous?" Her laugh was a cackle, an accusation of sorts.

"You're the one who plans everything out, who has to be in control," he said.

She glared at him. "I like spontaneity. I love surprises!" she said. "But you ..."

"How can you say that?" he asked. They'd strayed far from the original topic.

They were married *because* he'd been spontaneous. They'd been dancing at a Legal Aid fundraiser, an all-night dance-a-thon at

Harvard and he'd asked if she was tired and wanted to stop. She said, "I could dance with you forever," and he'd said—spontaneously—"Will you?" She jumped into his arms, and he held her up for just a second and then everyone was dancing around them, congratulating them. Yes, he was plenty spontaneous.

"Going up there was spontaneous," he said.

"Kind of a command performance, wasn't it?" she said, her eyebrows scrunched skeptically over a crooked smile. "This Harmony person suggests Ted needs help and you jump in to save him. Big hero. Can't even wait for me to go with you."

Really? She'd practically told him to go alone so she could go shopping in Chicago with their daughter. He'd taken her at her word. "So I shouldn't try to help him?"

"I can't say anything," she said. "What happened up there? Did he catch you stealing his work?"

"I didn't steal it." He rattled his ice cubes. He wished he'd kept his mouth shut.

She shrugged. "So, he doesn't know." She sounded conciliatory. "Well, are they good?'

"I haven't read them. I read a few pages of *Absolutus Amor.*" At the mention of the title, Sydney broke into a toothy grin, as if at some private joke. Stone continued, "But just enough to get interested in the characters and see that I wanted to read more."

"Yes, that's what a good opening does," she said.

"But of course I can't read them. You're right. It's technically an invasion of a person's privacy, even if the person is your brother." He lifted his iced tea to his lips.

"Oh, it's more than technical, but perhaps not as terrible as it could have been," she said.

He put his glass down. "You changed your mind?" he asked, both aghast and hopeful.

"I don't see the great harm," she said quietly, her eyes darting around the room as if afraid someone might be there, recording their conversation.

"Until he finds out," he said.

"He won't."

"If he does?" he asked.

"We'll deal with it. Maybe he'll punch you out," she laughed. "Or you'll convince him to publish them, they'll make a movie or two and he'll make a lot of money."

"That's what I was thinking originally!" Stone said. "When I was being spontaneous." She rolled her eyes. "So they can fix up Harmony's house," she teased.

"If I read the *Amor* thing, will you?"

"We'll see," she said.

"It's probably about you anyway," he said.

"Me?" she said, as if surprised. "I didn't even get a cameo in the first one."

"Then you're due," he said. Ted had admitted that the first novel, *Pater Noster*, had been a roman à clef. Stone thought Ted had drawn on Sydney for the lovely dead wife in that story, but obviously neither she nor their father had recognized themselves in the characters. Perhaps Ted had saved Sydney for this novel, and maybe that was why Harmony didn't deem it ready for publication. Perhaps she was jealous. Insecure. It would explain a lot.

"I'd have to kill him," she teased. "Besides: your crime, your time."

He hesitated. "You know it's not right," he said. He was dying to read *Absolutus Amor*. She probably was, too. At the very least, he might be able to understand why Ted deferred so easily to Harmony about not submitting the novel for publication.

"He'd never believe you took them and didn't read them." She took his plate to the sink. "We won't call it wrong. We'll call it spontaneous."

10

"Rise and shine!" Sydney said, waking him in his recliner where he'd fallen asleep. She handed him a cup of coffee, her expression expectant. Her hair was brushed out full and her breath smelled of mint. She was such a morning person, from dead asleep to full throttle in ten seconds. He needed more like forty-five minutes to become fully conscious.

Sydney pointed to the manuscript on the end table next to him. "That good or that bad?" she asked.

"It's really good," he said. "Beautifully written. You know how he is."

"What's it about?" she asked.

"Complicated. Well, not *complicated* so much as *complex*."

"Yes, but what's it about?" she asked again, the way a teacher might prompt a student who was having trouble organizing his thoughts.

"It's about ..." The plot wasn't complicated. "It's about two brothers who are secretly in love with the same woman," he said.

"Autobiographical then," she said, obviously pleased.

"No, not at all," he said. He wasn't as egotistical as the younger brother in the novel and not as weak as the older one.

"You're not in it," he said. Stone was relieved. He wanted to believe that second novels were more mature: the author, presumably having used up all the good stuff on his first, would be forced to be wholly creative.

"How do you know?"

"The woman is brilliant, drop-dead gorgeous, kind of ethereal...." Her morning energy wilted abruptly. Immediately he knew he'd made a huge mistake. He didn't mean it the way it sounded. Sydney's eyes were wide. He didn't think she was the type to cry over such a thing — fiction, for goodness' sake! — but she stood now in her courtroom pose: arms at her sides, posture yoga-perfect, jaw set against the impending verdict. "I mean," he started to correct himself, but Sydney looked away. Stone could see she had decided not to acknowledge any cause for insult, and he should do so as well.

"Does she know they're fighting over her?" she asked.

"They're not actually fighting," he said, thinking that in fact he'd never considered pursuing Sydney when she was at Madison. When he was in his first year at Harvard and getting used to the gravitas of it all, she was back in Madison, dating Ted. At the time, she seemed to him somewhat flighty, too much of a free spirit.

"Are the brothers polar opposites?" she asked.

"No, I wouldn't say that," he said. He'd already made one mistake in describing the characters. If it turned out Sydney liked the younger brother in the book better than the older one, he wanted to be that one. "More like two guys in the middle facing slightly different directions."

"So, very different," she said, as if she knew. "Even if they start with a one-degree difference, the further they walk, the greater the distance between them."

He didn't know why he was so annoyed. "Well, in the book they are more or less standing next to each other and both are looking at the same woman, so their paths are bound to collide."

"And she has to choose," she said.

"Everybody has to choose," he said. "What they want. How much to fight for what they want."

"Sounds a little melodramatic for brother Ted," she said. "I bet Miss Perfect chooses the bad boy."

"Who said one of them is a 'bad boy'?" he asked.

"Wouldn't be much fun if one wasn't wild and totally bad for her and the other was a nerdy, overly responsible, ideal husband type."

She was getting some revenge for his description of the heroine. "Nerdy?"

She shrugged. "You said it was fiction, didn't you?" she said.

"You'll have to read it," he said.

• • •

At work, Stone found it difficult to focus, still preoccupied with Ted's novel and its subject matter, but also the very fact of its existence — a highly entertaining, insightful and marketable product, one that his clients would call a non-performing asset. Stuffed in a drawer, with no apparent future, no purpose, no monetary value to a man with no money to speak of. As the older brother, didn't Stone owe Ted something? Encouragement and a safety-net, of course, but what about business advice or a financial plan? On the other hand, what did Stone know of the publishing business that Ted didn't know himself? The problem was diverting his attention from his own work.

He called Sydney, hoping she could meet him for lunch. She answered after six rings; usually her admin would've picked up after three. "Hope I didn't interrupt something," he said.

"I'm on my cell," she said. She must've forwarded her office phone.

There was a fair amount of background noise. "In court?" he asked, although he knew she wouldn't have answered if she were.

"No," she said. "What's up?"

She said she'd have to move some things around but agreed to meet him at a new French bistro across town from her office, a cab-ride away from his. He figured she must not be having a very busy day.

She was almost ten minutes late, but full of energy when she arrived, smelling fresh, as if she had just come out of the shower. He felt buoyed by her good spirits — see, he told himself, it pays to be spontaneous. They found a wooden booth at the window.

Stone scoured the menu. The word "organic" appeared eighteen times, describing everything from bread to lemonade, as well as granola, brown rice, butter, walnuts, bananas, "chia seed pudding" (whatever that was) and eggs from "happy hens." Stone looked around and felt twenty years too young for the place.

"No *pommes frites*?" he asked, slightly let down that she'd chosen a place quite so in-your-face healthy.

"Sorry," Sydney said. "However, they do have cream puffs." He was surprised she would volunteer that. Of course, she wasn't as tempted as he was by all the foods that suddenly had become "bad" for him. Must be why she looked so healthy, her skin smooth and taut, her hair thick with a lively bounce to it.

"Then you're forgiven," he said. She certainly looked younger than he did; with a starched white shirt open at the neck and a simple gold chain necklace, she looked younger now than she had even that morning. They ordered a turkey and brie sandwich for him and a chicken and walnut salad for her.

"This place was voted the best new Madison bistro," Sydney said. She tucked her hair behind her ear.

"Of course it was," he said, offhand.

"Meaning?" she shot back.

"I know you love 'the best' is all," he said.

Sydney put her coffee cup down and searched his eyes until he looked away. "Not on *my* account," she said. "*You*. Your family. They're the ones obsessed with the 'best.'" She sounded more annoyed than he thought warranted by his comment.

"I wouldn't say obsessed," he said, although he thought it close to accurate. Why else wouldn't Ted publish another novel?

"You have to be obsessed to be the very best," she said. "No one gets to be recognized as the best without something in play — either effort or a gimmick, or a lucky break of some kind."

"Your 'best' tailor didn't believe in 'bests,'" Stone said. "He believed in the one customer in front of him."

"A good philosophy," Sydney said, "but not the Hunnicutt way. As I recall, the family motto was '*Citius. Altius. Fortius,*' just like the Olympics." She ran her hand through her hair and shook her head slightly.

"'Smarter,'" Stone said.

"Oh yes," she said with exaggerated precision. "I forgot. 'Faster. Higher. Stronger. Smarter.' But not '*Scitius,*' in case the general public is too stupid to know '*scitius*' means 'knowing' or 'smarter.'" She was getting worked up. He put his finger to his lips.

"Don't shush me," she said, louder than necessary.

"Sorry. I just wanted to say that that was my father's idea of humor," Stone said. "If you knew what *scitius* meant, you might be *scitius* yourself. I do realize he was obsessed," he added, "but he only wanted us to do our best."

"He wanted you to win," she said. Just then a busboy walked by in a black tee shirt with the motto, "Don't Panic. It's Organic."

"Ted was gold medal all the way," Stone said.

"You brought home your share of honors, too," she said, calmer now. She rested her elbows on the table and cupped her chin in her hands, framing her face. He didn't think he'd bragged that much over the years about school accomplishments, but maybe he had. It was nice of her to remember. She was her sparkling best today; much more like the love-object of Ted's novel than he'd suggested that morning.

"Most Improved. Sportsmanship," he muttered. "A for effort." Even to say it brought back some embarrassment, which he recognized now as smacking of resentment. Their father hadn't valued effort; he was much prouder of Ted's As, based solely on his smarts, than of Stone's, earned by hard work and enormous effort.

"That counts," she said.

"Not as much as winning," he said.

"Winning is overrated, honey. It can take the fun out of it. Some of us just like to play the game for our own satisfaction." Of course she'd understand Ted better; despite her Harvard education, she wasn't nearly as driven as Stone. He wondered if she would rather live like a hippie in a trailer than in a stately brick home with someone who had to work as hard as he did. Maybe, if she had had the chance, she'd have made the same bad choice as the heroine in *Absolutus Amor.* Maybe that was what had been bothering her. He thought he should find a way to use his words from this morning — gorgeous, brilliant, ethereal — about her.

The waitress placed their food in front of them. Sydney dug into her salad and Stone took a bite of his sandwich before continuing. "So tell me. Like Ted, you're brilliant and although things come easily to you, you work hard and you're productive." Sydney didn't react. "Even if we're not talking about winning, what about productivity?"

She didn't seem to care about his intended compliment. "What about it?"

"Look, Ted's got a publishable novel, his girlfriend is asking us and God knows who else for money, and he's sitting around, not making an effort, not being at all productive."

"The effort went into writing it," she said. She stopped eating, as if to mark the importance of her point,

"Writing is easy for him," he agreed, "Why write a novel if you're not going to sell it?"

"For his own entertainment. For his own satisfaction."

"But how satisfying can that be?" he asked.

"For some people, it's all they need. They don't need outside validation all the time."

"Well, I do. Otherwise, I think a person's just kidding themselves."

"I know you do," she said. "You bought into the whole class rank, awards and money thing so you would know how you're doing."

"Didn't you ever want to win?"

"Yes, I suppose I liked to win as much as the next person. But I was never pressured to be first. The only things my folks ever said were 'did you have fun?' and 'did you do your best?'"

"And they didn't push you to do better?"

"They were so supportive. Always. Almost to a fault. Hell, it took me years to realize that pink was not a winning color."

He shook his head, not understanding.

"Swim team. I was terrible. Tenth place, but I finished." She shrugged and dug into her salad.

"You'd not settle for pink in someone else. You're always consulting those 'best' lists to tell you what you should like."

"Not true," she said. "I like my haircut a lot, even if my husband doesn't notice it."

"I ..." He tried to remember exactly how long it was before, whether it was this smooth and shiny or not. "I knew there was something! Honey! It's great! I was thinking earlier — honestly! — how young you looked, how naturally you fit in here." He swept his arm around the room, the tables filled with twenty-somethings, men and women all with perfectly chestnut, obviously bleached, unbelievably jet black or absurdly chartreuse hair.

"A little late," she said. "But see, I like it. Especially the new color. And I don't need you to notice or to tell me you like it."

He was going to say the color (brown, but in the realm of chestnut) was wonderfully natural-looking — that her hairdresser was no doubt on a list of "bests" in town — but he was already in trouble.

"I didn't know you were getting it done this morning," he said.

"Neither did I," she said, and he realized that his not identifying her as the gorgeous heroine of Ted's novel must've triggered her urgent make-over. He realized he'd never shared the picture he'd taken of Harmony, or else she could've seen for herself how very beautiful they both were, in different ways. Of course, he couldn't show her the picture now.

"I'm sorry," he moaned. "I'm an idiot." He reached across the table to touch her hand, but she'd withdrawn it. "Well, I like it," he said with finality. "You're gorgeous."

She worked the last of her salad with her fork, making sure the final leaves of lettuce were dressed, a smile tugging at her lips. She took a deep breath and looked up. "So it grieves you that Ted could publish, probably without much effort."

"Yes. He could get published any day of the week, yet he leaves his talent in a drawer," he said.

"You don't know for sure," Sydney said. "He's the one who has to try. Either he has tried, been rejected and won't admit it or he hasn't tried."

"He hasn't tried," Stone said. "Because of Harmony. It's not because of his own dissatisfaction with his work." An idea occurred to him. "But *I* could send it to Andrew. Ted wouldn't have to know. I could spare him the embarrassment of rejection."

Sydney bit her lip, a sign, he thought, that she was at least intrigued by the idea.

"He might not want that," Sydney said.

"Nonsense," Stone said. "Everyone wants recognition."

"Maybe in *our* world, honey. Lawyers thrive on competition. But Ted, Harmony, those folks up there ..."

"You haven't met them," he interrupted. She probably was right, but he counted on her not being quite so certain.

"No, but I know Ted. He's just a humble guy, Stone. It's who he is."

"You can't be humble without an objective standard."

"He doesn't compare himself to any standard," Sydney said, her hand half-raised, as in surrender.

"Exactly. And that's not humble. That's saying, 'I'm too good for your standard.' *That*, I'm saying, is *hubris*."

"Or freedom," she said. She was too good and incisive a lawyer for him to win this argument.

"Or just plain laziness. Letting other people do the work for you. Succeeding without any real effort," he said. He felt his heartbeat quicken, agitated.

"Yet, you want to try to do it for him. Make up your mind, do you want to help him or teach him a lesson?"

"I want what's best for him," he said. That sounded like the right answer.

"And you think you know what that is." Now she sounded like a judge, rendering her final decision.

"Yes," he said. "Yes, I think I do. Ten years ago, Ted *did* want to play. He *was* published, *and* he got good reviews."

"Maybe that wasn't all it was cracked up to be," Sydney said.

"Or maybe he's scared and he needs someone to drag him back into the game."

"Involuntary servitude," she chuckled. "I think you're taking a big risk, butting into your brother's life."

"His life is lived in a trailer," Stone said.

"*His* life," she answered.

"I don't understand it," he said, tired now.

"I know," she said. "It's a little ethereal for you."

He resented her use of the word. She wasn't right about him, but he didn't want to seem an idiot again, so he let it go.

11

The next morning, Jay Shore called and insisted on coming into the office with what he said was an urgent matter. Stone's most lucrative client, Jay Shore was Wisconsin's largest developer of consumer real estate, specializing in mid- to upscale "communities" offering a choice of twenty to forty "personalized" designs, mostly in suburban Milwaukee and Madison but also in Janesville and along the Illinois border. Immediately, Stone cleared his calendar of two meetings that could easily be handled by one of the junior partners and pulled some strings to make a last-minute lunch reservation at The Capitol Chophouse, a steakhouse he knew Jay liked.

"Good to see you, my friend," Stone said. He always met his clients in the reception area himself, rather than sending his admin to greet them. The offices of Gordon & Newman, a firm founded just after World War II, had been recently redecorated in a traditionally elegant style — gray carpeting, South American mahogany, early American chairs and couches with green-gray Japanese silk. Even though your clients were paying for the palace, you never wanted to rub their noses in the gold filigree. Stone, who had been of the old, maroon-leather-and-dark-wood school, appreciated the streamlined and modern look the designers had achieved. In fact, he'd asked them to update his corner office in a similar style. From a small round table where he sat with his most important clients for intimate meetings, two glass walls permitted a view of Lake Mendota. Behind his desk there was a built-in mahogany bookcase with a matching credenza and file drawers. He only kept a few books there, mostly leather-bound with gold-leaf on their spines.

His admin brought a tray of decaf to the table. Gloria, now in her late forties and still single, had been working with him for almost as long as he'd been married to Sydney. She was both independent and indispensable, never in need of instruction or reassurance. "Good to see you, Mr. Shore," she said. She smiled coyly. To her, Jay was a celebrity. Sometimes he could be seen on Madison TV, mostly home shows but occasionally in his own commercials, and Stone knew that Gloria boasted to her friends that "her firm" represented Jay. Stone himself was slightly embarrassed by Jay. To Stone's chagrin and Jay's regret, his outsized, treeless developments were lumped by environmentalists and architecture critics under the heading, "Garage Mahals."

"Trees?" he'd huff. "You try putting five bedrooms, six baths, a great room and a three-car garage on a quarter acre. These are *Executive Homes.* My buyers demand wine cellars, for gods' sakes. You, Stone, should sell that old firetrap shack of yours and move to Garland Lakes."

"If there were a lake, I'd think about it," Stone would joke light-heartedly, eager to change the subject. What Jay called a "lake" was nothing more than a retention pond. Sydney would be embarrassed to live in such a development. She wouldn't even patronize a fast-food restaurant.

Jay stared at his coffee but didn't stop pacing in front of Stone's windowed walls. "Thank you, Gloria. Hope this one's treating you right," he nodded toward Stone. "You know, if he steps out of line, you'll always find a place at Shore Homes." Gloria nearly curtsied as she closed the door and left the office.

"What's up?" Stone asked, dispensing with any further social banter. It had to be urgent for Jay to tell him to drop everything and make time for this meeting.

Jay finally sat down, reached into his briefcase and brought out a stack of documents about a half-inch thick. "It's a smear campaign. It's ruining my reputation. Damn, it just might cost me that development in Walworth County." The Walworth development was to be built on a small "lake," with an executive golf course and a hundred upscale vacation homes — Jay's most ambitious project yet. He needed some routine zoning variances to make it happen and some of the county's commissioners were, in Jay's words, "rabidly anti-progress." He raised his voice. "I want this assault stopped. Today!"

Stone grabbed the documents as Jay continued to rant. "Consumer reviews. They can't do this to me! How am I supposed to defend myself?"

Stone read:

> "Our new, $575,000 dream house has a leaky roof, and Jay Shore won't fix it."

> "Only guarantee from Jay Shore is a guaranteed nightmare."

> "Cheap construction, not up to code. The place will collapse before I pay off the mortgage."

> "Avoid construction with this dumb ass of a contractor."

"From a newspaper?" Stone asked. If there were any defendant he wouldn't want his firm to sue, it would be a newspaper. Stone was a fervent believer in the First Amendment. One of the accolades he'd received at the pro bono dinner was based on just that: he advised alternative newspapers, drafted legislation protecting student rights, advocated in the press for free speech and freedom of association, including the right to march in downtown Madison in support of gay marriage, against fracking and for the recall of a governor.

"No, no," Jay said, and Stone was relieved. "A website, ImJustSayin. There are nine of these now and counting."

Stone let out a long sigh. Thank goodness it wasn't a newspaper. "Out of how many?" he asked, trying to gauge Jay's actual damage. His firm oversaw construction litigation in addition to financial matters for Jay Shore, but he couldn't remember ever having litigated a case by a disgruntled consumer.

"Thirty-six reviews. But that's not the point." The artery in Jay's neck was throbbing, and his cheeks were flushed. He consistently received A ratings from the Better Business Bureau, but whenever an urban planner criticized the jungle of rooflines, chimneys, dormers, and columns in his developments, he would be inconsolable for a week, especially if it dropped to an A-. He wanted an A+.

"You've built a hundred homes in just the past year," Stone said. "You have a sterling reputation."

"Had."

"*Have.* Really, Jay. ImJustSayin? How many people read this crap anyway?" He felt that Jay had lost all perspective. Weren't consumer complaints a normal part of doing business?

"*One* would be too many," Jay said.

"There's always one, Jay," Stone said. "You know that. It's the majority that matters." Jay stiffened. Stone realized he was reacting like a protective friend, trying to soothe Jay's injuries. There was no surer way to lose clients than to minimize their concerns, whether real or imagined, so he backtracked. "I mean, you can't stop people from venting, right?"

"Stop them!" Jay demanded. "I'm one hundred percent innocent." Stone studied the papers rather than meet his client's eyes. No one — nothing — was one hundred percent he thought, and Jay's exaggerated response to the exaggerated claims suggested as much.

"I hate to ask this," Stone said, "even though I know the answer: Any grain of truth in any of this?"

"Absolutely not," Jay said. He scratched the back of his head.

"No leaky roof, ever?" It seemed to Stone impossible to achieve that level of perfection.

"There might've been a nail-hole or two in this one place, or a flashing issue on a chimney. I don't remember exactly. It was a couple years ago and we fixed it right away. The customer was happy as a clam. I fired the sub-contractor."

"Of course," Stone said. It was possible the customer wasn't as happy as Jay had thought. The fact that Jay fired the roofer suggested there *had* been some substandard work. Defending Jay based on the facts — given the antipathy juries had for contractors — would pose no small challenge in the courtroom.

"No code citations that I recall," Stone said, hoping to restore a sense of solidarity with his client.

"No," Jay said. "Anything not up to code means no occupancy permit, no sale." he said.

Stone lifted his chin. "That's it. That's right." There were, of course, cases of crooked developers and inspectors on the take, but Stone was confident that Jay Shore was not one of those. He'd given generously whenever Stone asked him to support one of his causes, but those were civic and charitable, not political or legal.

"Enough with the cross-examination. I want you to force them to take down those fraudulent reviews."

"I have a vague recollection that there's a federal statute of some kind that might address your situation," Stone said, "but ..."

"Oh, c'mon already," Jay shouted.

Stone knew for certain that there was such a statute, and thought to say, "It's a free country," but thankfully didn't. His friend had clearly lost all sense of proportion.

"I'm a little out of my area of expertise," Stone said, which was true as to the tactics of litigation, not the substance of the applicable law. In Stone's view, litigation — although profitable for the firm — was expensive, drawn out and often not in a client's best interests. He was a business lawyer and treated these kinds of matters as business problems with economic consequences.

"Get Lou in here," Jay demanded. "I'd like to hear what he thinks. Someone with balls."

Offended but eager to give Jay time to cool off, Stone dialed Lou. "Jay Shore needs an opinion," Stone said. "You got a minute? We'd like your perspective on a problem." Stone hoped the words "perspective" and "problem" would tamp down Lou's inner warrior. The more difficult the case, the better Lou liked it. Indeed, his success with "loser" cases was at least half the reason for Gordon & Newman's remarkable growth and success. Litigation and business deals fed all the people in the firm, from senior partners to the mailroom. Business advice that resulted in *not* doing a deal or walking away from a fight didn't generate the same kind of fees.

Lou bustled in, straightening his club tie. His sleeves were rolled up, as if he'd literally been up to his elbows in earth or dishwater. Apparently on a deadline — litigators were always battling the clock; it seemed to be their font of inspiration — Lou filled the room with energy, ready and eager for battle. He was a big man, more than six feet tall, and stocky, but not fat, much like a weightlifter or shot-putter.

With his fingers he combed his thick, mostly brown hair and listened as Jay repeated his story, getting more agitated at the injustice of it all. When he finished, Stone jumped in. "I've told Jay I thought the law might not be on his side." He nodded to Lou, expecting his agreement.

"Well, I don't know that we need to be quite so negative," Lou said gregariously. Stone's stomach tightened, as if for a blow. "There may be a couple of avenues here to pursue. You can always demand money damages from the reviewers themselves for any defamatory statements — like the one about being sub-code — provided the statement is false and injurious to your reputation. That assumes, of course, that the reviewer has some cash."

"I don't want their damn money, Lou. I want them stopped."

"I'd hate to see him waste his money and not obtain the right result," Stone said, trying to dampen Lou's enthusiasm.

Jay rolled his head back and closed his eyes with a grimace. "You're killing me," he said.

"Stone has a point, Jay. Litigation is never a sure thing, although I've won more than I've lost, and I've won some pretty close horse races in my time." With a sharp glance at Stone, he added, "I'll give you as good a chance, Jay, as you're going to get."

"That's the spirit," Jay said.

"We'll need to take a deep dive into the law to establish some parameters for our chances of success," Stone said, digging his eyes into Lou. "And there are business ramifications to be considered," he added. Any battle that pits a consumer's right of free speech against a millionaire real estate developer who crammed oversized homes on undersized lots would be a public relations nightmare — even if there were a legal leg for Shore Homes to stand on.

"We'll give you our best thinking Monday," Lou said.

Stone wanted to suggest that they explore alternatives to litigation, but it was clear that Jay was hell-bent on action. "Just draft the complaint," Jay said. "Stop the bastards."

"You betcha," Lou said with his usual bravado.

"I made a reservation at The Capitol Chophouse," Stone said, eager to regain some control over his client. "Shall we?"

"Not today, thanks," Jay said. "This business is giving me an ulcer. Add *that* to the complaint."

"Emotional distress," Lou said. "I like it." Together Lou and Stone walked Jay to the reception area and shook hands.

"What the hell?" Stone demanded of Lou as soon as Jay was out of earshot. "Wasn't I clear enough? We *cannot* bring this lawsuit."

"Why not? The man's reputation has been damaged."

"It's a tempest in a teapot."

"If he wants to sue, we'll sue," Lou said, not so jovial now. "That's what we do here," Lou said, waving his arms around the reception area. "I win cases for my clients."

Casting a glance at the receptionist, Stone lowered his voice. If he and Lou were going to get into it, they should do so in private. "Come on, let's go to the Chophouse. Before *I* get an ulcer."

They signed out at the front desk and walked the three blocks to the restaurant, Lou commenting with equal enthusiasm on the sunny weather and on the young women who passed by.

"Wish I was twenty years younger."

Stone smirked. "It would still be statutory."

"Trouble with you, my friend, is you think too much." They arrived at the restaurant and, even though they'd eaten there countless times, Stone hid behind his leather-bound menu, angry at his client's puckish demand for a needless legal battle and his partner's belligerent willingness to oblige him. Neither of them would back down, Stone knew. Lou was such an eager litigator — the kid who begged the coach to put him in the game even when he was too small, too slow or too likely to get hurt. For Lou, it wasn't about winning or the love of the game. It was the pure love of conflict.

"Get the lunch filet and we'll split the broccoli and a baked potato," Lou said. "Then put the menu down and tell me why Gordon & Newman shouldn't make a million bucks making our client happy."

"He's *my* client," Stone said, "and, it won't make him happy to lose."

"We'll get relief from the worst of it," Lou said. "He just wants some kind of satisfaction."

"You'll get overturned on appeal on First Amendment grounds,' Stone said.

"So *that's* what you're worried about?" Lou asked. "The First Amendment?"

"I happen to believe in free speech," Stone said. "Even when it's hurtful to someone's feelings."

"And when it allows a retention pond to be called a 'lake,'" Lou said flatly.

"Both sides," Stone said stubbornly.

"Hate speech?" Lou challenged.

"Different issue," Stone said. "Right now we're talking about a consumer's right to comment on services rendered."

"In crude language that ruins a client's reputation," Lou said.

"Ruins?" Stone took a long sip of ice water.

"Oh, I get it," Lou said. "*Your* reputation as a white hat lawyer, the darling of the liberal, do-good bar?" He drew out "rep-u-ta-tion" as if it were something bogus. Lou was liberal when it was easy to be. But he wasn't married to a Legal Aid lawyer.

"I just think," Stone started before Lou interrupted.

"Right. You *think*. These guys pay you when they want *thinking*. They pay me when they want *doing*."

Stone shook his head. His best friend obviously was itching for a fight. They were like an old married couple, finally admitting, after all this time, "I never liked your meatloaf," or "I haven't had a good night's sleep in forty years." Stone gathered himself, his anger rising. He said, "You shove papers around and file dilatory motions and you call that *doing*?" A hostile smile tugged at Lou's lips. "I help companies grow and make stuff and create jobs," Stone said. "*That*'s doing."

"That can be lucrative for us, too," Lou said. "The point is that Jay needs a fight now. He feels wronged and he wants us to agree with him. To be his advocate. He can *pay*. He *wants* to pay. And we *like* to be paid."

Stone sighed.

"We won't put your name on the papers, if it makes you feel better." Lou called the waiter over. "Bring us a couple house reds," he said.

"Don't celebrate yet," Stone said. "When you give him the fee estimate, we'll see how badly his feelings have been hurt."

Lou held up his glass. "To Jay's reputation," he toasted. "Priceless."

• • •

After the lunch with Lou, Stone wasn't hungry for a big dinner, so he picked at a salad Sydney threw together with whatever she found in the refrigerator, reminding Stone of Ted's Saturday night crab cake challenge. Tonight she'd found carrots and apples, almonds and dried cranberries and a single serving carton of cottage cheese. She added a bit of ranch dressing. Sydney'd brought home a baguette from the bakery near her office.

They sat at the glass table on their backyard patio. "What's on your mind?" she asked when they fell into an uncommon silence. Even though she liked discussing the law, Sydney chastised him if he brought work home to do after dinner instead of assigning it to junior lawyers. He countered that his diligence was what made him the "Best Business Lawyer in Wisconsin" and perennially on the lists of "best" lawyers that had become so popular in recent years. Sometimes he was cited in categories where his expertise was, in his own estimation, merely competence. He was an M&A guy and a secured financing guy, putting companies together or buying and selling off their assets — not, as some lists incorrectly had it, a securities lawyer. He knew the most about family-owned companies and a good deal about publicly owned ones, as well as a lot about loans and lines of credit. Even if his briefcase wasn't bulging with papers, Sydney knew when he was distracted by a deal.

"I would hate to be in a business where your whole livelihood depended on positive consumer reviews," he said, trying to understand Jay's position better.

"Like a musician?" she asked. "Or a novelist?"

Art was so subjective. Stone couldn't think about Ted at the moment — his kind of case in defense of his artistic reputation would be so different from Jay's. Without naming names, he outlined Jay Shore's grievance.

"One way or another, we're all dependent on customer reviews," Sydney said.

"Not really," he said.

"Best Company Lawyer's not a popularity contest?" she challenged.

"It's peer-reviewed," he said. "By other experts." Stone could hear Jay saying building inspectors were experts and homeowners weren't.

"Aren't consumers authorities on the goods and services they consume?" she said.

"No," he said stubbornly.

"I'm not entitled to say what I like or dislike in music or movies or books?"

"Best-seller lists aren't always filled with great literature," he said. Distaste for a narrative style was quantifiably different from finding fault with misaligned joists. In fact, he'd be willing to bet that very few recent Nobel Prize winners had been best-selling authors before winning the prize. "You can get a great review and not sell out your first printing, and *vice-versa*."

"All you're saying then is that professional reviewers can lead us to water but can't make us drink." She laughed. "And if we discover booze on our own, to hell with water."

He loved the way his wife's mind worked, the way she wasn't a prisoner of her exceptional education — she could go from a blues bar to the opera, perfectly comfortable in the same black slacks and sweater, with or without a hunky, artsy necklace, or a classic strand of pearls, and be familiar with most of the composers and artists in both venues. She could lose herself in the Chicago Symphony but still find high praise for the efforts of the local high school jazz band. He, on the other hand, was somewhat of a snob — and she knew it.

He said, "All I'm saying is that in certain fields, it takes an expert to evaluate an expert. Brain surgery, for instance."

"What I'm saying is that I know good customer service when I see it," Sydney said. Stone remembered her blasting the oven repair guy last year. As he recalled, the guy had to come back twice. Sydney'd taken the morning off both times.

"He should've carried spare parts," she said now.

"So you gave him zero stars, when the poor man had no control over what the company put in his truck. You probably cost him his job."

"He was rude," she said.

"You berated him. Insulted him," he said. At the time, he'd been appalled. It wasn't like Sydney to pick on the little guy. He was beginning to see Jay as Jay saw himself, a victim of circumstances not of his own choosing.

"I did not," Sydney said, aghast. "I didn't want him fired. I wanted his company to be smarter."

"We don't get to determine how people react to our words," Stone said.

She shrugged. "Bottom line is, I'm entitled to my opinion. The internet gives me a place to share my own experience as a consumer. I don't have to be an expert to know if my roof leaks or the brain surgeon has a lousy bedside manner, or my salon colored my hair too red." He was surprised how close she'd come to the actual problem. He felt uneasy and should change the subject. Of course she knew Jay Shore was his client; occasionally, they'd socialized as couples.

"But when the consumer is wrong?" he persisted.

"Truth will out," she said. His thoughts reverted to his original misgivings about Jay stifling the truth, stifling the press. She continued, "One bad consumer review of a popular product isn't nearly as devastating as a bad review from an expert, like a bad book review in *The New York Times*. Ted may have lost a little confidence because of that one bad review he received in some minor journal, but he didn't stop writing."

"He had good reviews," Stone rushed to his brother's defense. "I don't remember any bad reviews."

"It wasn't bad," Sydney said. "I think it said something like he hadn't reached his full potential."

"It was his first novel."

"Exactly," she said. "But you know how Ted is."

"He never talked with me about that review," Stone said. He tried not to sound jealous.

"But don't you think that's why he hasn't tried to publish since?" she asked.

"Is that what he said?" Stone asked, somewhat concerned that Ted had confided in Sydney and not him.

"I don't know," she said. "You're the one who was up there. You said it was Harmony's fault."

Stone thought for a minute. "You've just admitted reviews affect a person, both emotionally and in their business, even the writing business." Stone said. "Maybe a person doesn't publish and so doesn't make money. You're saying that if there's financial harm, there should be a remedy." Perhaps Lou's position wasn't such a strain on the First Amendment after all.

"I'm sure that's the popular perception," she said. "But as an expert," she tweaked him, "you know that not every harm is a legal harm, and not every harm has a remedy. We the people still enjoy free speech."

A good lawyer could argue both sides of any proposition. Could Wisconsin's best?

• • •

On Sunday afternoon, still nagged by the possibility of Jay bringing a case that would not repair his reputation and might injure his own, Stone called Mark McCray, the junior partner Lou had asked to prepare the case outline and budget. Mark had dug deeply into the case, even though he'd only had a weekend for his research. He'd uncovered news stories from fifteen years ago about a deck collapse in one of Jay's Milwaukee subdivisions. No one had died, but a six-year-old girl's leg had been badly mangled. The deck collapse might have ruined Shore Homes, if the building inspector had not granted the occupancy permit and certified that the deck was up to code. The family had overloaded it at their housewarming with twice the rated weight limit.

"Real dumb asses," Mark said after repeating the story for Stone. "Still, we'd hate to have to rehash all of that — either in court or in the press," he said.

"What your research doesn't show is that Jay set up a scholarship fund for the kid and she's now at UW-LaCrosse. But you're right, the media will have a field day. Squelching freedom of speech and all that," Stone said.

"Lou says we can position it as stopping defamation of character, not stopping the dissemination of information," Mark said.

"I'd rather Jay be dissuaded from bringing the case at all," Stone said. "I'm guessing that your budget estimates will ice the whole thing."

"I'm at about a million right now," Mark said, "assuming no appeal. So you're saying I shouldn't try to streamline it?"

That was exactly what he was saying. Make it so lucrative for the firm that Jay would be shocked to his senses. "Lou is all about scorched-earth," Stone said. "We don't want there to be any surprises."

• • •

Monday morning, Jay sat at the head of a Gordon & Newman conference table, surrounded by Stone, Lou, Mark and three young associates. The associates were weary from a long weekend preparing a case Stone hoped they wouldn't bring, but it thrilled them to be in the presence of the firm's management and one of the firm's most important clients. Mark had cued up a PowerPoint and the first slide burned, "Potential Defamation Lawsuit — Jay Shore and Shore Homes, Inc., plaintiffs."

"Look it, guys," Jay said, unable to remain seated long enough to hear all the introductions. "It's the principle of the thing." Stone felt he could say the same thing about freedom of expression, but he waited patiently. "I wasn't guilty in the deck situation and I'm not guilty here."

"But Mr. Shore, that's the problem," one of the young women said. Fools rush in, Stone thought, secretly applauding her gumption. "These reviews for the most part are just opinions, not accusations of criminal conduct. There must be a false statement of *verifiable fact* that harmed your reputation."

"They called me a dumb ass," Jay said, trying to stare her down,

"I found a case …" She'd found an exact case on the use of the words, "Top Ten Dumb Asses." Mark clicked through the power point to the relevant citation. "Insulting you is not the same as saying something factually false about you." She stared back at Jay.

"The allegation that your work is sub-code might be defamation,' Stone said, glancing at Lou to show he understood the need to appear sympathetic to his client. "But I suppose there would be a question whether the public would understand 'sub-code' as a literal statement of illegality or the same as 'dumb ass' in another context. After all, consumers don't usually know or understand the building code."

"Sub-code!" Jay paced at the front of the room, the PowerPoint lettering bouncing off his body.

"Very clearly actionable," Lou said.

"Jay, you know Lou's the best, and if anybody could make anything stick, it would be him," Stone said.

Lou interrupted, "Negligent misrepresentation, interference

with business expectancy, breach of contract, nuisance, intentional infliction of emotional distress, libel per se, defamation, unfair competition ..."

Stone interrupted back. "Exactly. Could be lots of smoke. But mark my words: they will answer with fire. They'll pull up every complaint you've ever had from any customer, including the whole deck thing again. They'll arm themselves with the First Amendment, with the blogosphere, with consumer advocates from all over the damn country." By saying "we," he felt he'd publicly aligned himself with Jay, but Jay was studying Lou's face and Lou was studying his fingernails. He raised his voice. "They'll solicit complaints. People you've never heard of will jump on the bandwagon. People just love to complain."

"And we'll fight fire with fire, Jay. You can have your day in court," Lou said, his voice stronger yet. He sounded triumphant.

Jay turned his back to the room and stood apart. He turned resolutely, his heels clicking together. Stone's heart sank.

"A million bucks," Jay intoned. Stone held his breath. "Let's do it."

"Attaboy," Lou said.

"Well we don't need to nuke 'em right away," Stone said, shocked that Jay would put that much of his hard-earned money at risk. "We don't have to spend the whole million on the first day." He chuckled nervously. "Let's start with the cease-and-desist and go from there."

"Of course," Lou said. "We always start with an opening salvo, demanding they take down the defamatory comments and provide us with the identities of any persons using pseudonyms."

"Which of course will get their hackles up," Stone said.

"It gets the ball rolling, and the court will want to know that we were open to a private resolution of our differences before filing."

"It's in your hands now," Jay said. "Whatever you guys say. Just get the bastards."

Stone, Jay, Lou and Mark went to lunch at The Capitol Chophouse. "I don't want to see this on my tab," Jay said, laughing as the waiter left the check between Stone and Lou. It was a hefty one: apparently cured of his ulcer, Jay had ordered the he-man portion of prime rib. As a reward for his ruined weekend, Mark had started with the crab and shrimp cocktail — almost the size of an entrée. To top it off, Lou had chosen a very nice bottle of burgundy.

"You've known us too long for that," Stone said. "You know how much we value our relationship."

"Priceless," Lou said, picking up the check and handing it to Stone. "We also have our reputations to uphold."

12

Stone read the draft ImJustSayin cease-and-desist letter that one of the associates had drafted while the partners were at lunch. You could tell she'd been trained by Lou, who favored inflammatory war whoops rather than the "come let's reason together" tone Stone preferred in these opening gambits. Everyone understood a lawsuit was the threatened endgame, and the name "Gordon & Newman" on the letterhead implied a scorched-earth, take-no-prisoners, terribly expensive litigation. No need, Stone thought, to fan fires barely lit; with his fine-tipped pen, he deleted every "-ly" word he could — "flagrantly," "deliberately," "recklessly," "irresponsibly," "blatantly," "wantonly," "egregiously." The text was stronger for his edits; he'd learned from Ted's muscular prose style that just plain "wrong" was stronger and more persuasive than "demonstrably wrong."

He asked Gloria to take his marked-up draft to Lou, who would, Stone knew, restore half of his deletions and probably make a few unnecessary corrections of his own, like a dog marking his territory. To give him something to change, Stone corrected the letter's demand for a reply within seventy-two hours to seven days; in return, he hoped Lou would let the letter end with Stone's added olive branch, a veiled reference to the First Amendment: "Because our clients both respect the expression of honest opinions by consumers, we hope this matter can be amicably resolved without the need for litigation." Lou could add "deeply" to "respect," but he'd probably leave the offer of amicable settlement. Judges always appreciated a stated effort — no matter how insincere — to clear their dockets.

Unlike Stone's neat, in-line markings, Lou would bleed all over the page with a red felt pen, drawing a line from a word in the first line to a change he'd scribble at the bottom of the page and crisscrossing the text again from a word in the last line to the correction at the top of the page. By the time the edited version was returned to the associate, it would look like a bloodshot eye, from which the associate might conclude she'd failed the assignment completely, outraged the two most powerful partners at the firm and should consider an entirely different profession. If an associate had been around for a couple of years, she knew it was one of the training exercises she had to suffer on her way to partnership and her own reign of terror. While young attorneys thus developed their own style, Stone hoped that this one would learn to go easy on the "-ly" missiles.

Even though Shore Homes was Stone's client, Lou's name would appear on the letter. He would be the one to take the case to trial, if — God forbid — it got that far. At least on paper, Stone wouldn't be the one inhibiting freedom of the press.

His next item of business was to call Andrew at White Pelican Press. As he waited for Andrew to pick up, he hoped that Ted would accept his publisher's opinion that *Amor* was ready for publication. Surely, Andrew had more literary credibility than Harmony.

Andrew answered on the third ring. "You still answer your own phone," Stone said.

Andrew laughed. "This is publishing, not law, my friend. Speaking of publishing, how's your brother?'"

"I was up to see Ted the other week, and guess what?"

"He's written the next Great American Novel."

"So you know," Stone said, deflated. "He told me it wasn't ready yet, so he didn't want to share it with me. He didn't say you had it."

"I don't," Andrew said. "Just a guess. But back up. Where is he? Still in hippie-ville?"

"In a trailer, out back at Harmony's Peace & Joy."

"Is he working?" Andrew asked.

"Nobody up there has any apparent means of support," Stone chuckled good-naturedly.

"I meant working on a novel. 'No apparent means of support' sounds like you think he's dealing."

"No, no," Stone said. "They have a farm stand. And a pumpkin patch. They share resources. Maybe the artists sell some of their pieces. I don't know. Harmony has a nonprofit foundation, ostensibly to restore this historic mansion she lives in — alone, with her cats — and she gets people to give her money. All pretty scammy if you ask me."

"Harmony Miller?" Andrew asked. "I met her years ago. Talented writer, as I recall. Another one who crashed and burned." Stone flinched at the word "talented." Maybe Harmony was right and Ted's books weren't ready for publication. Maybe Stone had underestimated her literary acumen. If Harmony was right, maybe Ted wasn't a literary genius after all and was wasting his time rather than getting a real job like a normal person.

"All I know is, she's the one calling the shots for Ted on whether his stuff is ready for publication. Apparently, Harmony says no."

"She could be jealous," Andrew said. "Or holding him back for some reason or other. Doesn't matter. The thing is, there are a lot of good writers out there who want to be published. Poor publishers like me don't have to fool with reluctant authors."

"Even if the reluctant author is naturally more talented?" Stone asked.

"It doesn't mean he'll sell more copies," Andrew said. "You know that's the bottom line."

"How *do* you make a go of it?" Stone asked, momentarily sidetracked.

"I have two solid mystery writers with a nice following, a young adult writer who's getting some attention from librarians, a couple of local history — meaning Packers — perennial bestsellers, and a couple of glossy gift books: *Cooking with Cheese, Fish Boils Made Easy*, that sort of thing. Not exactly the stable of Theodore Hunnicutt literary geniuses I aspired to when I set out in this business, but they sell."

"Genius?" Stone felt the sting of an old rebuke. Ted, the genius, Stone the plodder.

"Over-used these days, but I always thought Ted was special," Andrew said.

"Special" was a much better word. Their mother would say, "We're all special in our own way," and Stone would be temporarily comforted. "There are at least four new novels," Stone said. "I've only had time to read one, but that one is really good."

"Good?" Andrew asked.

Stone knew he was being chintzy in his praise. Part of him knew he withheld the more lavish "great" because Ted was his brother, his competition. Quickly, he added, "Better than the first, actually."

"That would be something," Andrew said. "But you said he didn't want to share them with anyone."

"He doesn't. But maybe if I made it sound like he would be doing you a favor," Stone said. Andrew was silent. "I know you don't need one, you're doing fine," Stone hurried. "But he wouldn't want to think you were doing *him* a favor." Andrew didn't respond. "You know how proud Ted is," Stone said, picturing Ted's trailer and thinking "stubborn" was a better word than "proud."

"I'm not one to stand on ceremony," Andrew said, conciliatory. "If you can pry it loose, of course I'll read it. Isn't Peter Bankman still his agent?"

"I don't know," Stone said. "I don't think he's in the picture right now. All I'm trying to do here is spare Ted an unwanted rejection. If you don't like it, you tell me, not him. Then we'll know that Harmony was right and I was wrong."

"He'd probably see through all that," Andrew said, "but I know what you mean. As a small publisher, I get very close to my authors. Sometimes I feel like their shrink. For as much as they reveal their blood and guts in their books, these guys have very thin skins. By the time they get to me, they've usually been rejected by all the big houses, so any negative review takes on *New York Times* proportions."

"Ted only got that one bad one, and, as I recall, it wasn't even bad. It wasn't the *Times*. Something about 'flaunting his talent.' Didn't sound particularly negative to me."

"Because you're a lawyer, Stone. That's what you guys do."

"We get paid to flaunt?" Stone said sarcastically.

"If the shoe fits, Stone. The point is, Ted took it hard. Writing that draws attention to itself, is show-offy, not in service of the story," Andrew said. "I thought the critic was wrong on that score."

"What I remember," Stone said, "is that the reviewer said he had stunning technique and had mastered his craft." He felt himself slipping into his deal-making mode, an advocate for a client too proud to defend himself.

"Exactly, but then it said that all that craft disguised a lack of passion and human empathy. That was for Ted the killer blow," Andrew said. "He's a sensitive guy."

Stone paused. He didn't remember Ted's work lacking passion, or the reviewer's accusation along those lines. If Ted had any glaring fault line in his sensitivity to others, it would be not understanding, on a gut level, how difficult some things — so easy for Ted — were for others, even for people as mildly "special" as Stone. "Strikes me as highly unfair," he said, as if he agreed with Andrew wholeheartedly. "Our father used to say Ted was highly sensitive. Frankly, I thought he was a crybaby." He laughed.

"The review was unfair and untrue, both," Andrew said. "I'd love to rub that guy's nose in it."

"You know I want the best for both of you," Stone said.

"You can think of yourself as a power broker," Andrew chuckled. "Resuscitating a legendary literary duo."

The last thing Stone wanted was to be accused of being as obsessed with "legendary" success as his father, but he had always relished his role as a lawyer who could make things happen, who could "save" a deal when others said it was going down the tubes. "Fair enough," he said. Andrew and Ted would be good for each other.

* * *

Andrew called five days later, thrilled, and eager to meet for lunch.

"That was quick," Stone said. "Lunch for sure, but you've got to tell me now what you think."

"You've got a problem," Andrew said, and Stone felt the blood coil in his veins. He held his breath: what if his assessment of the novel was wrong. What if Ted had lost it? What if he *was* a one-and-done, his genius spent? Stone tried to squash a vague feeling of satisfaction. Success was earned by hard work, by going into battle every day, taking your knocks and punches, and getting back on your feet, not hiding out in the North Woods and drinking homemade wine. But his stomach tightened when he thought of the possibility that Ted was not a success. If Ted hadn't fulfilled his promise as a genius, his father's legacy — *citius, altius, fortius* — would fall to him, even if he wasn't *scitius*. And how much more could be expected of him?

"So here's the problem," Andrew chuckled. "Who's going to be your client? Me or Ted?"

Stone blew out a breath of relief and resignation. His brother was still the genius. At the same time, Stone felt his body relax into a familiar zone, second place to his younger brother. The pressure eased as quickly as it had come on. "I'll get Ted pro bono representation," Stone said. "You know what Lincoln said …"

"The law firm who discounts its fees for friends and family goes broke?" Andrew laughed. "Seriously, he hardly needs a lawyer. I'll send over the same contract we used last time."

"He'll want a higher percentage," Stone said reflexively. "He'll want you to address e-book rights, too." He was a born negotiator.

"How much more do you *think* he'll want?" Andrew asked.

"I'd guess he'd want an advance," Stone said. If Andrew was going to propose the deal, Stone was automatically cast as the advocate for "the other side," representing the best interests of the author, who in this case happened to be his brother.

"He knows I don't offer advances."

"So, he'd probably want a couple extra percentage points on the first five thousand copies," Stone said.

"We should be so lucky," Andrew said.

"And double the rate for electronic. Foreign and the rest to stay the same. Pub date within eighteen months. A realistic out-of-print reversion right based on print copies, not POD."

"So when's lunch?" Andrew asked.

Stone checked the giant combination blotter/ calendar he still used on his desk, a reliable back up to the calendar on his phone. "Friday?"

• • •

Sitting down to lunch on Friday, Andrew handed Stone a manila envelope. "You drive a hard bargain," he said, "but fair enough." He winked. "I think your other client — sorry; I mean your brother — will find this acceptable."

Stone slid White Pelican's standard agreement out of the envelope and quickly turned to the most relevant paragraphs. "Generous enough," Stone said. "If I were *his* lawyer, I'd recommend he jump on this."

"It's a two-book deal with a first look at the third," Andrew said.

"As *your* lawyer, I'd have to ask if maybe you want to offer less to start and negotiate up?"

You know I hate lawyer games," Andrew said. He picked up the menu and quickly closed it. "I'll have the Dover sole," he told the waiter, beaming, "and a glass of white Bordeaux."

"Excellent choices," the waiter said.

"Well-played," Stone said. The sole was the priciest item on the menu. "The same." He looked back at Andrew. "For the purpose of business expense tax records, he's my brother, but you are my client."

"I think all of our interests are aligned here," Andrew said.

The waiter poured Andrew a taste of the white Bordeaux — also one of the more expensive selections on the menu — and he held it to the light, then sipped. "Very good," Andrew said. The waiter poured two glasses. "So when will he sign?" he asked.

"As soon as I can get up there," Stone said.

"Can't I just email him the contract?" Andrew said.

"I don't want to risk interference from Harmony," Stone said.

"Right. I forgot about her," Andrew said. He held his wine up to toast Stone. "So, you will earn your fee after all."

"No fee on this one," Stone said and clinked his glass with Andrew's. The thought of reuniting Andrew and Ted and saving Ted from the clutches of Harmony was more satisfactory than any modest fee he could reasonably charge either Andrew or Ted. But Ted remained a problem. He hadn't asked for a deal or known about the negotiations — he might feel sold out rather than grateful. He might even be angry about the behind-the-back activities on his behalf. Any satisfaction in cutting the deal was going to be hard-earned.

• • •

That night he and Sydney went for fish fry at Randall's, a place just out of town that was popular with the locals as well as tourists. It was renowned for its outlandish decor: walls of old, tongue-in-groove pine paneling covered with hunting trophies, some of the best taxidermy in Wisconsin. Stone had been going there since he was a kid when he and Ted competed to give the best names to those beheaded beasts. Stone opted for alliterations like "Sturgeon the Surgeon" and "Mister Moose," while Ted appealed to a more adult sensibility, the sturgeon, "Sylvester" and the moose, "Toulouse."

Nothing much had changed at Randall's. The same families came every Friday to celebrate the end of the school and work week. The same group of aging singles welcomed the weekend at the square bar in the center of the room. If you ordered the House Special — a double perfect brandy Manhattan (two ounces of brandy and one-half each of sweet and dry vermouth) — the bartender rang a ship's bell.

If the food wasn't as good as it was, and the atmosphere so small-town Wisconsin comforting, Stone probably couldn't have convinced Sydney to patronize it. But over the years she'd come to imagine a nineteenth-century settler felling each animal with a single painless shot to its unsuspecting heart, so that its meat might fill the bellies of a camp-full of starving babies. That was the only way she could work up any sympathy for the hunter; any other reality was too bloody, too macho, too cruel. Stone advised her that the wall-mounted trophies wouldn't stare at her if she didn't stare at them. Instead, she should concentrate on the two huge photographs in wooden frames that occupied the lower half of one wall, and which, in fact, were changed twice a year in opposition to the seasons: iceboats in the summer and sailboats in the winter.

Helmut, the son of Randall's original owner, was getting ready to turn the restaurant over to his own kids. He seated Stone and Sydney at their favorite table, a booth under a menacing black bear that Ted had once named "Bartlesby."

"Hi, Bart," Stone said as he sat down. Within seconds, a young woman approached. She greeted them with all the pep of a high school cheerleader. "Hi, I'm Peggy. What can I get you to drink?" Peggy was fortyish and new to Randall's and, apparently, newly blond. She was wearing the restaurant uniform — khaki shorts, tennis shoes and a blue golf shirt monogrammed with an exuberant white trout. Sydney ordered her usual splurge — a House Special — and Stone a light beer.

Stone was still studying the familiar menu, as if it might possibly have changed, when Peggy bounced back with the drinks and a detailed explanation of the Friday night all-you-can-eat cod special. The walleye and perch options cost two dollars more, but all the fish dinners came with minestrone or clam chowder; green salad or slaw; potato pancakes and applesauce, or steak cut fries or corn fritters. Peggy also recommended their special BBQ ribs — the most expensive item on the menu — the duck, and her personal favorite, the charred chicken.

"You get a whole half chicken," she said. Sydney must've raised a skeptical eyebrow, because Peggy quickly corrected herself, "without the head." When they ordered their usual cod, Peggy said, "Right," as if insulted by their "unspecial" choice.

Sydney leaned on her elbows and gave Stone an inquisitive smile. "You're looking particularly happy for a Friday night," she said.

"Especially for someone forced to order the broiled," Stone said.

"You could have had the headless chicken," she laughed. "Either way, you can enjoy your favorite, the potato pancakes," she said encouragingly. "That seems OK to me."

"Easy for you to say," he said. Peggy plopped their salads in front of them, the dressing in a little plastic cup on the side.

"Half of that," Sydney said as he reached for his bleu cheese.

"Not fair," he said. Sydney could eat anything and still fit into the size ten she wore when they were married.

"I can't help that I have better genes," she said. Stone winced.

"You could be a tad more sympathetic," he said. He was supposed to be grateful to her for watching out for his health — over the years she'd made sure he hadn't grown paunchy, like Lou — but sometimes he wished she wasn't so consistently strict. "Give a guy a break now and then."

They were half done with their salads when the fish was delivered. "The plate is hot," Peggy said, a second after Stone had thoughtlessly centered it on the paper placemat in front of him.

They put aside their salads and Stone looked longingly at the crispy brown filets on Sydney's plate. Sydney could be a bit like Ted — not cold, exactly, but sometimes more head than heart. That might have been what made it impossible for Ted and her to remain a couple. With Sydney, Stone at times had overcome that tendency in himself. He'd been crazy about her — his heart didn't care if she'd once been

Ted's girlfriend — after all, he'd won her fair and square.

"Everything OK here?" Peggy asked.

"Great," Sydney said, much too enthusiastically for Stone, who was happy enough with his potato pancake, but found the broiled fish bland. He was feeling like a spurned lover when Sydney cut off a two-inch piece of her fried filet and put it on his plate. "Now do you love me?" she said.

"A little," he said. "So, guess what happened today?"

Cocking her head, she gave him a sidelong look. "I knew there was something."

"A two-book deal for Ted. The richest deal Andrew's ever offered for a literary novel. I have the papers in my briefcase."

"Wow," she said. "That's great!" She squared her shoulders. "Does Ted know?"

"No," Stone said. Of course Sydney had homed in on the crucial issue. He was delighted with Andrew's contract, but he wasn't sure how to break the news to Ted without getting him all riled up. "If the damn documents weren't dated, I could try to get Ted's agreement to show Andrew *Amor* and *then* produce the contract."

"As Andrew thinks you did," she said.

"Don't say I told you so," he said.

"I didn't *tell* you anything," she said. "Although, I might have suggested something of the sort."

"What am I going to do?" he asked.

"I think the only way to go is straight up. Tell him you did it because you love him. He should get that."

"Think so?"

"You do love him, right?"

"Everyone loves Ted," he said.

She looked at him with that "play nice" tilt of her chin.

"What?" he asked.

"You sound jealous," she said, a crease forming between her eyebrows.

"Jealous? Why would I be jealous?" He raised his glass to her. "I got the girl."

"I didn't know I was a trophy," she said. He followed her gaze to the moose over the bar. She added, "I didn't know there was a competition."

"There wasn't. Isn't." She shrugged. "But it's hard for poor schmoes like me to compete with those sensitive writer types. How do I compete with a puppy?"

"Oh my God," she exclaimed. "You're asking me to compare lovers?" Her mouth dropped open in disbelief. She stared in the direction of the photos of the ice boats.

"Lovers?" Of course he'd known they'd dated, but by the time they'd met at Harvard, Ted was a footnote in Sydney's past. He'd always assumed that Ted was too shy to move from boyfriend status to committed lover. He'd never asked Sydney because some part of him didn't want to know. Why would Sydney now be thinking of Ted as a lover?

"You knew that," she dismissed him with a wave of her fork. Another waitress leaned over them to light the votive candle in the red plastic globe on their table.

"Not the specifics," he said. It horrified him to think that Ted might know about that special place behind her ear, the spot that made her giggle like a coquette.

"You're asking *now*?"

Peggy came back. "Another beer?" she asked.

"Yes, please," he said, just as Sydney said, "no."

"No," he said. "Make it a House Special instead." Sydney glared at him as Peggy announced, "One House, coming up." Emboldened, Stone held Sydney's gaze, waiting for an answer.

"Yes, Ted was my lover," she said, then softened. "In a twenty-something sort of way." Stone wondered if that meant clumsy or drunk or high or overly anxious, but he held his tongue. He didn't want to remember being a nervous college boy himself. "And perfectly adequate," she added, jiggling the ice cubes at the bottom of her glass.

"It's none of my business," he said, hoping to smooth things over. The less he knew the better. The ship's bell rang.

"Right. None of your business," she said. "Kind of like Ted's publishing life." She put the last bite of fried cod in her mouth.

Peggy came by with his drink and offered seconds. "Sydney said, "Can we please get another potato pancake?" Stone looked at her, grateful that she had decided to stand down.

"Thank you," he said to her, and poured some of his fresh drink into hers.

She sighed. "So, what are we going to do?"

"It's not 'we,'" he said. "This is on me, not you. Even if he doesn't love me, all I've done is given him a choice. Andrew won't do anything without his signature, so no harm, no foul."

"Of course he loves you," she said softly, as she did when she knew how fragile he was feeling. He hadn't realized what he'd said. It was supposed to be about his love for Ted, not Ted's for him.

Her tone turned matter of fact. "But he *is* going to think you're interfering. Imposing your bourgeois standards of success on him."

"Bourgeois?" The truce hadn't lasted long. The damn ship's bell rang again. "Bourgeois? Is that your word or his?"

She sighed. "A word. In the dictionary," she said.

"A word that means conventional, middle-class, not very exciting," he said.

"I didn't say that. I was preparing you for what Ted might say."

"Because you think Ted is exciting, living on the edge of survival as he does, and I'm boring because I work hard and make money and provide a more than adequate living for myself and my family?"

"Don't pull that crap on me. Don't put words in my mouth — or Ted's — so that you can feel superior because you've done the traditional, expected thing. All I meant was that Ted is going to think you are imposing your middle-class standards of success on him." She busied herself with her drink, fishing out the maraschino cherry and placing it on the napkin, where it bled brightly like fresh blood. "You think you know what's best for him, based on your assumptions about success and material wealth." She reached over and moved the half-full container of bleu cheese dressing out of his reach.

Stone waved at Peggy. "I'll take another piece of fish," he said, not daring to look at Sydney. "Fried."

"Such a child," Sydney muttered.

"He should be grateful to me. I've done for him what he couldn't do for himself."

"He might call it playing God," she said.

"That would be absurd," he said. He knew he'd won a point.

"He might be furious. You might be best off not telling him."

"I have to," Stone said. "Andrew made an offer."

"Andrew has enough problems without adding Ted to them," she said.

"Ted shouldn't *be* a problem," Stone said. "He should thank me."

"I know you mean well, honey, but there's a fine line between helping someone and controlling him. I tell you what. Let's go up there and see how he's doing. How he feels about his writing and this Harmony person. If you get a bad vibe, you don't tell him." Now she sounded to him more like a mediator than a lawyer choosing sides.

• • •

"Twice in one summer?" Ted asked when Stone called the next afternoon. "What's up?"

"Nothing's up. Why does something have to be up?"

"It's just that …," Ted started. "Say, are you OK? You're not coming to say goodbye, are you?" For a moment, Stone was touched that his brother would be worried about him. "Because you know I'm not good at goodbyes."

Stone wanted to say no, he didn't know that, and from his point of view Ted was a lot better at goodbyes than Stone.

"I promised Sydney," Stone said gamely.

"Well then, come on up," Ted said with a bawdy enthusiasm. He must've noticed Stone's silence because he returned to his normal, quiet tone. "You two might be a little crowded in the trailer," Ted said. "I could …"

"Of course, we'll book a motel," Stone said.

"I assume she still likes her creature comforts," Ted said.

"Like Harmony and her house," he said jokingly. Now Ted turned silent.

"The Starlight is the best we have," Ted finally said. "The *only* one we have, really. It's just down the road. You go past the campgrounds on the left …"

"I know," Stone laughed. "I have GPS."

• • •

They set out for the White Caps Saturday morning. Even though it was only late August, some of the trees were already tinged with yellow.

"Way too early for this much color," Stone said.

"Still, it's pretty," Sydney said.

"We should have a couple more months, yet," Stone said. He dreaded November, turning the clock back, the onslaught of holiday commercials and the obligations and expectations they implied. "Maybe we should go away for Christmas."

"Maybe after," she said. "Just in case the girls want to come home. I want to have our traditional Christmas," she said. To her that meant caroling with a local theater group; a Christmas Eve roast; a Christmas Day brunch; a turkey dinner with all the trimmings; at least three presents for each girl; the red felt stockings they'd had when they were young, stuffed with trinkets like lip balms and breath mints; a new Brooks Brothers shirt for Stone, who was so very hard to shop for; decorating pressed butter cookies; house decorations; spices constantly simmering on the stove. It was lovely, but it sometimes made him sad and nostalgic for his own early childhood, when his mother was the most important person in his life and Ted was just an infant; when they were in primary school and the toys were trucks instead of chess boards.

And before he knew what Ted's genius implied.

"What if it's just us? What if they can't come home, or don't want to?"

"Of course they'll want to, if they can," she said. Personally, he dreaded the day his girls chose to go to a boyfriend's house for the holidays, but he also wanted them to feel free to do so. It was just a single day, he rationalized, an annual event; they saw their adult children several times a year — more often than many parents. They'd also made it clear that they'd welcome their friends at family celebrations and on sailing vacations. They usually had four cabins and so there would be plenty of room. As he and Sydney got older, they could use the help hoisting the sails and setting the anchor. Still, he knew that in time the girls would leave his house for homes of their own.

"So, would you like to go someplace after Christmas? Maybe for New Years?"

"That sounds better," she said, "although again, it depends on the girls."

"We should try to get a read on that," he said. He checked his rearview mirror and passed a truck that had been holding them to a mile below the speed limit.

"It's a bit early," she said. "I don't want to pressure them. You know what happens when you push too hard." She leaned over to check the speedometer.

He eased back on the accelerator to five miles over the limit. He didn't push. He never pushed.

They sat in silence for a while, Sydney periodically pointing to a colorful moraine or a stand of purple coneflowers down the middle of the highway meridian. When they got close to the White Caps, there was a drive-in restaurant off to the right, and a large sign displaying the breakfast specials. It had been tampered with. Sydney laughed. "I love a place where the kids' idea of a prank is to steal the 'i" in 'Croissants.'"

Stone remembered how, in their teens, the game of naming the trophies at Randall's had taken a turn for the prurient when the boys discovered the double meanings of names like Dick the Deer and Layla Elk. He was still smiling when they came upon a farmers' market just off the road. There were several wagons of corn and a play fort made of haystacks. Children were crawling all over it, and under an open-sided barn, families sat around sun-bleached picnic tables.

"Let's stop for a snack," Sydney said, and he turned into a gravel parking lot. As soon as they got out of the car, they were greeted by the sweet smell of fried dough, and, upon entering the picnic area, they saw a young man dribbling batter into a vat of bubbling oil.

"Let's bring some house gifts," Sydney said, pointing to the elephant ears.

"I'm shocked," he said, even though his mouth watered. "They're fried. In pig lard, no doubt. Harmony would probably have a heart attack just looking at them." He paused a beat. "On second thought," he said.

"She can't possibly be as bad as all that," she said, laughing.

"Time will tell," he said. "Maybe some of this?" He held up large jars of homemade peanut butter and orange marmalade.

"May I help you?" A young man approached Sydney, then looked quizzically at Stone, who felt caught in some kind of illicit act.

"Mark?" Stone guessed. He recognized the young man from Harmony's.

"David," the man answered. "Half right."

Stone apologized for his mistake and introduced Sydney. "David and Mark organize the farming and beekeeping at Harmony's" he explained. "This is their product."

"This isn't our usual gig," David said. "Local festival. Ted's in the back barn with Harmony." He pointed to a red barn a short distance from them. "It's story hour. I can get them for you."

Sydney said, "No, don't disturb them. We're meeting up later." She looked around. "We were going to take some corn to Ted for dinner, but I guess that doesn't make sense."

"We don't grow the melons," David encouraged. "We're only resellers — on consignment." He sounded to Stone more like a businessman than he'd expected to find at Harmony's. "So if you'd like to buy a crate or so, that would help us out."

"A crate?" Stone choked as Sydney promptly said, "Of course."

David picked up the closest box of honey dew. "We love these," he said, and carried it to their car. "We'll be home around two," he said.

"Thanks," Sydney said, but even with stops at a nursery and another farm stand and checking in at The Starlight, they arrived at Harmony's around one. The women known as "the Girls" were in the kitchen of the big house. Large raw beef bones were strewn about the counter, where Heather was sawing and swearing, her cleaver getting stuck on strings of fat and flesh hanging off the bones. "We're making beef stock," she said. An institutionally large soup pot and a copper kettle sat on the stove, both steaming.

"Very ambitious," Sydney said. She used canned stock, or, in a pinch, bouillon cubes. Homemade stock was, she thought, a bit more "gourmet" than necessary.

"Like boiling water," Sunshine said, giggling. "And I'm making a carrot cake." Stone shot Sydney a look that said, "You've got to see this."

"Girls," he said, "I'd like you to meet my wife, Sydney," Stone said.

"Super!" Sunshine said. Sydney went to the counter to inspect the Girls' projects while Stone left to leave a note on Ted's door. When he returned, he put the box of melons next to the giant refrigerator in the corner of the room. "Great for breakfast!" Heather said.

"Or even melon soup," Sydney said.

"Gourmet!" Heather exclaimed, and high-fived Sydney. Sunshine brought them tea and muffins at the kitchen table. While they worked, the Girls chatted with Sydney. Stone watched in amusement as Sydney tried not to intervene in their efforts. "It's harder than it looks," Sydney whispered to him, just as a bone rolled off the counter and Heather scurried after it. Sunshine fished shells out of a bowl of beaten eggs and started to grate a bunch of carrots. When she swore and drops of blood fell from the tips of her fingers, Sydney jumped up from the table to help. Sunshine was more than happy to let Sydney finish the job as she held her bloody hands under cold water. With Sydney at the helm, the rest of the process — measuring flour, sugar, raisins, walnuts and spices — went smoothly.

Once the cake was safely parked in the oven, the Girls started to clean up. As they did, Sydney said, "Stone can do that." Surprised, but happy in a way to have something to do, Stone took an apron from a peg on the wall and moved to the sink. Sydney said to the Girls, "Why don't you sit down for a moment and tell me what it's like to live here?"

Heather, the novelist, sat down opposite Sydney at the kitchen table while Sunshine squeezed in beside her.

"Harmony's pretty amazing," Sunshine said. At the sink, Stone glanced back at the door as Sydney persisted. He knew she would. He also knew that Ted wouldn't like to hear the women gossiping about Harmony and him.

"How so?" Sydney asked.

The Girls looked at each other. They each began to answer, then giggled, "you first." Stone could see by the tracks between her eyebrows that Sydney was having trouble taking them seriously. At their age, she'd been nearly done with law school, if not already a practicing attorney, not tucked away in the North Woods playacting at becoming a novelist.

"She's so free and independent," Heather finally said.

"Yes!" Sunshine said enthusiastically.

"Free?" Sydney asked. The Girls sat back in unison, as if dumbfounded.

"You know, free," Sunshine insisted, as Heather tried to fill in the thought. "She's single and she's made all this happen pretty much by herself. She always tells us to 'live free.' To make our own decisions." Stone tried to catch Sydney's eye, to see if she might challenge such a blatant falsehood. With a slight tilt of her head, Sydney encouraged them to say more.

"And she's very spiritual," Heather said.

"Not religious," Sunshine added. "She's very much at one with herself and with the universe."

"At one with herself," Sydney mused. Stone rinsed the cake bowl a second time.

"You know. Authentic. Integrated. Individual. What's the other word, Heather?" Sunshine asked.

"Whole."

"Complete unto herself," Sydney observed, her tone solemn. Stone turned toward them, wiping the bowl with a terry cloth. The Girls shot him a glance and giggled. Sydney caught Stone's eye as if to suggest she didn't know what was funny.

"Of course she has a man," Sunshine said.

"That's another thing," Heather said. "She shows us how to have a steady relationship with a man and, at the same time, not be dominated by him or dependent in any way." You can't be dominated if you're the dominant one, Stone thought, as he put the dry bowl on the counter with an unintentional thud.

"Careful," Sydney said. "Those old bowls are brittle."

Stone raised his eyebrows in acknowledgment. Sunshine went on, "She doesn't place demands on anyone."

"Everyone here knows Ted is her lover, but they don't flaunt it. She's kind of cool with him in public, actually," Heather said.

"What a hunk," Sunshine said.

"He's a sweetheart,' Sydney agreed. Stone sighed loudly, a mocking swoon.

"Oh, you," Sydney said, glancing at Stone.

She turned her attention back to the Girls. "I dated Ted a long time ago, but I married his brother." The Girls stared at Stone. He guessed they were trying to figure out how Sydney could've made such a mistake. Annoyed, he looked at Sydney with furrowed brows. She waved him off.

"Who is *also* a doll," Sydney said, and winked.

It was close to two when Harmony and Ted arrived, each carrying two cloth bags. The Girls eagerly took the satchels from them so that Ted could reach out to Sydney for an enthusiastic hug before shaking Stone's hand and slapping him on the shoulder. Then, he introduced Harmony to Sydney.

"I hope the Girls took good care of you,' Harmony said. Her hair was pulled back in a loose ponytail, exposing some gray at her temples. She looked older than Stone remembered from his earlier visit. In the harsh kitchen light, her straight nose dominated her face, but her hands were loosely tented, reverent and pointed toward Stone. She was wearing a long full black skirt festooned with colorful ribbons and flower appliqués. A low-cut scooped tee shirt stretched over her breasts while a gold and diamond pin drew his eye to her ample and inviting cleavage.

"Delightful," Sydney said. "We had muffins and tea."

"She really wants to see the house," Sunshine said.

"Did I say that?" Sydney asked. "I hope I wasn't that obvious." She turned uncharacteristically crimson. "But it does look fascinating," she recovered. "Stone says you're looking for contributions to restore it?"

Ted looked at Harmony as his face tightened. "It's been Harmony's dream," he said. "But there are no firm plans right now." He put his hand on Harmony's shoulder. Stone thought it was not an altogether affectionate gesture. Sydney must have noticed as well; she gave Stone a cautionary glance. Perhaps Ted hadn't known or approved of the letter, in which case they should drop that subject right now.

"Make no little plans," Harmony said. She marched to the stove and turned the gas back on under the copper kettle.

"They have no magic to stir men's blood," Ted said, completing Harmony's quotation. "It's so good see you, Syd," he said. "Looking great, as usual." Stone inadvertently caught Harmony's eye; she demurely put her hand over her pin. He suppressed the urge to count the number of gems.

"Here, sit," Ted said, distracting Stone. He pointed to the kitchen table. The kettle whistled, and Harmony offered more tea. Stone and Sydney declined, but Ted said yes, gently touching her hand. Harmony joined them at the table.

Heather came over with a jar of honey in its comb and a wooden spiral honey dipper. "Finish your tea," Harmony said to Sydney, "and I'll show you the main part of the house."

Stone heard "part." Calculated. Mysterious. A stingy spirit, he thought.

"We'll let the brothers bond," Harmony said.

As they left, the women looked back at the men as if they expected them to immediately do something to "bond." Stone idly twirled the honey spiral. Left alone with Ted, he knew he should tell him about Andrew's contract, though originally he thought they could raise it at dinner, perhaps over a post-dessert cordial. But this might work. At least Ted would be free from Harmony's direct influence and even if he still deferred to her, there might be a better chance of Ted's telling him why that was.

Harmony and Sydney went off — two peas in a pod, Stone thought, except Sydney was prettier, smarter and clearly more grounded. Watching them go, Stone said, "I knew they'd get along."

"Harmony's not the jealous type," Ted said.

"I wouldn't think so," Stone said. "I can't imagine her wanting Sydney's lifestyle. All that competition and pressure." He almost added, "Sydney doesn't drive a Mercedes" but he checked himself. Harmony might be jealous of Sydney because Sydney was, after all, Ted's first love — if Harmony knew about that chapter in his life. But as a spiritual guru she was supposed to totally forget the past and live in the present, with the man she now loved.

"Women like Harmony and Sydney often prefer the company of men," Ted said. "Sometimes the lionesses don't get along; they can be even more territorial than the males."

"Who is she protecting?" Stone mused. He thought Harmony was in some sense sheltering Ted, perhaps guarding his talent, but instead he asked, "The residents?"

"She's not as strict as you might think," Ted said. "Here, pretty much everyone does his or her own thing."

So everybody did their own thing. Except Ted? It seemed to Stone as good a time as any to explain why he'd come back. "Good," he said. "Because Andrew wants to publish you again."

"When it's done," Ted said gamely. "So you've seen Andrew lately? How is the old guy?"

Stone felt his heart pulsing in his ear, loud, alert to danger. "I still do some work for him from time to time," Stone said. "He's OK actually," Stone stole a deep breath from his diaphragm. "He could use a financial boost right now."

"He needs a best-seller," Ted said.

"That's what I was thinking," Stone said, nearly forgetting that he hadn't told Ted the whole story yet.

"Then you also know he doesn't need a Theodore Franklin Hunnicutt," Ted said.

"Andrew thinks he does," Stone said, his breath labored. "You had him with the title." As soon as he said it, he realized his mistake. He'd thought he might get Ted nodding as he would during a negotiation. Stone wanted Ted to agree to give him a manuscript which he would take back, wait a week, and then send along Andrew's contract with a congratulatory note. He would have to think fast to save that plan.

"How does he know the title?" Ted said.

"You told me last time," Stone lied.

"I'm pretty sure I didn't," Ted said. "Did Harmony tell you?"

"I don't know. Maybe," Stone said. He swallowed hard. This was going to be more difficult than he'd imagined. So far, Ted didn't seem excited about the possibility of publication. "But wouldn't it be great to have another book out there? Wouldn't the money also be good?"

"Andrew never pays advances," Ted said. "Besides, I don't need the money."

"What about fixing up the house?"

Ted's face darkened. "That's her gig. She shouldn't have asked you."

"Figured," Stone said, as if it were no big deal and he hadn't been annoyed by her letter. "I'll do whatever you want on that score," he added.

Stone thought he'd been highly diplomatic in his response, but Ted seemed offended. "My financial situation is none of your concern. Nor, for that matter, is my writing career."

"I just want what's best for you. So does Andrew. He thinks the book is ready for publication." As soon as he said it, he realized he'd compounded his initial mistake.

"What?" Ted stood up, planted his hands on the table and bent his face to within inches of Stone's. "How does Andrew know it's ready?"

Trapped, Stone studied his tea. "To tell you the truth," Stone started. He was a good negotiator, but a terrible liar. "Last time I was here, I was looking for more coffee, and I came across the manuscript. *Amor.*"

"You couldn't see the difference between a coffee can and a manuscript box?"

Stone shrugged. He turned away.

"You read it?"

"The *Wall Street Journal* wasn't handy," Stone said.

Ted stood motionless. "But how could Andrew know ...?" As if in a panic, Ted took three giant steps away from the kitchen table. Stone studied the brown scars in the blond wood of the table and traced a singed semicircle where someone had placed a hot pot.

"How could he, unless," Ted could hardly get the words out. "Unless." He slammed the counter with his palm. "You took it! You copied it!"

"I wanted to help," Stone mumbled. Then he gathered his wits and stood up, hoping to plead his case. "Look, I'm sorry," Stone said. "Maybe I shouldn't have given the manuscript to Andrew, but he loves it, and he is offering you the most generous contract he has ever offered anyone."

He waited. He had nothing more to say. Of course Ted would see the wisdom of publishing with Andrew and would forgive him. It was Ted's turn to say, "thank you," sign the contract and shake on it. As a wry smile spread across Ted's face, Stone relaxed. Ted stepped slightly back on his right foot, then threw a solid right cross at Stone's face.

"God damn," Stone shouted, instinctively touching his battered nose and then reaching back to retaliate, "Son of a bitch!" Stone lunged at Ted, but Ted landed a powerful jab at Stone's stomach.

The door to the kitchen burst open and Harmony rushed to Ted's side. She flung one arm across his stomach, like a wild crossing guard.

Sydney yelled "Stop!" and grabbed Stone's elbow. "He hit me!" he shouted. He was breathing hard and shook her off.

"What's going on here?" Harmony demanded. At the same time Sydney ordered, "Outside!" her arm outstretched and pointing like a rifle at the door.

"No violence," Harmony said in a strained imitation of serenity. "Peace." She clasped her hands together, Krishna style.

"Tell *him* that," Sydney demanded, pointing to Ted. "Stone arranges for Ted to publish all four of his novels and Ted belts him in response?"

Ted shouted, "Four?" He took another swing at Stone, but only caught the top of his arm. "Outside!" Stone snarled, blood spurting from his nose, spotting his shirt and splattering the white tile floor.

"Here," Sydney said, handing him a flour-sack dish towel, her eyes squeezed nearly shut. Stone grabbed it and pushed past Ted to go outside, letting the kitchen door bang in his wake. Outside he wiped his nose again and spat on the grass. The blood was salty on his tongue, but not bitter.

He shook his shoulders, dancing like a boxer in his corner. "Come on out," Stone shouted again, holding up the towel, a displaying a large red stain the size of a grapefruit.

Alone in the yard, waiting for another round, Stone felt foolish. Having been prevented from landing the impulsive retaliatory punch to which he'd been entitled, he was now losing some of his fire to his natural, rational and nonviolent self.

Ted didn't come out. Stone waited. An ant carrying a crumb slowly circled the toe of his loafer and hesitated before rounding a drop of blood. It disappeared near a blade of yellow grass. In the silence, he felt the sweat beading on his forehead and wiped it with his long-sleeved tattersall shirt.

An insect buzzed in his ear, needling him out of his daze. This wasn't over. He shuffled his feet to remain alert and ready, remembering his father's Golden Glove instructions. *Lead with your left hip. Firm fists, not tight. Elbows tucked. Aim for the soft spots, the floating ribs, the nose. Quick, sharp jabs.*

He was ready and then he was lost again, rescued from his reverie by the bang of the screen door and the sight of Ted slowly descending the stairs. He seemed so much younger. Tan. Slim. Healthy. In fighting form. He walked toward Stone and stopped fifteen feet away.

Harmony and Sydney followed him but remained standing on the stoop. Harmony again stretched out her arm as if to hold Sydney back. Sydney swatted it away. They both crossed their arms like drillmasters.

"Truce?" Ted offered. He held his hands up in front of him. His fingers were patrician — thin and long, like the hands of a pianist, not like those of someone who worked in a garden or threw damaging, unanticipated punches.

"How about a ride to the emergency room?" Stone said. His nose had stopped bleeding, but he could feel the bruises rising in his cheeks and under his eyes.

"Don't be a baby," Ted said matter-of-factly. He folded his hands in front of him, prayer-like.

"It feels broken," Stone said.

"It's not life-threatening," Ted said. "Trust me."

"*I* have insurance," Stone said haughtily. He rubbed his nose and then bent down to rub his bloody hands in the grass. He didn't take his eyes off Ted.

"I'm sorry it hurts," Ted said. He crossed his arms on his chest.

Stone pointed at Ted. "I'm sorry you sucker-punched me."

"I'm sorry that you deserved it," Ted said evenly. "And more! All four of my manuscripts?"

Stone trembled. "I apologized already," he said. He crossed his arms, aware that they now looked like matched bookends.

"What good is that?" Ted asked.

"As good as you're going to get," Stone said. "What's the big deal? There's no harm done here. Only Andrew and I have read the books, and they're not going to see the light of day if you don't want them to. So get over yourself."

"What's done can't be undone," Ted said.

"*Nothing's* been done," Stone said coldly.

"Right. Nothing. *I* didn't do anything. We didn't *want* anything done. We weren't ready yet." Ted rubbed the knuckles of his punching hand. Stone stepped back, fearing that Ted's anger was reigniting.

He noted Ted's use of "we," and felt helpless, his role as big brother and protector replaced by a woman with unknown motives. He could see the two women near the house, like two moms shoulder to shoulder, supervising the truce. "I said I'm sorry, Ted," he said again. "I don't get it. You obviously need the money. I still don't get why you don't believe Andrew, but if you don't sign the contract, this is all over anyway."

"I told you. I'm not obsessed with money like you are. I don't need it. I don't want it. " Ted said, his voice low and threatening. "I want you to destroy all the copies, yours and Andrew's."

His nose ached. "OK, I'll send them to you."

"I want them burned."

Why would they want to spend any time together after this? If he never saw his brother again, it would be too soon. "Hell, no," Stone said.

"Burn them," Ted said.

Stone threw up his hands in disgust and ran them through his hair. He looked away from Ted to Sydney, hoping she might intervene. Surely she would see how ridiculous Ted was being.

As if reading his mind, Sydney stormed down the stairs and stood between them, facing Ted, her back to Stone. "I'll make sure you get the copies," she said quietly, her voice judge-like.

He loved her.

He hated his brother.

They should go.

Now.

Sydney turned to Stone. "Let's go," she said, and with Stone at her side, marched to their car. "You guys can work this out another time." She didn't look at Ted and she barely looked at Stone. She opened the driver's side door and got behind the wheel. Stone followed her to the driver's side.

"I'm driving," she said.

He didn't want to fight in front of Ted and Harmony. "Just to the motel," he said. He walked around the car to the passenger side.

She didn't wait for him to buckle his seat belt. Without looking, she backed up, nearly broadsiding Harmony's Mercedes. She barely stopped at the entrance to the two-lane road in front of the house.

"What?" he cried. "It's not my fault. I'm trying to help him, for gods' sakes. And *he* hits *me*? Don't you dare say 'I told you so.' Don't you dare take his side in this!"

Her jaw was set and a vein twitched along her neck. She was angrier than he'd ever known her to be: she didn't turn toward him, or contradict him or respond, "Or what?" He didn't know what to say: "Or I'll never speak to you again"? Or "I'll move out"? Or "I'll file for divorce"?

"Dammit," he said and turned toward the window. The road was lined with pine, but little else. She drove like she knew where she was going. As they approached the town of Upson, he said, "Take me to the hospital."

She pulled over at the green road sign that introduced the town and pointed to its white lettering: "Upson. Unincorporated."

"Hurley, then," he said, though it occurred to him that with only 1,500 people, it, too, might lack a hospital.

Sydney flipped on the emergency flashers and turned to him. "Look at me." Her eyes darted left and right, comparing his pupils for signs of uneven dilation. Then she lifted an index finger and moved it right and left in front of what he was certain was a broken nose. His eyes focused on the metronome of her glossy French manicure. It occurred to him that he might fake a concussion to make her feel sorry for taking Ted's side. Traumatic injury to the head! At the hand — no, the fist — of his own brother!

He was still considering how best to mimic a concussion when she put the car in gear, and declared, "You'll live."

He said, "Turn off your flashers." She delayed a cycle of three on-off blinks before complying.

At the motel, she parked in front of their room and put her hand out for the key. He stared ahead at the rows of alternating blue and yellow room doors, the silver metal numbers starting ambitiously at "101," each slightly askew. The battered gutter hung loose at one end. "We're not staying," she said. "I'll get our things."

"I'll get them," he said reluctantly. She turned off the motor and together they retrieved their bags. He took the key to the office and returned to the car. He was surprised that Sydney was again behind the wheel. He felt like he was having his driving privileges taken away. He was the one who'd picked out the Audi — upscale but not too flamboyantly so — and he almost always drove. He hated being a passenger.

She turned the key.

"Come on, I'll drive," he said. She didn't respond. "I said I'll drive," he said again, more insistently.

Turning sharply to him, she said, "Do you not see me?"

Yes, he saw her. In profile, her brow was lowered and her lips drawn tight. Her jaw dropped a little, suggesting the start of a second chin, but he had the impression she was trying not to smile. "I want to drive," he pleaded.

"So do I," she said simply. Her shoulders were relaxed, comfortable with her anger and confident in her position.

He hesitated. She never begged to drive. It was his thing, not hers. Now she filled the driver's seat like a deployed airbag. She revved the engine. "You don't get to do everything you want. Other people may want the same thing, or something entirely different. The world doesn't revolve around you and what you want."

He stomped to the other side of the car, got in and slammed the door shut.

"Are you sure it's closed?" she asked. He rubbed his nose with his handkerchief.

"Don't," she said. She sighed, as if forced to do something she didn't want to do. "It'll start bleeding again, and you know I...." She might be a strong woman, but she'd been known to faint at the sight of blood.

"Don't look then, if you can't stand it. It's not all about you, either.

This is *my* nose. I'll rub it if I want to."

"Ohmygod," she half-laughed. "Go get the room key back."

"What?"

"We're not going anywhere tonight," she declared. "Get the key, we'll go inside, look at your nose and work this out."

He was grateful that she sounded at least halfway reasonable. Still, he didn't move.

"Go," she said. "In the morning, we'll flip for driving privileges."

He soon returned, opened the car door for Sydney and extended his hand. "The front desk thinks we're nuts," he said.

"Astute observers," she said. The metal door had a dent in it that could've come from a baseball bat. "I'm sure we're not the craziest guests they've seen." She got out while he gathered their overnight bags from the back seat. She opened the trunk.

"I have the bags," he said.

"I have the medicine," she said, holding up a bottle encased in a silver foil bag. "I brought this for Ted's celebratory toast, but obviously, we didn't get that far."

Inside, she took the clear plastic wrap off the two chubby glasses on a tray next to the TV. "You don't need ice, do you?"

"I think it's a little late for that," he said.

"I meant for the brandy."

"Of course not," he said. "Straight up."

She poured Stone a hefty amount and handed it to him. He sat in one of the orange Naugahyde chairs near the window. He got up and dragged it close enough to the bed to put his legs up on the paisley bedspread, moved her matching chair closer and swept his arm out, urging her to sit. He held up his glass. "Thank you," he said. He took a sip and swirled it in his mouth before letting it trickle down his throat. The fumes warmed his nose. "OK let me have it, and then you can pour me another."

"Finish what you have, and then we'll see," she said. She took a sip from her glass. When she'd swallowed, she waited a few seconds, as if reluctant to break the temporary truce.

"The book thing is not such a big deal," she said, as if informing a client that the minor charges would be dismissed. "This can't be about the book."

"What else could it be about?"

"You're brothers. It could be anything," she said. Did she think he was jealous of Ted? No way.

"I don't know, could be about Harmony or the house or ..." she continued.

"This is not a piece of cake," Stone said in his best faux professorial voice. "So, what did you think of the manse?"

"The house is not a historic landmark," Sydney said, imitating his tone. "Not yet. It would cost a fortune to restore it and she's not moving in that direction. I liked the parody art. But you should see her bedroom!"

"She took you upstairs?" Harmony had withheld the upstairs from him; showing Sydney her private space seemed unfair, perhaps conspiratorial.

"Yes. And it's all modern and designer and, I'd say, overdone. Her bedroom has a king-size canopy bed. Canopy! With curtains. Sheer white curtains, with gold pullbacks, like you see in the movies. It's covered with quilts and sheets and coverlets and pillows and shams and it would take an hour to make the thing, if you even remembered what went where." Sydney was a very practical person, and not particularly fond of making the bed in the morning, a job that fell to Stone, to whom a made bed was as essential as brushed teeth.

"Hmm," Stone said. He knew better than to speculate on what Ted and Harmony were doing in the king-size playground. Perhaps Harmony was just showing off for Sydney, marking her territory.

"Such a fraud," Sydney continued. "How many diamonds are on that pin?"

"What pin?"

"That disco-ball sparkling on her boobs." She eyed him over a long sip of her brandy.

"The Aquarian?"

Sydney's eyes bulged.

"What?" he said, slowly catching on. "I know my constellations."

"And?"

"I'd thought once about getting you something like it — the Pisces version," he said.

She looked up at the ceiling, where an amoeba-shaped water mark on an acoustic tile was outlined in brown. She dipped her chin and looked at him. "But you knew I wasn't a diamond kind of gal," she said, her tone riddled with coy sarcasm.

"One of the many things I love about you," he said, raising his glass. He hoped she'd accept his apology. Would it have been better if he'd told her there were twenty-one stones glittering between Harmony's breasts?

"Always keep it simple," Sydney scoffed. "Guru Harmony! Live off the land, my ass. Live off every idiot who's smitten with you and will give you what little money they have."

"I'm not smitten, and I haven't given her a dime," Stone said. "For your information, the pin alone is worth thousands. And I only have eyes for you."

"So we know Ted didn't buy the Aquarian," she sighed. "I wonder. Maybe she tells Ted his work isn't ready just so that he'll stay on with her. Or maybe Ted needs her. If he had his own money, surely he'd pry himself loose."

Stone sipped his brandy, considering her comment. "He seems very devoted to her. You could be right about her wanting to hold on to him. Certainly not for the money. Maybe for the canopy bed!"

She smirked. "I don't remember him being all that great." Stone smiled broadly.

"So what's really going on with him?" she asked. She sounded genuinely concerned.

"I wish to hell I knew," Stone said. He tried to think. What had been the worst rift between them? Kid stuff, mostly. Stone had been terribly hurt when Ted chose to attend a writer's conference rather than his law school graduation. Although not number one, Stone had graduated *cum laude* and had been elected by his peers to speak for his class. Their father had been there, of course, though reserved in his congratulations. Ted should've been there. It was a once-in-a-lifetime experience; Ted would have the opportunity to go to hundreds of writing conferences.

This rift was all Harmony's fault. If Harmony hadn't asked for money, he wouldn't have wondered what was really going on up here, wouldn't have visited, wouldn't have discovered the manuscripts, wouldn't have sent them to White Pelican, wouldn't have tried to help Ted.

Ted was a loyal guy, but also a private one. Growing up, he'd had few close friends. Stone wondered how many of them could understand or appreciate him. Ted wasn't the kind of guy to share all his feelings; it was one of the ways he protected his genius mystique. Did Harmony know him as well as she thought she did? Was it possible Ted was hiding something from her? "You know what?" he said to Sydney, not sure what it meant, but certain it meant something. "I wonder if Harmony knows there are *four* novels. He seemed even angrier when he hit me the second time."

"That could explain it," she said. "Maybe he really does want them published, but is afraid to cross her."

"She's a wacko," Stone said. "He's got to get free of her."

"Doesn't seem very likely," Sydney said. "Like you said, for whatever reason, he's very loyal to her."

Stone rubbed his nose. "Too bad he doesn't feel that way about his older brother."

13

There was only one choice for breakfast in Upson the next morning, The Sunny Day Diner. Inside the place was old and drab, years of cigarette and griddle smoke and grime dulling whatever attempt had once been made to live up to its name. It suited Stone's mood perfectly. While Sydney searched the thick plastic menu for a healthy choice — oatmeal? Special K? — Stone didn't bother. From their table across from the U-shaped center counter, he had a good view of the back sides of middle-aged men who spend too much of the year sitting in a Boston whaler with a six-pack.

Ever the health advocate, Sydney asked the waitress, "Do you happen to have fresh grapefruit?"

The waitress, a tired-looking twenty-something, eyed the ceiling and said, "Fruit cocktail. Canned." With an undertone of severe disappointment, Sydney ordered oatmeal and orange juice, although she must have guessed it wasn't freshly squeezed. The waitress furrowed her brow at Stone and quickly tapped her order pad. Stone was decisive. He ordered the biscuits and sausage gravy with an order of links on the side and extra cream for his coffee. Sydney could say whatever she wanted; he was tired of being corrected, of being second-guessed. He was a good and well-intentioned person and did not deserve to live under the critical eye of other adults — not his brother, his wife or that charlatan Harmony. None of them were close to his equal in terms of professional and personal accomplishment. Well, maybe Sydney was. But what he ate was his business.

Sydney sighed. He met her gaze, daring her to say something about his breakfast order. Last night the pain and brandy had overwhelmed his anger, but it was simmering now. He fully expected that when the platter arrived, Sydney would finally object. Then he would feel justified in issuing a new tirade against the great unfairness of it all.

There was a small chip on the edge of the pale oval plate, overflowing with two huge biscuits drowned in thick white gravy loaded with generous bits of pork sausage. Sydney stared at the plate for a second, but only said, "You don't look too bad, considering." He shrugged. That morning he'd decided not to shave, afraid to aggravate the patchwork of purple, brown and yellow that marred his usually healthy complexion. "Still sore?" she asked.

"I'll live," he said, which, he realized too late, was her point exactly. Whenever either of their girls had suffered a defeat or setback during school — usually over a broken romance — on the second day of mourning, Sydney would tell her, "Enough. Off the pity pot. You'll live." He cut a piece of sausage, mopped it in the gravy and lifted a forkful with some bits of biscuit, cooling it while Sydney busied herself with her oatmeal. He couldn't help but notice when she stopped stirring and held up a spoonful, blowing over it longer than he deemed necessary, then licked her lips. Good for her for choosing the heart-healthy option; what *he* needed was comfort food.

He paid for breakfast, left a generous tip, and they headed for the parking lot. When they got to the car, Stone stood back. "Do you want to drive?" he asked, aware that such an offer was his best defense against losing his driving privileges for the day.

"You're good," she said. He appreciated the possible ambiguity of her response, but he didn't hesitate to jump into the driver's seat.

Sydney smiled. "I'll back-seat," she said, her tone playfully menacing.

Stone sat paralyzed behind the wheel.

"What's wrong?" Sydney asked. "Did you forget something?"

"No, but I'm not sure where we're headed." Sydney shot him a sardonic look. He hadn't meant it as a philosophical question, just a practical one. "Do we really have to go to Andrew's and pick up his copies?" he asked.

"We could, I suppose. Get Andrew's copies, then get ours, box them up and have them delivered overnight. He'll have them Tuesday at the latest."

"A pine box?" he said. Where we're all headed, he thought.

"He can build his own fire and make his own ashes," she answered.

"I don't get what's the big deal," Stone said. "He still has the originals."

Stone dialed Andrew's number, apologizing for calling on a Sunday, and asked if they could stop on the way home from Upson. Andrew had started White Pelican in a former jewelry store in a strip mall in the northern suburbs of Madison. Andrew said to meet him there. The front door was still set off by two white pillars, suggesting a wedding chapel. There were two businesslike leather chairs anchored against one wall, directly across from the reception desk. Two more chairs were set against a white lattice room divider topped with a planter of tall mother-in-law tongues. A glass coffee table featured his bread-and-butter baseball and local history moneymakers, and a few literary-looking titles Stone knew nothing about.

"Coffee?" Andrew offered.

"We're good," Sydney answered for both of them.

Stone decided to keep it simple. "Ted doesn't want to publish right now. He's a bit paranoid about copies being out there and wants me to return them. He's pretty steamed at me for showing them to you."

"And now, so am I," Andrew said. "You got my hopes up."

"You've gotten along so far without him," Stone said. Andrew made a face.

"You seem to be very busy," Sydney chimed in, nodding at the reception desk, where there were two tall stacks of large manila envelopes, manuscripts apparently awaiting review.

"Those would be long-shots," Andrew said. "I was hoping the discovery of the long-awaited second Hunnicutt novel would breathe some new life into this tired business. I actually engaged a P.R. firm to make a plan for Ted's comeback."

"I'm sorry, Andrew. I'll try to find a way to make it up to you," Stone said.

"Why don't *I* talk to him?" Andrew asked.

"No!" Stone nearly shouted. "That would make things even worse."

"How could they be worse? I'm his publisher, after all. He trusts me, doesn't he?" Andrew leaned toward Stone, as if realizing that the brownish tint around his eyes wasn't caused by shadows.

Stone raised his eyebrows. "I'm told I deserved it," he said.

"Usually it's the author who takes a beating for his work," Andrew said. "What aren't you telling me?"

"He didn't know I had the manuscripts," Stone mumbled.

"What?" Andrew raised his voice.

"It's a long story, Andrew," Sydney intervened. "Best told when this is all over. For now, we've been sent to collect all the copies and supervise the deletion of files from your computer."

"Nothing's ever really deleted from a computer," Andrew said.

"I know," Stone said. "Ted knows, too." He wondered how computer-savvy Ted actually was; he himself felt totally dependent on the firm's IT department. "Or he must know. This is all a stupid ego trip on his part."

"So if I give you a couple of thumb drives with files labeled *Amor*, he'll be satisfied?" Andrew asked with a hint of mischief.

"Hell, I don't care if you give me a thumb drive with the Encyclopedia Britannica on it," Stone said.

Sydney cleared her throat. "I think he trusts you both do to the right thing." "Clients can be so naive," Andrew said, and smiled at Stone.

• • •

Stone drove home as slowly and carefully as he'd ever driven — two miles under the speed limit, not cheating on yellow lights, signaling the length of a football field prior to making a turn.

"Taking away all my fun," Sydney mocked when she reminded him to turn when the light changed to green just outside their neighborhood. "You know, you're just going to have to let this go," she said wearily.

"Yeah," he said.

"We're just going to forget about it," Sydney said.

"I'm not senile yet."

She yawned. "Change the movie. Stop thinking about what you should've said or not said. It's over. Forgive him and move on."

"But," he said.

"There's more important stuff to worry about than whether or not Ted publishes another novel."

"Like what?" he said. He was ten miles over the limit and checked himself.

"Like something you *can* do something about. One of your own deals. Where to take your wife after Christmas."

"Seems so trivial …"

"Look," she said, and he slowed again. "Truth be told, the world will continue to spin whether or not it gets to read *Amor*. It's just a book. Can you think of any book that changed the world?"

He still wanted to finish the twelve rounds with Ted. An argument with Sydney would have to do. "The Bible?" he said.

"Doesn't count," she said. "Many writers. Many ideas. Did any of them change the world?" When he didn't answer, she said, "There's still more wisdom unwritten than written. We get by." She reached over and patted his knee.

When they got home, he left his bag unpacked on their bed and immediately searched his closet for a shoebox to use as a coffin for Ted's manuscripts. He thought he'd line it with a satin pillowcase and strap the thumb drives in, but then realized he had all that paper to add. Sending ashes wasn't proof—they could be any manuscript or a pile of scrap paper, for that matter. He should shred the copies and bury the thumb drives under mounds of manuscript. The gesture would more than comply with Ted's "send-the-ashes" edict and would also, he hoped, convey his ongoing anger.

He went to his study, located the files on his computer, and with his phone took a video of himself as he deleted the novels. He hated the way the selfie bloated his profile, but when he saw that even in bad light the camera captured his swollen black eye, he held the phone directly at his face and said, "It really hurts me to have to do this." He grimaced into the camera—baring his teeth in a pained smile. If Ted were going to hit him like an uncivilized animal, he needed to show his brother that he, too, could act like an animal. He pointed to his computer with his middle finger, then transferred the video to a thumb drive. He added a tag that said, "WASTED" and put the stack of manuscripts and the drives in a grocery bag. In the morning he would ask his assistant to shred the documents and ship the boxes overnight to Ted.

"Feel better?" Sydney asked when he climbed into bed beside her.

"Done," he said. He tried to sound upbeat, as if he'd indeed put it all behind him.

"We don't know how Ted would've felt if it had all unfolded differently," she said.

"If I were a genius author and I was offered publication, I'd take it," Stone said.

"Most rational people would," she said. "I'm glad you told Andrew that other factors were involved."

"When you plead guilty, you still do the time," Stone said.

"But you've made it right by him. Or at least as right as it can be," she said. "Now, it's up to him to forgive you."

"Damn right. My conscience is totally clear. You can call it interference if you have to be all legal eagle about it, but I'm OK with it. I'd do it again. That's just who I am."

"Lucky for you, I love you," Sydney said.

"You're the best," he said, taking her hand so they could fall asleep as they always did, side by side, holding hands. "I love you, too."

• • •

The next morning he was back in his office at the law firm, restless and itching for a fight.

Lou stood in the doorway of Stone's office. "We filed this morning. They should be served in the next day or two, and we should develop a statement for the press. Do you want to take a crack at that, or should I?"

"Your lawsuit," Stone offered, knowing Lou's request was just a courtesy.

"Your client," Lou countered.

"Your specialty," Stone said. "Lipstick on a pig." He was feeling a little guilty about his shenanigans with the manuscripts the night before. He'd compromised his good intentions with the mean-spirited video; he probably wasn't the right one to take a wrong-headed but legitimate lawsuit and make it sound like they were saving the world.

"Yup," Lou said. "The press is going to be in an uproar over the freedom of speech issue." He sounded like a prize fighter trash-talking his opponent at the pre-fight press conference.

"I'd hoped they'd settle and not let it come to this," Stone said. "Opinion versus libel can be a very thin line."

"That's the angle," Lou said, and left. Stone grabbed a couple of antacids from his top drawer, even though he knew they couldn't begin to soak up the anxiety he felt about the looming legal battle.

On Wednesday, the *Madison Reporter* picked up the story and ran it on page one. "Jay's ecstatic about the coverage," Stone told Sydney at supper. They were at their kitchen table having grilled cheese sandwiches.

"He shouldn't be," Sydney said.

"Can't get him to see it in that way," Stone said. "Hardly anybody saw those reviews in the first place, and now they're front-page news, as if they're verified facts. Even the sub-code allegation isn't true, according to Lou."

"You'd think Jay would want to bury the negative ones," Sydney said.

"He'd rather bury himself than have someone — anyone — say they didn't like him, or his work," Stone said.

"He's so thin-skinned," Sydney said. "But we've agreed to let it go. Right?"

"I was talking about Jay," he said.

As if suddenly deaf, she concentrated on a gooey string of melted cheese that oozed from her sandwich.

• • •

On Friday morning, Lou came charging into his office while Stone was hanging his coat jacket behind his door. "What's wrong with your brother?" He slammed the *Madison Reporter* on his desk. It was folded open to the editorial page, home to a regular guest column entitled "My Opinion." The headline read, "Lawsuit Condemning Consumer Website is Arrogant and Stupid."

Stone looked at Lou. "Ted?"

"You have another brother?"

Stone skimmed through the short essay, written in aggrieved-citizen, letter-to-the-editor style. Ted was usually even-tempered but must've skipped his meditation to work up this head of righteous indignation. "This isn't about the suit," Stone said.

"Oh?" Lou positioned himself in front of one of Stone's windows, blocking Stone's view of the shimmering lake in the near distance. He boomed: "The Shore lawsuit, filed by Gordon & Newman, is signed by supposed Pro Bono Lawyer of the Year Stone Hunnicutt and his partner-henchman, Lou Desmond. It is an arrogant, shameful and stupid legal action."

Stone felt his ears burning. *Stupid.* How dare his own brother sling the one invective that had always had the power to eviscerate him.

In his deepest and most sonorous voice, Lou bellowed, "I am not your henchman."

Stone nearly laughed, but Lou's voice was menacing. "I didn't say you were," Stone said.

Lou ignored him. "Apparently," he continued, "I'm trying to put a gag order on Paul Revere. I quote, 'What redress do any of us have against rude service, shoddy and tardy workmanship, or price-gouging scoundrels? We have each other.'" Lou snorted. "Crap."

Stone bit his lip. Lou was on a roll. "And listen to this bit of highfalutin plagiarism: 'In the hour of darkness and peril and need, the people will waken and listen to hear the voice of these fellows, a knock on their door, warning them. It is not too much to say the fate of a nation depends on our freedom to sound the alarm.'"

Despite the lilt of the language, Stone was still fixated on "stupid," and the words that preceded it.

"Who does he think he is, Longfellow?!" Lou demanded.

"It's beneath him," Stone agreed. "Much more like him to slip in 'ass.'"

Lou quickly skimmed the article. "He said stupid," Lou said. "You're projecting ass."

"Arrogant. Shameful, Stupid. That spells 'ass.' It's a little in-joke of his he occasionally slips into a piece, a secret message for those in the know."

"Juvenile," Lou said. "Plus, he knows jack-shit."

"Right," Stone said, feeling vaguely taunted. "We didn't talk about the suit at all," he said. "It won't affect the case. It's just his opinion."

"Damn right it won't affect the case," Lou said, storming toward the door. "You can stake our reputation on that." Abruptly he stopped and plopped in one of the armchairs in front of Stone's desk. "Where'd you get those bruises?"

"Oh, you noticed," Stone shot back, then relented. "Another story. They're nothing."

Lou shrugged. "So, if it's not about the stupid, shameful case, what's it about?"

"It's not like him to stick his nose into other people's business. Especially in such a public way," Stone offered.

"That's what I meant," Lou said. He paused. "It's not really 'other people,' is it? So who's the ass? His big brother?"

Stone shrugged him off. Even the glitter of Lake Mendota failed to calm him. He *was* a stupid ass.

"What happened up there?" Lou asked.

"Nothing," Stone said.

"It had to be something," Lou said.

Stone shook his head. Even though Lou was his best friend, he wasn't about to confess about the books or his shame at having been sucker-punched. "What are we going to do, Lou?" he asked.

"I know a guy ..." Lou offered, and Stone had to look up to make sure his partner was kidding. He worked his lips as he studied Stone's face. "It's not really all that bad," Lou said in a conciliatory tone.

"My face or the letter?" Stone asked. Lou waved his hand. Of course, Lou, the consummate litigator, would never cede an adversary an inch of satisfaction. "For one thing, it's way over the heads of most of the citizens he wants to warn. And, more importantly, he didn't raise a single legal argument we can't respond to. He's a writer. We're attorneys."

"So we let sleeping dogs lie?" Stone asked.

"Unless you want my guy's number," Lou said. Having blown off his customary head of steam, Lou got up and rapped twice on Stone's desk. "I don't care what you do," he said, "just do something."

When Lou left, Stone realized he needed to talk to Sydney. Remarkably, she answered on the first ring.

"What took you so long?" she asked.

"So you saw it," he said. He drummed his best writing pen, a Visconti, against a yellow pad in front of him.

"Not until I got to the office. Hey, a lot of people feel the way he does. Even you." That was a huge part of it. Basically, he agreed with Ted, even if it was a closer call than Ted made it out to be. Having his name on the filing papers was embarrassing. Having attention focused on his role was even worse.

"He deliberately tried to humiliate me," Stone said. He drew an elaborate "J" on his yellow pad, framed in an ornate, curly-cued rectangle.

"He vented," Sydney said in her most calming voice, the one that usually worked to separate the girls when they were young and squabbling with each other. "It doesn't change anything. By his own choice, he lacks a following, or any notoriety to speak of. He had to borrow yours, and the Gordon & Newman name, to get the paper to print it. The case will stand or not on its own merits."

"Don't panic," Sydney continued. "I'm sure that fewer people read the op-ed page than the ImJustSayin website." She was probably right. "I'm sorry, honey," she said. "I have a nine-thirty court call. Let's go for fish fry tonight and we can talk some more." He ripped the spoiled page from his legal pad and tore it into small yellow pieces. He knew Sydney meant to comfort him with the promise of "fish fry," and he hoped she wouldn't make a fuss if tonight he actually ordered the "fried."

• • •

"Asshole." In a padded workout room at his social club, Stone confronted the hundred-pound Everlast punching bag hanging in front of him, chin down, hands up. He limbered up, dancing back and forth, then fired rapidly, right, left, right, left, as if he could break the bag with enough determination. He punched ten, twenty, twenty-five times until his arms ached and he was gasping for breath. He stepped back: Ted and Harmony splayed on the canvas before him, down for the count. He'd never hit a woman in his life, and never would, but Harmony wasn't a woman in his eyes. She was *The Cause. The Enemy. The Meddler.*

He remembered the drills he and Ted had practiced with their father at his gym. Five low kicks. Five high. Twenty punches. Five hooks right, then left. Five knee strikes. Repeat. He was younger then, but he was much angrier now. He kicked with his right leg, martial arts style, five times low, then high. He was breathing hard, and on his third — or was it his fourth? — high kick, he stumbled and fell onto his back. Lying flat-out, he saw scattered pinpricks of white light. His ears were plugged. He gasped for air. He couldn't feel or hear his heartbeat. He willed himself not to black out — it would be an hour before the lunchtime crowd arrived. He tried to call to Javier, the gym attendant, but couldn't form the words.

He came to with an oxygen mask over his mouth. Directly overhead there was a square white light, flush with the ceiling, one of many in the gym. This one was perfectly centered over him, as if he were in surgery. Uniformed young men asked him questions that Javier answered. *Stone Hunnicutt. Big lawyer in town. Late fifties? Sixties? Pretty good. Good. Comes here a lot. Not too often on the bag. Weights.*

"Any heart problems?" the paramedic asked.

Stone scrunched his eyebrows together and mumbled "no" under the mask. Why didn't Javier tell them? He was fifty-five. In good shape, good health. This was no big deal.

"Did you fall?"

Stone dropped his chin, yes.

"Where does it hurt?"

He didn't hurt, as far as he could tell. He was numb; he had no will to move. Stunned, he supposed. Stone pulled the mask down. "I'm fine, gentlemen. I slipped and fell. That's all."

The paramedics prepared the gurney next to Stone.

"No, I don't need that," he pleaded. He strained to see Javier, but he wasn't in his line of sight. "Protocol requires that we let them take you to the hospital," the club manager said. When had he appeared?

"I just bonked out. Really, George, no. I'm fine," Stone insisted. "Ask Javier."

"Most people don't pass out when they fall," George said. Petty bureaucrat. Worry wart.

"I'm not going to sue you, George," Stone said. "It was my own fault. I fell."

"You could have a concussion," George said. "You need to be checked out."

"Mr. Stone, I don't know how long you were on the floor. Let them take you," Javier said.

"Jeez," Stone moaned. It couldn't have been long. For sure, he'd passed out. He was in a dark tunnel, periphery vision impaired, depth perception skewed, too weak to protest. His sense of space was off and he knocked the kneeling paramedic next to him in the chest.

"Okay, Rocky," the paramedic said. Stone felt foolish. They lifted him onto the gurney and levered it up. He'd been a competent boxer — not as good as Ted, but pretty good. Why was this happening to him?

"I'll call Mrs. Hunnicutt," George said as they wheeled Stone away.

"Don't," he said.

"Protocol," George said again. Stone wanted to punch him.

• • •

Sydney met him at the emergency room of the community hospital. He'd been stored in one of the curtained-off beds that lined one wall and held the patients for observation or diagnosis. In contrast to the gym, the space was dimly lit, as if to encourage him to rest while waiting this turn. Beyond the curtain, he could hear a thin, high-pitched call for someone named "Joe;" a hacking dry cough that wouldn't cease and made him glad he hadn't smoked since college, and a drunk's slurred denial, "sure a drop of brandy never hurt no one." When he recognized Sydney's voice in the hallway he had to keep himself from shouting out, "Behind Door Number Three!" He wanted to laugh it off and apologize to Sydney for being called away from work, but he was touched by the panic on her face. For a moment he feared that she knew something about his condition that he didn't. Sydney wasn't the type to panic easily.

"I'm fine," he said, testing the waters. "It's nothing. I'm fine." She didn't say a word, but leaned over him. Then she raised her reading glasses from their chain around her neck and inspected his face and eyes. She drew back, put her fingers on the inside of this wrist, closed her eyes, and mouthed the count of his pulse. Unceremoniously, she dropped his hand and burst into uproarious laughter, one wave after another, catching short breaths in between. Her glasses dangled on their chain while she wiped her eyes.

"Ohmygoodness. It's not funny. I'm sorry, honey, it's not funny. I know. Really. What were you doing boxing in the middle of the morning?" When he didn't answer right away, she said, "Did the punching bag punch back?"

"I just slipped on a kick," he said, annoyed at her and at all the fuss. "Not as young as I used to be."

"You're not going in the ring with Ted," she said, a slight question at the end of what otherwise sounded like an injunction.

"Not *with* him," Stone conceded. "*Because* of him."

She sat on the side of the bed and looked at the IV bag dripping fluids into his right arm.

"Is it spiked?" she asked. "Do they have you on painkillers?"

"Tylenol 3," he said. "I'm OK"

"Well that's a relief. But really, honey, enough drama. You've got to get over this thing with Ted. We've done what he wanted. The ball's in his court."

"I was just letting go," he said.

• • •

In the next few days Stone read all the follow-up articles the *Reporter* ran on the founder of ImJustSayin, the top ten similar sites, the Better Business Bureau, and the success of its own "Consumer Action" column in which a reporter investigated a citizen complaint and printed the company's apologetic response, even if the consumer was dead wrong. The business section ran an article on the top five residential real estate developers in the state and the number of Better Business Bureau complaints against each. Jay Shore was at the bottom of the list of complaints, but the reporter managed to dredge up the old story about the collapsed deck.

Although it depended on the same statutory immunity as the defendant website, it occurred to Stone that the newspaper might not mind differentiating its professional journalism from the populist rants on the website. After all, the paper employed knowledgeable, professional real estate financial and consumer reporters, all of whom were threatened by amateur reviews of the ilk posted on ImJustSayin.

Over coffee at a nearby diner after church on Sunday, Stone was reading the business section and Sydney the Arts and Leisure section of the paper. The sermon had been entitled, "Be Doers of the Word." It had been, of course, a coincidence, but Stone was taking it personally. He read to Sydney from a recap of the Jay Shore matter quoting a law professor on the protection of the First Amendment for consumer speech and Bar President Jackson Wood on an attorney's duty to advocate for his or her client.

"In civil cases, you're not generally required to advocate for clients whose positions you don't subscribe to," the paper quoted Jackson. "It is surprising that Stone Hunnicutt's firm [Gordon & Newman] would take this on." The story said some unidentified members of the Bar Association were suggesting that Stone's Pro Bono Award be taken away.

"That's bull," Sydney said when he finished reading the story. "If there were such a movement, people in my office would be all over it and I would've heard about it. The paper's just trying to drum something up."

"Maybe your colleagues are keeping it from you," Stone said.

"Not a chance," she said, folding her section of the paper and putting it aside. "They'd love to tease me about something like this. And some, at least, would argue that the First Amendment protects you and your right to represent Jay as much as it protects the folks who want to sue him."

"Of course I have a *right* to represent him. *The Doers vs. the Sayers.* But perhaps I have a *duty* not to. There are lawyers who would take his case and would probably charge him less."

It would be one thing if Jay's case had been brought to the firm by one of his partners. Stone could then distance himself while defending his partners' rights to defend anyone they chose. At least within reason. There could be some extreme criminals or terrorists that the firm might not want to take on, but they'd never had to confront such an issue, and Jay Shore wasn't a terrorist or an arms dealer, just a run-of-the-mill businessman who hugged the middle of the political road.

"Lou isn't troubled," Sydney said. She propped an elbow on the table and cupped her chin in her palm.

"That's right," Stone said. A single, red-tinged white carnation stood in a cheap glass bud vase between them. Stone remembered that the brother-in-law of the shop owner ran a funeral home a couple of blocks away. It seemed a better use of extra tributary flowers than throwing them on a grave.

"And all the business folks likely to be your clients in the future are on Jay's side," she said. "They don't care, realistically speaking, about the pro bono side of things."

He knew she was right. He felt his mood lighten and darken at the same time.

• • •

The associate who'd found the "Dumb Ass" case came by Stone's office Monday morning. Her blond hair was pulled back in a snug ponytail and she was wearing a black pantsuit and heels. She fit his notion of what a professional should look like, except for the light blue nail polish, something he just couldn't get used to. When she wore polish at all, Sydney wore a bright red. Sometimes, one of those foreign manicures with the white tips.

"Lou said I should talk to you, if you have a minute," she said. These days, he was mildly annoyed that everyone called everyone else by their first names, no matter how senior or important they were. He was struck again by her youthful confidence and enthusiasm. He'd once had that enthusiasm, the excitement of finding the exception to the regulation that benefited his client, the right analysis, the new client seeking representation. It probably wasn't surprising that now that he was at the top of his game, maintaining that enthusiasm and his competitive edge felt like work. Running a law firm and being responsible for paying the rent and the salaries of young lawyers and the support staff — no wonder he'd become jaded. He looked at the document the young woman pushed toward him.

"These are print outs from ImJustSayin. After the articles in the *Madison Reporter*, they started posting reviews about the firm." It took a few seconds for Stone to process what she was telling him.

"Which firm?"

She looked at him as if he were someone in a memory care facility who needed her to speak more slowly. "Gordon & Newman. The first one, for instance: 'Overpriced. Always getting or giving extensions so they can rack up the fees.'"

"Doesn't sound like one of our business clients," Stone said.

"Take the next one," she said. "'Arrogant know-it-alls. Will give the store away to stay friends with their golf buddies rather than go to the mat for their client.'"

"I don't play golf," Stone said, which seemed to unnerve her.

"Lou — Mr. Desmond — was outraged," she said. "He said you'd want to know."

"Sticks and stones," he said.

"But this is the same situation as Jay Shore. Gordon & Newman is entitled to the same redress," she said.

"Not all entitlements are necessary and not all deprivations thereof require redress," he hedged, being deliberately pedantic. "Words can't hurt us unless we let them." He was aware he was quoting his father's unwavering belief in the adage, "Sticks and stones may break my bones, but words will never hurt me."

"This could hurt us in recruiting," she ventured.

Fools rush in, he thought. This one twice. He wanted to shout at her, lambaste her for her fearlessness, her tenacity, her lack of understanding. How dare she question him!

"There's one more you should look at," she said. Unflappable. Perhaps arrogant. But Gordon & Newman quality all the way.

She read, "'Gordon & Newman thinks it stands for the Wisconsin business community. They think they are outstanding corporate citizens. But they are only out for themselves and will sell their few remaining principles down the river for a buck. Exhibit I: Stone Hunnicutt, Pro Bono Lawyer of the Year and Best Business Lawyer in Wisconsin. A serpent speaketh with forked tongue.'"

"Thank you," Stone said, waving his hand toward the door. She looked a little startled. He was blaming the messenger and he knew that was unfair. "What's your name again?" he asked.

"Alice Woodland," she said.

"Good work," he grumbled as she left.

His father was wrong. Words *could* hurt you.

14

I hit him.

That had been Ted's only entry Saturday evening in his special black notebook, the one he'd told Stone was reserved for his big ideas and best thoughts. In fact, sometimes he wrote down spiritual aphorisms that he found comforting or just average ideas that might write big someday. Needing solace, he looked at the book now, five nights later, alone in his trailer, dusk falling slowly, a single light shining on the second floor of the house across the way. He stared at the new page on which he'd written that single sentence, a stark recording of a moment not yet fully processed. *I hit him.* It had shocked him. There had been no thought between the impulse and the impact. Each time he replayed the scene, his fist tingled: furious, cheated, frustrated, humiliated; proud, justified in standing up for himself; embarrassed at his spiritual failure, a pacifist flop.

He'd gone to his black book because of the front-page story in the day's Madison paper. Brother Stone was in the headlines, making himself rich by representing Jay Shore while attacking the media. Bad enough that Stone represented a man who squeezed seven sub-standard homes on a single virgin Wisconsin acre without a thought to Sacred Water; now Stone was trying to prevent disillusioned homeowners from saying so.

He flipped back through the pages.

> *You have turned my mourning into dancing;*
> *You have stripped off my sackcloth and wrapped me in gladness.*

Hogwash. The psalms were lovely poetry, but ultimately unrealistic. Harmony wasn't dancing with him and he wasn't glad. The way she was acting, you'd think he'd hit *her*, not Stone. Since last Saturday, she'd addressed him directly only when no one else was around or she was asking him to pass the salt and pepper. He hadn't once spent the night in her canopied bed. She let the others know at dinner that she was in a highly creative phase and needed her "alone time." Her sudden dedication struck Ted as calculated and flat-out false. She wasn't really that inspired a poet.

Love is rare.
Life is strange.
Nothing lasts.
People change.

When had he written that? Was it some long-forgotten piece of advice from a former girlfriend? From a poster on a college dorm room wall? Or from that guy who'd first told him about Harmony's Peace & Joy — perhaps Harmony's ex-lover? He should've known better than to fall in love with his spiritual guru, his creative muse, his best friend, his harshest editor. Any single one of those roles was fraught with peril; combined, they were a minefield, not so much for the guru/mentor — who called the shots — but for the devotee. A lover should comfort you in times of spiritual failure, not be the one to judge it. A lover picked you up when you stumbled. Defended you. Forgave you if you failed her. Didn't assume for herself the injuries you inflicted on others. Didn't presume to forgive what was not hers to forgive. Lovers weren't supposed to change overnight.

But she had changed, hadn't she? Stripping their land with a mine? Using his fight with his brother as an excuse to punish him for not signing the lease, when, really, he was the one who'd been wronged. She'd written to Stone *behind his back*! At least hitting Stone had been out in the open. Spontaneous. Honest.

The star that guides you might not be there. Billions of light years away, it could have exploded eons ago, and who would know? What difference does it make to the journeyman?

Sounded like something from one of his disaffected, existential phases. So far, little in the black book was providing comfort. He looked up just as the light in Harmony's bedroom went out. He flipped a few pages ahead and read:

You're in the right place.

More irony. But this suited him. It had taken him a long time and hours of meditation to fully understand what Harmony had meant when she'd welcomed him with those words upon his arrival at Peace & Joy. He'd been driven there by dissatisfaction with his wandering, purposeless life and that dissatisfaction had motivated him to try something completely different. Now he understood that if he didn't like his life at Harmony's Peace & Joy, he could do something about it, actually change things. If he felt he was in a terrible, depressing fugue state, he could practice patience and be alert for the guidepost pointing to what was next. Perhaps the white deer was pointing to something, telling him to save the land?

He *was* in the right place. He had the right skills. He closed the book and patted its cover. People have a right to speak out. They were right to complain about environmental rapists and two-faced lawyers who would shut them down just to earn a robust fee. What a phony Stone was, pretending to be one of the good guys. He'd show him! He took out a college-ruled notebook and began to write.

He wrote as if the fate of the republic depended on his freedom to sound the alarm. He wrote for an hour, stopping only briefly to remind himself of Longfellow's glorious language. Six-hundred and fifty words spilled onto the page. After a quick edit, he hit "send" without hesitation and emailed it to the *Madison Reporter.* A digital Paul Revere raising a pixilated alarm.

Having given vent to his frustration and his surfeit of anger, his Thursday morning meditation was not as serene as he'd hoped — perhaps he should've proofread his letter one more time before sending it. Still, Harmony seemed to have let go of some of her anger, as well. When they had breakfast after mediation, she appeared cordial. She'd put her hand on his back when he'd been at the stove, waiting for Mark to serve him some scrambled eggs with basil. But she disappeared after the meal. He didn't see her again until dinner, and then, only at a distance. Harmony was such a sensitive soul — it occurred to him that perhaps he'd not let go of *all* his anger. He resolved to be patient.

He spent the next morning helping Mark with his bees — a self-imposed penance, given his childhood fear of insects. He almost made it through the morning when, on the walk back from the hives, he felt a sharp sting on his forehead, just above his nose. He swatted at the bee, too late. It had already dropped to the ground.

"Damn!!" he cried.

"Here," Mark said, removing his gloves and pinching the bite before Ted knew what was happening. "You're not allergic, are you?"

"No," he said. "Damn."

"No good deed goes unpunished," Mark intoned.

"Aggressive little monsters," Ted muttered.

"Sorry, pal. Usually they don't attack like that unless their hives are threatened. Only the female worker bees sting," Mark said.

"Right," Ted said. "The females. Of course. What can I do for it? Shouldn't I put something on it? Toothpaste or baking soda or clay?"

"Old wives' tales. The venom is too deep for topical solutions to help. You could take some Benadryl. Or you could grin and bear it."

Ted rubbed the welt he was sure was blossoming like a bindi in the middle of his forehead and grinned.

"Come on," Mark said, "I'll buy you lunch."

They washed up at the kitchen sink in the house. Ted was happy to see someone had made a large pot of squash soup, along with some fresh bread and cheese. He sat down next to Mark. Harmony arrived and asked if she could sit next to him. He was certain she had noticed the welt on his forehead, but she didn't ask about it. When Mark offered him honey for his bread, Ted said in a low voice but loud enough that she might hear, "I think your bees have done enough damage for one day," and passed the jar to Harmony.

Just then David, Heather and Sunshine came bounding in, Heather waving the morning paper.

"You're the best," Heather squealed. For a novelist, Ted thought, she had a limited vocabulary. The way she expressed herself, you were never quite sure what she was talking about.

"I'm sorry your brother's partner is a henchman," Sunshine added, which at least gave him a clue. "I think you're so brave for saying as much"

"It's a good piece," David said to Sunshine. "But in this country, the First Amendment is *supposed* to protect us. It shouldn't require bravery to say whatever you want to say about a company or even about your brother."

"Thank you," Ted said. "I didn't know they'd publish it so soon. Or at all, really. Can I see?" Heather passed him the paper, folded open to the op-ed page. Harmony busied herself with her soup while Heather prattled on about how great it was to get published in a "big city" newspaper. Her enthusiasm was a bit embarrassing. Publishing in a Madison paper wasn't a big deal. And, seeing his words on paper under the "arrogant and stupid" headline, he felt a prickle of shame for condemning his only brother. Perhaps he should have paused before sending his midnight missive.

The corners of Harmony's mouth were turned down, as if she were peeved. "The First Amendment is meant to protect artistic expression," she said, emphasizing "artistic" as if to dismiss Ted's defense of ordinary consumer speech. She always had to be different; to make a pronouncement as if she expected it to be the last word on the subject at hand.

"Not really," Ted snapped.

"The original purpose was political and religious," Heather said, as if hoping for Ted's approval.

Harmony stiffened. "I suppose it can also pertain to a case where an individual's livelihood is at stake," she said. Ted thought she wasn't assigning blame to Stone as much as he was.

"Art *is* a livelihood," Mark said, as if settling an argument. "Hey! It's not our lawsuit. Let's congratulate Ted on his publication." He raised a glass of water for a toast.

"Isn't toasting with water bad luck?" David asked, his tone curious rather than critical.

"Old wives' tale," Mark said, and shrugged at Ted. "Two in one day."

"Greek myth," Ted corrected. He didn't mean to show off. He just remembered stuff like this. "But I know you don't wish me bad luck or a watery death, and we're nowhere near the River Lethe. So, since water *is* sacred in these parts, let's toast to ourselves, our art and our friends."

He held his glass up to Harmony, who raised hers but didn't clink his. He shouldn't have brought the Sacred Water into it.

"Oh!" Heather suddenly exclaimed. "What happened to your forehead?"

"The queen bee stung him," Mark explained. Ted let the exaggeration stand, hoping his silent suffering would evoke some sympathy from Harmony, but she was remarkably quiet and apparently uninterested. Still, they were sitting next to each other, pretending to listen to all the stories around the table about bites and bee stings and old wives' tales. He worked up his courage so that, as they were clearing their places, he asked her if she wanted to take a walk.

"Only if we don't talk about your brother," she said.

"That would be a relief," he said. "I'd much rather talk about you. About us."

"We'll survive," she said, taking his hand. They walked out to the garden, giving the hives a wide berth, and then toward the woods.

"How was your writing this week?" he asked.

"Very emotional," she said. She never said more than that when a work was in progress. Most of her work seemed to be in progress. In all these years, he'd read maybe a half-dozen she considered "finished," although she hadn't, to his knowledge, sent them out. In his opinion, they were good, but not great. Few were truly original enough to be publishable. "Drafts of two poems."

Two. Not much production. He was glad he wasn't a poet. He couldn't imagine spending a solid week writing in earnest and having only two poems to show for the effort. He'd seen Harmony hover over a single stanza for two hours. He couldn't help but wonder what she was truly doing, thinking all that time. But as a prose writer he wouldn't understand. At her rate, a single chapter would take him a year. He didn't have that kind of patience.

"You know I'm sorry," he said.

"We agreed not to talk about it. It's between you and Stone," she said. "Yes."

"Although I will say this: you must apologize directly to him," she said. He made a face, and she added, "Eventually. For both things."

He nodded. Of course the article would be a second blow to Stone. He was proud of the op-ed, but a little embarrassed by its ad hominem tone. He shook off the guilty image of Stone's bloodied nose. "But no apology to Jay Shore," he said. "That's business. *His* bad business."

"Be fair," she said. "His houses aren't aesthetically pleasing, according to *your* aesthetic."

"Please don't say he creates jobs in the community," he said. She dropped his hand. He realized they were now on a topic more important to her than Ted's breach of the peace or Stone's representation of a real estate tycoon.

"I've been thinking," he volunteered, changing the subject, "that *Amor* is ready for publication. Yes, I'm angry at Stone, but I do trust Andrew's judgment." He looked to her for approval.

"More than mine?" she asked. Perhaps, he thought. He knew Andrew wouldn't coddle him. But he also wouldn't try to make him into a successful writer if he weren't already one. With Harmony, he wasn't sure if she was working to foster his vision of himself or her own. "You have more work to do on *Amor*," she said.

"I thought it would help you out financially. We wouldn't have to sign the lease if we published." He used "we" consciously, to compliment her for her considerable help to date.

"That's optimistic," she said. Of course literary fiction wasn't terribly lucrative, but Andrew's offer had been generous, and she had no right to insult him on that score.

He rubbed his forehead, the sting now raised, swollen and sore. "Maybe I should write an op-ed about the mine," he mused. "To clarify my thinking."

She narrowed her eyes. "Is that a threat?" she asked.

"I suppose *Rolling Stone* or the *Atlantic* or even the *New Yorker* would find the topic timely. Don't you?"

"It's not fracking," she said.

"But our mine raises similar issues, don't you think? Personal financial interests versus larger environmental concerns? Distractions from finding sustainable solutions to major problems?"

"Please," she scoffed. "That sounds like a high school sophomore's science thesis." She turned back toward the house. He hurried to catch up. A good night's sleep in her bed was unlikely now. "Five hundred words in the local rag and he thinks he's big time," she muttered.

"I know I'm not," he said. "But the *subject* — the Sacred Water."

She looked at him and her eyes filled. If it were money she wanted or needed, he'd offer what he had, and she'd turn him down. He'd ruined any chance of her receiving a donation from Stone, and, worse yet, hadn't really known that she felt such a dire need for money. He'd not appreciated the grandeur of her expectations. But he sensed there was something else at work.

"You still don't understand," she said.

"What don't I understand?" he let his voice rise in challenge.

"What we're doing here," she said.

He swallowed hard. She was right. *Love is rare. Life is strange.* "Let me try to understand," he said.

15

"Now you know what it feels like," Jay said. He'd agreed to meet Stone for a drink at The Madison Club, where all the Gordon & Newman partners were members, and many saw their fathers' oil portraits — faces earnest, serious, self-satisfied — hanging in gilded frames throughout the club's various lounges and reading rooms. Stone and Jay sat in a grouping of maroon leather chairs in a corner of the cocktail lounge near the second-floor entrance. Stone was telling Jay about the ImJustSayin posts on Gordon & Newman.

"They're disparaging," Stone said.

"Care to join my suit?" Jay asked.

"Of course not," Stone said.

Jay's face darkened as he put down his scotch. "*Of course not?*" Jay waited. Stone understood he'd belittled Jay's claim when in fact he'd meant to show that not all insults required a legalistic response. "*Of course not?* Are you saying you don't believe in the importance of my suit? Are you ashamed to represent me?"

"No, I'm not saying that." Stone said, although, in fact, that's what he was feeling. "I don't want to get your hopes up is all. You know we've always said the case was fifty-fifty at best." His mouth felt parched, so he took a long sip of his Glenlivet. Jay didn't appear mollified, so Stone tried to back off. "Juries dislike lawyers even more than real estate developers," Stone said.

"So you admit these posts damage the firm, but you don't have the balls to fight the bullies," Jay said. He pointed his glass toward Stone.

"Sticks and stones." Stone gestured to the waiter for another round.

"My ass," Jay said. "When your own brother calls you out, it more than hurts. It demolishes your reputation."

"That's yet to be determined," Stone said.

"To be determined?" Jay nearly shouted. Stone surveyed the other tables and scowled at Jay. He could feel the blood rushing to his face. Jay lowered his voice, which made him sound even angrier. "That's what *you guys* are supposed to prove — that *they've* irreparably damaged *my* reputation. Now they're going after *yours*." He shook the cubes in his glass while the server waited to set the fresh drinks in front of them.

"We'll do what we can," Stone said, offering his empty glass to the waiter.

"Look it, if you don't want the case, I'll give it to someone else," Jay said. "I'm sure there are a lot of lawyers in Madison who'd be happy to charge me a million bucks and actually act like they're on my side." Stone hesitated. Lou would kill him, but Stone would love to have the case go away. "Is that what you want?" Jay demanded.

Again, Stone was tongue-tied. Jay knocked back the last of his scotch, then stood up, towering over Stone. He looked down on him as if Sone were a defeated fighter whimpering in his corner. "I wouldn't give you the satisfaction," Jay said, and marched out of the lounge without looking back.

The waiter swooped in, cleared Jay's glass and asked Stone if he could bring him anything. A third scotch before dinner was unheard of. He looked up and nodded "yes."

He hadn't been in this situation before. Over the years of his career, he'd not been personally involved in cases or deals he didn't believe in. Yes, there had been times when, at his client's behest, he'd argued for a position on some tax liability or other expense allocation that he may have thought was over-reaching, but a deal was only a deal, an exchange of financial advantages between various economic powers which were by definition already advantaged. No one got hurt. Lives weren't in the balance.

He'd never been ashamed of a client or a specific case. It wasn't that Jay's interests were crassly commercial; most of his clients' matters were. But in those cases, his personal convictions and beliefs hadn't been at stake. He could honestly say he'd never "sold out," at least not outright. He felt like his personal integrity was at stake. But so was loyalty to a client and friend.

He'd barely touched his drink when Lou and Mark McCray, the junior partner in charge of the day-to-day preparation of Jay's case, entered the room.

"Jay sure was in a rush on the way out," Lou said. "He didn't even see us. Is he OK?"

Stone held out his palm, motioning for them to sit down. "He'll get over it," Stone said.

"What does he have to 'get over'?" Lou asked. The waiter put a clear drink with a blue plastic sword of stuffed bleu cheese olives in front of him and then asked Mark what he wanted. "Club soda with lime," Mark said. Stone, on his third scotch, felt mildly chastised. His father had always turned mean — meaner — after two.

"Gotta stay alert for fourth-grade math," Mark said unapologetically.

"Two and two?" Lou asked, looking at Stone.

"Depends on what you want the answer to be," Stone played along. It was a standard joke among corporate lawyers, who sometimes shopped for answers among the tax accountants, economists, investment bankers and venture capitalists who served their business clients.

"We're at rates," Mark said.

Lou laughed, "Start 'em young."

"Miles per hour," Mark said, and squeezed the lime.

Stone drifted off in his memory of story problems. When they were young, Ted always had the answers on the tip of his tongue without being able to explain his thought process, and so had been of no help to Stone. To Ted, the answers were always obvious.

"Drives me crazy," Stone said, turning to Mark. "If you've got five apples and four oranges, how many bicycles will you have in six months?"

Lou looked at Stone's scotch and smirked. "The man never could hold his liquor," he said.

"Depends what you do with them," Mark replied, and they both looked at him.

"That's why we pay you the big bucks," Lou said, raising his glass toward Mark. "So," he turned to Stone, "Alice told you about the ImJustSayin posts?"

"The girl's got balls," Stone said, surprised at his own vernacular. Sydney would be furious with his use of both words. He put down the scotch.

"I like her," Lou said. "She's going to do just fine with us."

"You're the chicken-shit who made her tell me," Stone said.

Lou smiled widely. "For practice. Part of her professional training."

Mark eyed them over a long sip from his glass, as if waiting for the sparring to land an actual blow.

Stone suddenly pictured Ted's fist coming at him, a blur the color of cookie dough but tough as a rock. "We should resign Jay's case," he said.

The waiter brought Lou's second double and a side saucer of additional olives. Mark waved off the waiter's offer of more drinks, as Stone shrugged. Lou sucked two olives from their spear. "Sorry you can't stay," Lou said to Mark, who was already standing up.

"Me, too," Mark said.

Lou watched Mark go. "Hell, no," he said. "We're not resigning anything. We're just getting started."

Stone studied his partner's profile — high forehead, aquiline nose, his once well-defined jaw, now doughy. "And look at the damage so far," he said.

Lou twirled his olive spear. "You mean a couple a-holes call us arrogant and you want to cave? Where I come from, arrogance is a virtue."

Citius. Altius. If you were in fact smarter, better, stronger, then it wasn't arrogance, according to Stone's father. Newton Thaddeus Hunnicutt *had* been truly arrogant, Stone thought, under the guise of promoting Ted's brilliance. As a youngster, Stone had understood that only someone as brilliant as their father could sire a genius like Ted. "It's a virtue to be confident in being the best if you *are* the best, but it's a fatal flaw if you're exaggerating your worth." Stone said.

"We *are* the best," Lou said simply. "Hell, you've got awards to prove it." That Lou had yet to be named "Best Litigator in Wisconsin" was a sore point between them. Stone knew Lou used Stone's father's logic to console himself: *who* was brilliant enough to judge Lou's brilliance as a trial lawyer?

"Our reputation as a firm is being trashed. They don't mean "arrogant" and "overpriced" as compliments," Stone said.

"So who cares? We *are* overpriced, but we get results."

Lou was right, Stone was overreacting. It wasn't the accusation that they were overpriced that bothered him — that was almost a badge of honor in the corporate community. Rather, what provoked him was the allegation that they routinely compromised their principles and that they didn't "go to the mat" for their clients. The firm *was* compromising its principles — Stone's, anyway — by having taken Jay's case in the first place. Stone couldn't go to the mat for Jay without losing some of his standing in the pro bono community.

"If you're worried about the firm's reputation — or more particularly, your own — then you should be naturally aligned with Jay," Lou said.

"But I believe in freedom of the press," Stone said slowly, adding some solemnity. He resented Lou's insinuating that injured pride was what was motivating him. "The case is a loser and we shouldn't bring it. We should let some ambulance-chaser take it on."

He was feeling self-righteous now, too.

"It's not a loser until it's lost and it's far from trial," Lou said. He pointed at Stone with the plastic cocktail sword. "We're not even ready for summary judgment. We're still tracking down who wrote the offending posts."

Stone hadn't been aware that tracing the posts was possible; at the very least, he knew it wasn't easy. "Surely freedom of speech doesn't depend on who the speaker is," Stone said, indignantly. He braced himself with a long pull on his scotch.

"Surely," Lou said, imitating Stone's inflection, "only the arrogant would make such an absolute statement prior to investigation."

Stone rubbed the lemon peel around the edge of his new drink. "What do you expect to discover that would render a statement like 'shoddy workmanship' unprotected speech?"

"The difference between you and me on this one, my friend, is that I am not blinded by the principles I hold dear. Principles, such as they are, require thorough investigation of all the facts that might *possibly* be relevant, if not to the law, at least to the predisposition of the defendants to settlement."

"Blackmail?" Stone asked, slowly getting a bead on where Lou was going with this: it was possible that some of the online critics might be embarrassed if their identity were known publicly.

"In the vernacular," Lou said, raising his glass in toast to his own insight, "it's called 'going to the mat.'" Stone studied the carpet, a maroon background with a geometric gray design of Celtic crosses interlaced with intricate patterns that looked luxurious but were in essence practical, all the better to obscure spilled hors d'oeuvres and drinks.

They sat in silence for a while, Lou standing several times to shake hands with opposing counsel, a fellow fundraising committee member and then a neighbor. Stone knew as many Club members as Lou, and Gordon & Newman was as much his firm as Lou's but sitting there alone while Lou glad-handed made Stone feel like second fiddle. He was seething about Jay's lawsuit and what it portended for the firm. When Lou finally sat down, Stone said, "I'm telling Jay we're resigning."

"You can't do that," Lou said.

Stone uncrossed his legs and leaned forward, resting his elbows on his knees. "It's my client. My firm. Of course I can," he said. He wanted to sound commanding, but he knew he sounded childish.

"*Our* firm, my friend. One we've built, in part, on the success of Jay Shore. How long have we represented him?" Lou leaned forward and folded his hands.

"It doesn't matter," Stone said, looking away.

"Twenty years, and what, fifty-plus million in fees, and it doesn't *matter*? As his lawyers, don't we have an ethical duty to represent him in all his legal matters, to the best of our ability?" Lou looked at Stone as if that should be the end of the discussion.

"How dare you talk to me about ethics," Stone said. He took a deep breath and continued, "I've always been the conscience of this firm — and God knows, we need one. Integrity and ethics are my only concerns here."

"Jay feels he's been wronged," Lou said. "I can get him some relief, probably without having to go to court and arguing about your precious principles."

"So, it's just our integrity at stake then," Stone scoffed. Winning Jay's case on the technicalities of the law would be bad enough, but would winning through intimidation be any better?

"Oh, give me a break, Stone. If nothing else, consider your fiduciary duty to your partners. They rely on Jay for a good part of their livelihoods and reputations. That's not to mention how generous Jay has always been whenever they or you or even Sydney have asked for a contribution to their favorite charity or cause. Sorry, friend, but it's not all about you."

Stone drew himself up, ready to explode in response, but Lou delivered a shot that knocked him off his pegs. "Resigning the case at this juncture would be just plain stupid," Lou said.

There it was, out front and center. "Stupid" was the word Thaddeus Newton Hunnicutt had used as a term of supposed endearment for his older son, the way some fathers used "Junior" or "Buddy" or "Kid."

Stone drained his glass. "Stupid?" He looked around for the waiter, thinking about ordering another.

"Jeez, Stone, what's got into you?" Lou looked truly concerned.

"My brother humiliates me, a wacko website says I'm an arrogant whore and you call me stupid. What do you think is wrong?"

"I really don't know, Stone. I do know that you're way too emotional about Jay's case."

"I'm not emotional," Stone said.

Lou slowly released his breath. "Look. You don't like the case, but it's an interesting one. A close one, to be sure. But potentially a lucrative one. The partners would be furious if you fired one of our biggest clients."

"Let's ask 'em," Stone said.

"Terrible idea," Lou said.

"I'll call a meeting for tomorrow afternoon."

"Don't do that," Lou said. "Please, don't. At least, give it some thought. You don't have to decide now. Come, let's go home."

"I can drive myself home," Stone said. "I've only had a couple."

"At least four, which is way over your limit," Lou said. "I'll admit you're holding it better than usual, but we don't need a DUI on top of everything else. In fact, let's both take a cab."

"I could drive," Stone said stubbornly, but as he stood up the room swirled. "I'll get my own damn cab," he said and sat back down.

"Your funeral," Lou said, and got up to leave. A few steps away, he turned and said, "Just sleep on it, will you?" and marched out of the room.

"I'm not stupid," Stone muttered. The waiter brought two glasses of water and seemed surprised that Lou was gone.

"Stupid" had been his father's word, even before Ted came along. Once Ted's genius had been discovered and routinely flaunted, their father had called Ted "Little Man," never "stupid." Stone drew his own conclusion about the meaning of the word. When Stone started calling kindergarteners he didn't like "stupid," his mother told him not to.

"Stupid isn't a nice word," she'd said one day when he was helping her bake cookies and Ted was taking a nap.

"Daddy calls me 'stupid,'" he'd replied. When the cookie scoop stuck, he used his finger to dislodge the dough, but she didn't seem to notice.

"That's different," his mother had said. "Your father loves you."

Stone's little mind had considered this, but skeptically. "Don't you love me?" he'd asked.

"Of course I do," she'd said, and he could feel the alarm in her voice. She'd bent down and put her face in front of his, so close he could see each eyelash, curled slightly up at the end. "I love you more than anything," she said.

"More than Ted?" he'd wanted to know.

She'd offered him a cookie, still warm, smelling of oats and melted chocolate. "Not more. The same as. I love you both equally."

"Daddy loves Ted more," he'd persisted.

"I don't think so, Stone," she'd said. "Think about it. You're older, so he's loved you longer, right?"

He'd felt comforted by that.

That night, he overheard her trying to discourage his father from using the word "stupid." "Sticks and stones," his father had said.

"You have no idea how a child reacts to such a thing," his mother had said.

"Don't be stupid," he'd said. So they both were stupid, Stone had thought, but to be honest, he loved his mother. More than his father.

Later, when Stone was wrestling with AP calculus during his

senior year in high school, his father had made generous use of the "stupid" word while trying to help him study. The more Stone struggled, the more frustrated the elder Hunnicutt became. Their discussions of first and second derivatives got so animated and loud that Stone soon understood that they weren't really arguing about math — who could care that much about the rate of change? — but about the fact of his mother's death two years earlier from pancreatic cancer. Thaddeus Hunnicutt was furious with the world in general.

What Stone hadn't understood then was how fearful and insecure his father actually was beneath the bravado of his prodigious mind and unswerving ego. Intimidated, perhaps, by his sons. Earlier, Stone had learned from his mother that his paternal grandfather had left his family when Thaddeus was eleven, requiring him to beg for the prestigious scholarships that ultimately paid his way through Macalester College with the help of menial jobs and a sparse lifestyle. Thaddeus had graduated with a sense of entitlement because of the loss of his father, and when the world wronged him a second time, Thaddeus knew for certain that he was entitled to raise a genius son.

Finally, two nights before the final calculus exam, his exasperated father quit "helping" his son, but Ted, on his way to the refrigerator for a glass of milk, had said something — Stone couldn't remember exactly what it was now but something about calculus being only a language for people who understood it. That had made the whole subject suddenly fall into place. As if in an instant, he "got it." It had been a moment of elation and gratitude, the proof he wasn't "stupid" after all. He'd aced the exam and the course, although he couldn't remember much of it now. "See," he'd dared to say to his father when he received his straight A report card. "You're stupid if you think I think you're stupid," his father said, and Stone stormed to his room. It was one of the few times since his mother's funeral that he'd cried. When his tears dried, he realized something else: Other people usually didn't call him "stupid," not even Ted.

• • •

Stone walked into the house through the kitchen door, expecting to see Sydney at the table with the newspaper or *The Economist* and perhaps a cup of tea. The idea of tea and toast suddenly appealed to him as he pictured his mother's rose-lined china cups and bread plates calming him as a child. He filled the kettle with fresh tap water and was about to take the English breakfast from the cabinet when he saw a lavender packet labeled, "STRESS RELIEF" in bold letters. He read the content listing while the water boiled. Ingredients he'd never heard of, none of them, "tea." What was a carob pod? A kava root? What was barley malt doing in "tea"? Organic barks, organic roots, organic seeds and oils. It reminded him of Ted and purslane and why his body still ached, even though he'd over-medicated with the Club's scotch. He took the tea bag out of its tell-tale wrapper, wadded up the lavender paper and put it in the waste basket under the sink.

Their everyday china was boldly colored, in four different solid colors, two plates, two bowls and two mugs in each earthy color: yellow, blue, green and red. He took a blue mug from the cupboard and warmed it with boiling water, the way he'd seen Sydney do so many times. He was not a tea-drinker, except when his stomach was upset.

He was bobbing the tea bag up and down, imagining his vindication at tomorrow's partnership meeting when Sydney arrived, dressed in her jogging shorts and a red-and-white Badgers tee shirt. With a sweatband around her head and a purple Fitbit on her wrist, she looked to Stone not a day over thirty-five. Despite having two children and a full-time job with high-risk clients, she didn't need scotch or calming tea to relax. How she got through Harvard Law near the top of her class with so little stress was still a wonder to him. During her second and third years, he thought he had contributed to her serenity, but after they were married, seeing her frost cupcakes for school while dictating her thoughts on an appellate brief, he knew he was more likely to be a disturbance to her serenity than its source.

In fact, sometimes she accused him of *creating* drama, which was ridiculous. He always felt his reactions and emotions were those that any normal person would have. He didn't *create* drama; he *recognized* it. When drama happened, it was like an ache in his stomach, even if he appeared cool, calm, in charge, the way a lawyer of his stature was supposed to look and behave. Sydney lived so much in the middle, no peaks higher than a molehill, no valleys deeper than a tire rut. She was as calming as vanilla, coaxing him off ledges which, she said, existed only in his imagination.

"Tell me you didn't let Lou lead you astray," she teased.

He sipped his tea. Sydney opened the fridge and poured herself a tall glass of orange juice. "Where's the car?" she asked. She didn't sound suspicious, but she did sound curious. It wasn't a typical question of hers.

"At the Club," Stone said casually. "I thought Lou needed to take a cab, so I decided to set a good example. We can get the car tomorrow."

"You didn't share a taxi?" she asked. She took off her sweatband and fiddled with the elastic holding her ponytail in place.

"He had someplace else to go," Stone lied. He was surprised she didn't lecture him on moderation. Maybe she did understand his current pain and discomfort.

"So how did it go today? Did you move around every hour like I told you?" she asked.

"I tried, but I did get a little stiff," he said.

She laughed, "I can see that." The toaster popped up, startling them both.

"You know," she said, "we need a new toaster. Only one side works."

He would've sworn he hadn't been told before about the toaster. "Which side?" he asked. She pointed at it, Stone's slice of wheat looking as fresh and soft as when he'd dropped it in.

"Your guess is as good as mine," she smiled.

• • •

While most law partnerships allocated votes according to the same formula they used to share profits, Lou and Stone had committed themselves to a one-partner-one-vote methodology. Although it appeared overly democratic, it did not produce overly democratic results. Lou and Stone were still recognized as the leaders of the firm and when the two of them agreed on something, which they almost always did, there was rarely a reason to record a formal vote at all.

Being presented with an actual disagreement — though highly civil and intellectual in tone — was a new experience for most of Gordon & Newman's twenty-eight partners. Without consulting Lou, Stone called the meeting, just as he'd threatened. He scheduled it for 4:30 p.m. in the partners' conference room in the southeast corner of their top floor. An oblong mahogany table stretched the length of the room, accompanied by twenty-eight plush gray leather chairs, a fresh yellow pad and sharpened pencil imprinted with the firm's name in front of each. Except for the compensation meetings, no more than twenty-two lawyers usually attended. Today, Stone counted twenty-one. They were surrounded on two sides by dark oil paintings of Messrs. Gordon, Newman, Reichart, Holt and half a dozen other long-dead early members of the firm who now gazed out of the floor-to-ceiling windows to the lake and city below.

Lou, Chair of the Executive Committee (it was Stone's year as Vice-chair; they alternated), convened the meeting promptly and promised they would be done in an hour. He then asked Stone to present the matter for review. Stone took a deep breath. He'd expected that Lou would present a neutral statement of the issue to be voted on; asking him to explain the situation might make Stone sound like a lone wolf. He stood up and smoothed his jacket. It occurred to him that he was also being given the opportunity to *frame* the issue. He positioned himself near the portrait of Edwin Holt and began.

"I bring this matter to you today because I believe our firm's reputation is at stake. Thirty years ago, I joined Gordon & Newman because it exemplified the best of our noble profession. My first cases were pro bono, working with Mr. Holt on sex discrimination and AIDS matters. As a firm, we are unsurpassed in corporate law, but we have also always been dedicated to representing the oppressed: civil rights cases in the sixties, reproductive rights in the seventies, sex discrimination in the eighties, gay rights in the nineties, and so on." He bowed his head in reverence to the image of Mr. Holt, and realized with a start that every leader on the wall was white and male. At this moment that was beside the point. "I fear that we are becoming nothing more than a big business. Our desire for ever-increasing profits-per-partner undermines our judgment in accepting certain cases."

Stone explained that Jay Shore recently had asked the firm to shut down a consumer review website and that the *Madison Reporter* and the publishing community were up in arms. He read *verbatim* the criticisms of Shore Homes on ImJustSayin and then cited the case law that supported the website's side of the case. "A website is entitled to the same protections as any publisher. To sue a publisher is arrogant, shameful and stupid." Out of the corner of his eye, he thought he saw Lou smirk. "I ask you to do the right thing and resign the case of Jay Shore vs. ImJustSayin."

He sat down, flushed. Not since law school had he had to make such a formal oral argument, and his heart was pounding as if he were before an actual court. But he felt momentarily triumphant. Eloquent, even. Lou-like.

Of course, oral argument was Lou's forte, and Stone was surprised when he demurred, putting Mark McCray in the role of "defense attorney." First, Mark said, it was a close and complicated case. Second, Jay Shore had been libeled and there was more at stake than what met the eye: in discovery, they expected some relevant facts to emerge that would completely justify Jay's suit. Third, Jay's concerns were the concerns of businesses everywhere, vulnerable to reputational slurs by a single disgruntled customer. Finally, but not to be overlooked, Jay Shore's business represented 10 percent of Gordon & Newman's revenue. Resigning the suit and its million-dollar payday would surely cause Jay to take the rest of his business — real estate, estate planning, employment, tax, and all its other corporate matters — elsewhere. Could anyone in the room say they were so ashamed of the case that they'd take a 10 percent cut in pay?

In rebuttal, Stone briefly repeated his key points and McCray his. Then Lou opened the floor for questions. There were only a few, all directed at Mark: what were Jay's actual numbers over the past five years? (Substantial.) What was the trial schedule of the case? (At least a couple of months until they could seek an injunction.) How far along were they in discovery? (Halfway). Were there any Ethics Committee rulings against this sort of thing? (None on point.) What was ImJustSayin's reach? (ten thousand Wisconsin subscribers.) Had the Wisconsin Press Association taken a position on the case? (Not yet.) What about the Wisconsin Chamber of Commerce? (No.)

It wasn't clear to Stone, who was trying to read their faces, whether any of his partners really cared about these answers, rather than just showing off their legal agility. He thought some of the younger, more idealistic partners would side with him, but they were — as expected — silent observers of the proceedings. At 5:15 p.m., Lou looked at his watch. "Unless there are any other burning desires to be heard," he said, "shall we vote? All those in favor of resigning the case of *Jay Shore and Shore Homes Inc. vs. IJS Inc., d/b/a/ ImJustSayin.com*, please raise your right hand."

"Shouldn't that be the left?" one of the smart-aleck, middle-aged corporate partners quipped.

Stone raised his hand and looked down at the deep tooth marks on the Gordon & Newman pencil at his place. He was horrified that someone's secretary had let that happen. He looked up and saw that his vote was joined by only two of the idealistic young litigators and two partners ten years Stone's junior.

Stone felt the first blush of humiliation, although he wasn't really surprised by the outcome. As he'd just said, his noble profession had become just another greedy big business. Lou perfunctorily asked for the nays, and declared the motion lost, 5-15-1, with the chair abstaining.

"Before you go," Stone stood up. "I'd like to state on the record that I will not participate in the profits from this suit."

"Duly noted," Lou said wearily. "The Compensation Committee will honor your wishes in that regard." How officious. There was a little twitter around the room. Everyone knew that Stone's gesture would have little actual impact on his take from the firm. When they calculated Stone's share of the tens of millions of the firm's revenues, they'd subtract the profits on one million of Jay's billings before applying Stone's percentage. As Stone had almost said at the pro bono dinner, before he thought better of it, "no one would starve."

The partners filed out quickly, most of them eager to finish some remaining business before going home, but some headed directly for the elevator. Lou and Stone were the last two to leave. One of the conference room attendants who no doubt was responsible for placement of the chewed pencils came by to clear the coffee cups and water glasses. In a moment of forbearance, Stone decided not to mention the teeth marks.

Lou leaned his hand on Stone's shoulder. "Shall we go back to the Club and pick up our cars?"

"Sydney said she'd swing by for me," he said. "I said I'd take her to dinner." In truth, Sydney probably wanted to make sure he didn't over-indulge two nights in a row. "Great," Lou said, accepting the offer Stone had made a point of not making. "I haven't seen her in weeks. You'll call me when she gets here?" Lou was acting as if Stone needed to save face, but he didn't need to. He was the one with principles, the one who was comfortable — and certain — taking the high road, following his own certain moral compass. "Come on, Stone. It's done. Can you really blame them for voting their pocketbooks?" He slapped Stone's back.

"I blame myself for not being more convincing," Stone said. He straightened his back as Lou removed his hand.

"Gotta get over yourself, my friend. The cavalry is coming for both of us. Burn and Winkel voted with you so that next to me they'd be the largest billers if you won, and then they'd bury you. There are very few people in this world you can trust. Just so you know, I'm one of the few."

When Stone went to his office to gather his briefcase, the Pro Bono Award on the corner of his desk taunted him. He was angry and wanted to smash it against the wall, but he couldn't bring himself to do that. He placed it in his briefcase, thinking he'd hide it at home.

In Sydney's car, Stone pouted while Lou charmed Sydney. Of course, Lou didn't mention anything about the vote, which was firm business and confidential. Stone hadn't told her either. Sydney laughed at all the right places, unaware that her good cheer was grating on every nerve of Stone's body.

When they arrived at the Club, Stone was afraid Sydney was going to ask Lou to join them, but as she handed the keys to the valet, Lou said he was late for a dinner across town and had to go. Whether he did or not Stone didn't really care; he was just glad that he would be alone with Sydney. They went up to the members' formal dining room, where it was white-linen quiet and they could talk. Passing on cocktails, they ordered the daily special, a shrimp-and-mushroom risotto. He figured his financial business was Sydney's business, so he told her about the vote at the firm.

She listened sympathetically, then simply said, "I'm proud of you. You were ready to make the big sacrifice for what you believed in. That's important."

He was so grateful, his eyes watered.

"Although I do think that in this case, your partners saved you from yourself."

"That's not what I would have expected, coming from you," he said.

A grain of rice had stuck to the corner of her lips and Sydney dabbed at it. "I can see both sides of this one," she said, checking her napkin for the rice. "I think Ted's op-ed is what got to you, not the Constitution or the yahoos on that website." He wanted to protest, but she continued, "Arrogant? Shameful? Stupid? The man knows how to push your buttons."

He flinched. He'd used the words in his presentation to the partnership. He wanted to change the subject. "You weren't on Ted's side?" he asked.

"Side? He's not a litigant in the case," she said, rather legalistically, he thought. "Neither, for that matter, are you. I'm on one side, and one side only: yours."

He slept poorly, Sydney's words rattling around like dice in his semi-consciousness. He appreciated her support but was troubled that she presumed too much about him. She'd said he'd been ready "to make the big sacrifice," but he hadn't been. If he'd really been ready, he would've told Jay to his face that he didn't want his firm involved in the case. He would've suffered the consequences, including protests from his partners. He could have, but he hadn't. He'd known that the partners would vote their self-interests and he could stand aloft — oh so safely — on his high and mighty principles. He suffered almost nothing by giving up his share of Jay's fees from the case. He could, if he wanted to, make up the amount easily by increasing his overall percentage. Sydney was wrong. He'd not sacrificed anything. He was a shameful phony, just as Ted had said. He didn't deserve the Pro Bono Award.

He slipped out of bed and went to the den. He found his briefcase and pulled out the crystal paperweight from the Bar Association. In the dark, it didn't look particularly impressive.

He rubbed his fingers over the engraved scales of justice and the inscription, "Stone Hunnicutt, Dane County Bar Association, Pro Bono Lawyer of the Year." He let out a long sigh, then took it to the kitchen. He wrapped the Award in paper towels and hunted in the garage for a box and old newspapers. He packaged the Award and returned to his den, where he searched for a piece of stationery. With his nose just a few inches from the paper, he wrote, "For personal reasons I regret I must return this Award." He thought of adding, "So you can give it to someone more deserving," but that would be stupid — the thing was personalized with his name.

He heard a floorboard pop and held his breath. He didn't want to explain himself to Sydney. Hastily, he hand-printed Jackson Wood's name on the box. He placed it in his briefcase. Gloria could messenger it to Jackson in the morning.

Slowly he climbed the stairs. He felt oddly relieved. No one was likely to notice the empty space on his desk, but *he* would know and that was, ultimately, what mattered — not what the Bar Association or Jay or his father or Ted or even Sydney thought of him. For once, he felt free from the judgment of others.

When he arrived at work the next morning, he gave the box to Gloria without any explanation beyond, "By messenger, please. Personal charge." Feeling unburdened, he entered his office and closed the door. Immediately he was struck by the fifty little squares and oblongs of crystal and Lucite, mementos from deals he'd closed, scattered on the bookcase over his credenza. Worthless dust-catchers. Fifty feathers — an impressive collection that reflected the *fact* of his vast experience but didn't — and couldn't — attest to the *quality* of his services on those deals or the importance of the deals themselves. Should he jettison those too?

Stone knew that in the law business he wouldn't land his next deal without having a reputation for the many he had done before. Nothing bred success like the appearance of success. His clients were terribly susceptible to name-dropping — it fed their egos to complain about Stone's exorbitant rates and to let their competitors know they were represented by the Goliath, Gordon & Newman. He'd given up enough for one day. At least the celebratory icons reflected actual achievement. That's who he was — a dealmaker. And he wasn't giving up his livelihood, as well.

He sat down to review a stack of documents on his desk. Lou knocked and simultaneously opened the door, then stood with his arms outstretched, as if holding up the doorframe.

"We're good?" he asked. Lou didn't seem to register the absence of the Pro Bono Award on Stone's desk. It struck Stone that these awards weren't top-of-mind for anyone except the recipient and possibly the overly ambitious next in line. Who remembers even the big ones, like last year's Superbowl, Stanley Cup or World Series champions?

Stone smiled. What a charmer Lou was. Sometimes gruff, out-sized, arrogant, but always eloquent. He was the most loyal person Stone knew. Business was business. Politics was politics. And neither defined him. Friends were friends. Even his ex-wives (both of them) were friends.

"We're good," Stone replied, "but the sooner you settle this case, the better."

"I'll have our PI brief you this week," Lou said. "We're getting there." As Lou left, Stone wished he could be more like him, impervious to the opinions of others. Stone had grown up defined by who he wasn't, by having to prove his father wrong through the testimony of teachers, employers and awards panels. "You're such a people pleaser," Sydney would say whenever he worried about something beyond his control, such as whether his daughters' boyfriends would like him. "Who cares?" Sydney said, always more practical and to the point. "They probably won't last, and if they do stick around, you can be sure it's not because of you. It's usually about the bride, Stone, not the father of the bride."

Alone again, staring at the gaping space on his desk — large only in his mind — Stone felt somewhat buoyed, as if he could put all this anxiety about the case behind him. Or at least rise above it. Either way, he had work to do, and he was eager to do it.

16

Sydney was chopping onions and celery for stir-fry when he got home that evening. Stone plopped down at the kitchen table, grateful for a return to the quotidian. She was wearing gray slacks and a starched white shirt that looked as if she'd just put it on, although she'd probably worn it to work under her navy blazer. He loved how young she looked, how fresh. She radiated optimism, which always kept him from slipping into the trough of mild despair that so often loomed over him, even when there really was nothing to worry about.

She'd left the mail on the table, and on top of the bills, ads and magazines, there was a brown cardboard box addressed to him in an unfamiliar hand. At once, he noticed the return address: a P.O. Box in Upson, Wisconsin. He started to shake it.

"Why do people do that?" Sydney asked.

"To guess what's in it," he answered, as if that weren't obvious.

"Could be breakable," she said.

"Doesn't sound like it," he said.

"You can't know that until *after* you've shaken it," she said. She raised her eyebrows in a way that said she'd won her point.

He laughed. She was right again. "But it doesn't say fragile," he said. She handed him a paring knife. The box had been sealed along all the edges with clear plastic tape. He was about to slice into the tape when he hesitated. "Upson," he said. "It can't be good."

"I'm sure it's not lethal," she said. "They don't allow explosives in the mail."

"Supposedly," he said.

"Or other toxins," she teased. "They sniff them out."

"Who do you suppose it's from?"

"One of them, obviously. Open it and find out."

Carefully, he cut the seam in the middle at the top of the box. It was filled with crinkly shredded paper straw. Under the swarm of straw there were two bundles of bubble wrap, bound with tape. Sydney brought him a pair of scissors. Stone snipped carefully.

Unwinding what seemed like yards of wrap from the first bundle, he discovered a blue pottery bowl. When he picked it up, it promptly fell into four pieces.

"That's impossible," Sydney said, just as he was about to say he hadn't shaken the package that hard. "It must've been sent that way."

"Why would anyone deliberately send broken pottery?" Stone asked.

"Maybe the other one's OK," Sydney said. "It could be a set."

Gingerly, Stone opened the second bundle. The second bowl looked just like the first but was intact. On closer inspection, Stone saw that it had once had four cracks, all now repaired with some kind of clay. Stone held it up for Sydney's inspection. "What am I missing?"

Sydney took the bowl and turned it around in her hands. "Artfully done," she said. She turned it over to see if it was signed. "No note? No message?"

Stone emptied the straw on the table. "What do you think?" he asked. "What does your intuition tell you?"

"On the one hand, not to think about it too much," she said.

"You sound like Lou," he said.

"On the other, I have to believe someone up there is sending you some message. Not so much because of the broken bowl — that could be an accident — but because of the one that's repaired." She thought a minute longer. "That's it," she said, excited. "Remember the exhibit we saw last year of broken Japanese ceramics at the Art Institute?"

"They used gold," he said. "It had a funny name."

"Yes," she said. "In Upson, apparently, they make do with clay."

Stone took out his phone and hesitated.

"Try 'Japanese art and broken pottery,'" Sydney said.

"Pretty broad," he said, but he tried it. Skimming his results, he said, "Wikipedia thinks it's *Kintsugi*. There's some philosophy behind it. Something about used things, even if broken, being more beautiful because they have a history."

"I remember it felt rather profound," she said.

"Everything in Upson is meant to be profound," he said sarcastically. "Maybe if I meditate over the broken bowl, I can miraculously make it whole again."

"You think they're from Harmony?" she asked.

"More likely her than Ted," he said.

"If they're from Harmony, maybe they represent restoration, like her broken house?"

"If she wants it to recover its former splendor, she's going to need a lot of gold," he said.

"Which could be the point," she said. "I'm just saying."

He choked on his coffee, which dribbled down his chin.

"Oh, no," she cried. "I didn't mean anything. I'm so sorry." She offered a paper towel, and he wiped his mouth.

"The next missive from herself will be another demand for money?" he asked.

"Request," she corrected him. "It could be the hook for another ask."

"After her boyfriend punched me? That would take a lot of gall."

"She *has* a lot of gall, and her boyfriend is your *brother*."

"Who in the past month has broken my nose and humiliated me publicly."

"Your nose isn't broken," she said, and kissed it.

"You always defend him."

"I don't."

"You do."

"The facts, sir. No broken nose. Yet."

"He humiliated me," he changed tacks.

"He criticized a case your firm was handling," she said, her tone suggesting that he was being a crybaby.

The next morning Sydney poured Stone a cup of coffee while she waited for a single slice of toast to pop up. "Maybe today I'll get that new toaster," she said.

"I could mend it with clay," he joked.

"Be sure to unplug it before you fiddle with it," she dead panned.

"Actually, you're psychic," he said. "I ordered one two days ago. Should be here today."

"I saw you crossed it off my list of things to do," she said.

"Random act," he said.

"Not exactly random," she said. Sydney kept a list of household projects on a small yellow legal pad on the counter under the wall phone. As a feminist, he knew she wouldn't call them "honey-dos," but they did seem to him to fall into that category — digging out a dead bush near the back door, power-washing the garage floor where one of the girls' beaters had leaked oil, calling the roofer for an estimate because they would take advantage of a woman's naivete. "But still appreciated."

"It has four slices," he bragged. "The Mercedes of toasters."

"And energy efficient?" she asked.

He hadn't thought to look. It was a toaster, not a refrigerator or a car. He didn't even know whether toasters came with energy guides. "Definitely," he said. "Just like Harmony's alternate fuel Benz."

"You sound jealous," she teased. The toast jumped up, nearly escaping the toaster.

"Of Harmony's car or Ted's woman?" he asked.

"Oh, you're bad," she said. "The point is, either Harmony or Ted is trying to get your attention. You're going to have to repair our relationship with them."

"Where is it writ?" he cried. "We can't help it that we are brothers."

"And you can't undo the fact that you are. Until recently, you'd found a way to get along," Sydney said.

"Sounds like you're the one who sent them," he said.

"Better put a private investigator on it," she laughed.

• • •

A round-faced man in an olive-green sports jacket and a green and yellow checked shirt was sitting in the reception area when Stone arrived at work. Stone assumed he was a pro bono client who'd dressed up for a meeting with his fancy downtown lawyer, probably a first- or second-year associate. Stone nodded pleasantly and hurried to his office. He was doing something right if the young lawyers were willing to give their time for such matters.

Minutes later, Lou's secretary called Stone and, apologizing for Lou's not calling him directly, asked Stone to come to the corner conference room. Because she sounded earnest, Stone rushed to the room, smoothing his shirt and straightening his tie on the way.

Lou, Mark, Alice, Jay, and the man in the olive jacket were waiting for him. Jay nodded sternly, as if he'd not forgiven him for their conversation at the Club.

"This is my guy," Lou said playfully, gesturing to the man Stone recognized from the reception area. "Ollie Streeter." Ollie's handshake was surprisingly strong. Lou gestured for everyone to sit down. "Ollie's got some news."

Ollie stood up and walked to the end of the conference table, where a large TV monitor displayed a replica of his card: "Streeter Investigations."

"It's a conspiracy," Ollie began. His voice was high-pitched and nasal. Stone leaned back in his chair and crossed his legs. In Stone's opinion, paranoia was not a good legal strategy. "Most of these posts trace back to a single citizen's organization."

"How is that good news?" Stone said, uncrossing his legs and leaning forward with his palms on the table, as if about to spring out of his chair.

"They're a bunch of shareholders and subcontractors of Citizen Builders," Ollie replied.

"Sons of bitches," Jay sputtered.

Ollie continued, "See, they wanted to build near Mr. Shore's property. Ya know what I'm saying?" He looked around the room. His voice rose. "They never got the zoning!" Stone shook his head.

"But, see, that was good for us," Ollie said, as if explaining simple arithmetic to a first grader. "So now they have to stop Mr. Shore. They started another project on the other side of town, but see, the town isn't keen on two developments at once. Get it? They figure if they raise a stink about Mr. Shore here, they'll stand a better chance themselves."

"So we just gave them a lot of publicity they otherwise wouldn't have had," Stone said.

"Or Ollie just uncovered deeper pockets for the suit," Lou said encouragingly.

Jay stood up, unable to contain himself any longer. "So we could sue the bastards, right?" he asked.

Stone muttered "Aw, c'mon," just as Mark responded, "Possibly."

Stone clamped down hard on his teeth; the last thing they needed was the publicity of another Jay Shore lawsuit.

"Citizens is a big contributor to the County Board President and a couple of the commissioners," Ollie said. Ollie flashed a few slides on the large monitor at the end of the conference table, purporting to show how he'd traced the posts, but he stood in front of the screen and the slide's content blurred across his chest. Stone didn't care about the technical details. Slowly, it occurred to him that if everything Ollie was saying was true, it was possible the suit *could* be settled. He interrupted Ollie's explanation. "Any overlap between the ownership of Citizens and the ownership of ImJustSayin?" he asked.

"No," Ollie said.

"That's it, then," Stone said. Everyone at the table turned to him.

"ImJustSayin doesn't want to be used like that. It undermines their credibility. Forget Citizens and their deeper pockets. ImJustSayin will settle."

Lou raised his eyebrows at Stone in a gesture of resignation, and then shook his head at Jay. "It would save you a lot of money," Lou said, his disappointment evident to Stone, if not to Jay.

"Can you make that happen?" Jay asked Lou.

"Stone can," Lou said.

Stone understood that Lou didn't mean to compliment him so much as goad him, but it was a softball. Stone was a dealmaker. Lou was confident Stone could make it happen.

"What about Citizens?" Jay asked. "Can't someone stop them from ganging up on me or buying the County Board?"

Lou leaned across the table. "That might be pushing it," he said. "Not every wrong has a private remedy. You wouldn't necessarily get much out of a civil suit against them. We'll turn everything we've got over to the state's attorney for possible criminal prosecution, and then we'll give it to the press. Free revenge."

"What about your fees? Couldn't I sue them for that?" Jay asked. The man was certainly pugnacious.

"Not more than a hundred at this point," Lou said, as if he considered the bill chump change. To trivialize a bill of one hundred thousand dollars for a few weeks' work was, Stone thought, consummate arrogance, Gordon & Newman style.

"We'll write it off," Stone said.

The room snapped silent. Lou turned slowly to Stone, who lifted his chin. Stone drilled his eyes into his partner's. If he wanted, he could be just as arrogant as Lou. He was the billing partner. It was his call. Writing off the fee would wipe the slate clean, as if they'd not made the mistake of taking the case in the first place.

Lou stretched his lips into a tight, lopsided smile. "My pleasure," he said.

Stone sighed heavily at Lou's use of "my" but was determined not to start anything that might upset Jay, who appeared to be satisfied now that he'd been well-served by the firm. And Stone was grateful that the case was going away. He decided to take the high road. "I want you to know, Jay, that this result would not have been possible without everything Lou and his team have done up to this point. I'm writing off their time not because it wasn't productive — in fact it was stunningly productive — but because of my own personal commitment to freedom of the press. And to you. We'll bill you for expenses, such as Mr. Streeter's fees and his bonus."

Lou gave Stone a look; Stone didn't often recommend bonuses to vendors. Recommending a bonus for Ollie was a tip of Stone's hat to Lou. At Jay's expense.

"Just my luck to have a choir boy for a partner," Lou sighed, but good-naturedly. "Stone has a reputation to uphold."

Ollie beamed.

Alice, the youngest associate in the room, jumped in, uninvited. "If it makes you feel any better, Mr. Shore, your case may lead to a more responsible use of these kinds of websites. Plus, you exposed a scheme to corrupt the county zoning process. I have to believe that it will be Citizens who won't be building in Walworth County anytime soon." Jay smiled at her gratefully, just short of lustfully.

"Well said," Stone said, trying to regain control of the meeting.

"Yes," Lou said. "I bet you'll have clear sailing as soon as we deliver our papers to the county."

"That's why I pay you guys the big bucks," Jay said.

"Or not," Lou laughed.

"Just don't try to make up the difference on my next project," Jay said.

"Haven't we had this conversation before?" Stone asked.

"We have," Jay said. "So today it's my treat at The Capitol Grille."

• • •

The terms Stone negotiated were relatively easy for ImJustSayin to agree to: ImJustSayin would 1) take down the Shore Homes comments in question; 2) provide an opportunity for companies to respond to any review with less than three stars prior to posting it, and 3) adopt a formal take down policy, reasonably acceptable to Shore Homes, for allegedly libelous statements. ImJustSayin would issue a press release which touted these terms as voluntary enhancements to the site's credibility. No money would change hands.

Tuesday morning, the parties exchanged drafts and by five o'clock three copies were signed and delivered. Gordon & Newman's public relations firm issued its press release. The ten o'clock news devoted two sentences to the matter.

In the morning, the *Madison Reporter* gave the settlement four inches on page five. Stone noticed the story while eating a bowl of oatmeal at the breakfast table.

"It doesn't mention your name, does it?" Sydney asked. She was scanning the business section.

"No," he said.

"Good," she said.

He was somewhat disappointed. He was proud of the settlement. "I hope Jackson sees it," he said.

"The legal papers will pick it up," she said. "They will name names, if it's your reputation you're worried about."

He tensed. He wanted to be free of his concern for his reputation, but he also wanted redemption. He got up and scratched in the junk drawer for the pair of small scissors Sydney kept there for clipping oddball news stories she liked to send to the girls. Stone cut out the story and then, inspired, snipped it into a dozen odd-shaped pieces.

"What are you doing?" she asked. "It was a great settlement." It wasn't just good for Jay, Stone thought, but also sound public policy. He was glad she'd finally complimented him on it.

"I'm sending it to Upson," he said.

She laughed. "And the message is?" she asked.

"Thinking of you," he said.

"Or one good *Kintsugi* deserves another?" she said.

He found a business-sized envelope in the drawer and addressed it to Ted. "Right back at ya," he said to the envelope, licking the seal.

"You're assuming it was Ted's message in the first place," Sydney said.

"They're one and the same," he said. "And it *was* his opinion piece." He quickly sealed the envelope. "She probably put him up to it."

"She's the troublemaker, that's for sure. She got you up there in the first place," Sydney said, and turned the page of the paper.

"I think it's pretty clear by now I'm not contributing to Harmony house or whatever she calls it. So I doubt she wants me back," he said.

"Unless she has an ulterior motive," Sydney said. She folded the paper and put it beside her cereal bowl.

"Like she wants to provoke me into doing something stupid, so she can sue me?"

Sydney passed her hand in front of his eyes. "Maybe she just wants the brothers to be civil to each other," she said. "After all, they *are* brothers."

"Happenstance," he said. "Biologic accident."

She didn't say anything.

What did she know about siblings? "Brothers. Sisters. Vastly over-rated," he said. Stone sat back down at the table. It was covered with a colorful blue and yellow cloth, which Sydney had bought in Provence. He'd not noticed before, but there were two different designs in yellow, sunflowers and stalks of wheat, in addition to the green olive branches. It was very cheery, and practical. Perfectly Sydney. He wasn't that much of a morning person. He thought about Ted getting up early to meditate, and then he thought about Lou, grumbling in the morning as he charged past his secretary with a paper under his arm and not one but two paper cups of expensive coffee, one in each hand, both for himself. Lou was the kind of brother he wished he'd had;

he understood what was at stake for Stone in settling the case. Lou was like a brother — his own man, of course, with his own style and peccadillos — but they understood each other and were fiercely loyal to each other. Lou was understandable by Stone in a way Ted wasn't.

"I get that you two are different," Sydney said, uncrossing her arms and sitting back. "Very different."

He suddenly felt angry and took the folded paper from her side of the table, opened it and straightened it out. "Maybe I was adopted. Maybe you married the wrong Hunnicutt," he said.

"Don't!" she said. She waved her arms in his direction and her juice glass flew across the table and shattered on the floor. They both jumped up. Sydney tossed Stone a sponge and then brought a wad of paper towels. He took the floor and she the table; together they swept the glass into a dustpan and Sydney tossed the pieces into a paper bag and into the garbage under the sink. Stone gave the floor a final wipe with more paper towels.

When they sat back down, Sydney smiled sheepishly. "Clay wasn't going to work," she said.

"Probably not," he agreed. "Too many pieces."

"Can I say something?" she asked, but he knew she would anyway. "No matter how different your DNA, you and Ted share history," she said. "You both lived through that crazy father of yours. That makes you *real* brothers."

"He wasn't crazy," Stone said, not sure why he was defending his father. She threw her head back in an exaggerated nod. "He had standards," he said.

"*Impossible* standards," she corrected him.

"*Our* standards," he replied. *Despite* their history, or *because* of it. Sydney had hit on something. How indeed did two people brought up the same way in the same house turn out so differently? How did they survive one Thaddeus Newton Hunnicutt?

"The same standards. But you adopted different strategies," Sydney said. "You are different people with different gifts and you adapted differently. One way or another, we're all just a bundle of survival mechanisms." His eyes stung. He felt on the verge of tears. She added softly, "Growing up isn't easy."

He wanted to say "wasn't" but a morsel of sympathy for himself and for Ted lodged in his throat.

She got up and stood behind him, her hands massaging the top of his shoulders. "I married a grown-up," Sydney said gently. "The other brother has yet to take responsibility for himself. Living off his supposed genius? Letting a two-bit guru support him and pretend she's managing his career? Please!"

Sydney had always seemed to Stone entertained or amused by Ted and his free and unburdened lifestyle; at times when she was crazy busy as a working mother, he'd almost been convinced she was attracted to it. He was surprised she was so critical now. "When did you draw that conclusion?" he asked.

"About the time he punched you," she said.

"So now what?" Stone asked.

"You mean after enlightenment?" she said, standing in front of him and folding her hands Zen-style in front of her chest, Harmony-style. "After enlightenment, one reheats one's uneaten oatmeal, rinses one's dishes, and chops wood." She took his bowl to the microwave and gave it thirty seconds. "The rest is up to you," she said.

17

It didn't take Ted long to pound out 2,500 words, but the piece had evolved from an exposé on small-site open-pit mining into a lyrical meditation on environmental justice and Native American cultural values. He discovered the issues were far more complex than mere water quality. Some of the news reports he read said that the mine's ripple-effects on natural habitats, endangered species, cultural preservation and sacred sites were more emotionally charged than their possible effects on human physical health.

On the practical side, opening a new mine was a nightmare, replete with federal and state regulations, overlapping jurisdictions, competing community zoning permits and various fringe interest groups. Permitting alone could take a couple of years, and then a few more before the mine could be productive, and then only if everything went well. And even after a successful reclamation, the Native American and environmental interest groups were likely to decry the disturbance of sacred, life-giving water and to host ongoing, disruptive demonstrations and occupations. When he'd finished writing, he was more convinced than ever that the mine would be a disaster.

Harmony and he had almost reconciled on the day he'd decided to write the piece, but then when she learned he'd written it but wouldn't share it, she'd considered it a threat and their rapprochement stalled. Harmony softened during that following week — probably, he suspected, to discourage him from publishing the threatened essay. Then, after an afternoon tasting one of Ted's new wines, they'd spent a lovely evening in her canopied bed. That got them back to their usual routine, Ted spending several nights a week at the house. The truce they'd promised each other settled in. He allowed himself to hope that she'd cooled on the whole lease idea. He decided not to show her his draft. She would only be discouraged by the legalities and challenged by the spiritual implications.

He was surveying the pumpkin patch one day in early October

when Dylan, the potter who hardly ever spoke, came out of one of the sheds and stood next to him. It always amazed Ted that the thick vines that blanketed the ground all summer seemingly withered overnight and revealed a field of oversized orange orbs. "I should've done them in orange," he said, looking at Ted for affirmation.

"Done what, Dylan?" Ted asked kindly.

"The bowls," he said. "Did your brother get them yet?"

"Must be a senior moment," Ted stammered. "I don't remember sending him any bowls. But I'm sure if you threw them, they were beautiful. I really like your most recent work." Dylan flexed his fingers as if massaging the air. Ted was afraid he'd given offense. "All your work, actually, but I especially like the earthy colors you've been using lately."

"Harmony sent the bowls," Dylan said. "Maybe you weren't supposed to know."

"She must've told me and I forgot," he lied.

"I made her two bowls." Dylan studied the ground in front of him and Ted noticed that one of the leather strips of the potter's huarache sandals was taped together with silver duct tape. Dylan continued cautiously, "Then she broke them each into four pieces but only asked me to put one bowl back together."

"How did you do that?" Ted asked, trying to buy some time while he figured out what Harmony had been doing behind his back — again — and why.

"I made up some more clay and used it as glue," Dylan said. "Old Japanese art form, except they do it with gold."

"North Woods *Kintsugi*," Ted mused, as Dylan bowed slightly in appreciation that Ted knew the term.

"I'm sorry if you didn't know," Dylan said. He tilted his head toward Ted. "You didn't, did you?"

It was impossible to lie to someone so guileless. "No, Dylan, I don't think I did. Sounds like Harmony wanted to send my brother a message."

"Sounds like she wants you two to get back together," Dylan said. He stared ahead at the pumpkin patch.

"It's really none of her business," Ted said, which made Dylan jerk his chin up and squint at Ted in apparent disbelief. The residents at Peace & Joy rarely criticized one another, and they never criticized Harmony. Dylan twittered, a hand over his mouth. Brown clay was caked under his nails.

"You don't need to quote me," Ted said.

"Wouldn't think of it," Dylan said. "But if you need a bowl to send to anyone, let me know." He touched his visor in a halfhearted salute and left.

Damn. Again, Harmony'd gone behind his back to contact Stone. She was acting like a mother, trying to make the boys "play nice" with each other. Their own parents had let the Hunnicutt boys work out their childish squabbles — few though they were — rather than force feeble reconciliations. Stone had been good at that, proposing a Solomon-like compromise that made them both slightly less unhappy than they'd been before the disagreement. Ted remembered one afternoon when Stone had refused to let Ted play with him and his new friend George because he was the "baby brother." To make Ted go away, he'd promised Ted he'd play with him the entire next day. The promise was enough to convince Ted then that he was happy with the proposed solution, although when he was older he realized that a "tomorrow" solution didn't solve his immediate need and didn't solve the underlying problem — that he would still be the "baby" brother. At the time, Ted had thought Stone forthright and justified. He wished now that he could say the same for Harmony.

After dinner that night, he lingered at the dining room table with Harmony, since it was not his night for kitchen duty and it was never Harmony's. He'd always assumed Harmony's exemption from domestic duties was fair, given her generosity in sharing her property with so many others. Her system, as he understood it, was a Marxist "from each according to his or her ability, to each according to their need." Dylan, for instance, probably didn't contribute financially at all. Today, however, as she lounged at the table during the after-dinner hubbub, he felt she was playing "queen bee," yet again lording it over everyone.

"What's on your mind?" she asked. There was no use denying it.

She could've registered any one of a dozen of his involuntary signs of distraction: an extra beat before answering a question at dinner, a hand-comb of his hair, a soft drumming of his left hand on the table while the dishes were being cleared. Harmony took serenity seriously; she said inner peace always stilled an anxious body and inner disturbance caused it to twitch.

Tonight, he'd noticed her own tells: her voice a half-tone higher, her pace an eighth note faster. "Same as yours," he said.

"You first," she said.

He leaned back in his chair and rubbed his hands along his thighs. "*Kintsugi.*"

"A beautiful concept, don't you think?" she said, her tempo betraying her.

"Maybe, if you're an artist, and the fix is to something of your own," he said.

She looked away. "I was a witness," she said.

"That doesn't make you responsible for him or for me," he said.

She turned to him, pointing to his chest and then hers. "Your resentment of him affects *us*. Doesn't that make it my business?"

"Actually, not," he said. He felt the serenity of the group lunch dissolving. The more she rationalized her meddling, the more his anger prickled under his skin. He wasn't sure he could control it. He knew that the best course would be to rise from the table, return to his trailer, welcome a moment of needed grace and talk about *Kintsugi* in the morning. But he couldn't. "Your only concern should be not letting *my* resentment of him — if that's what it is — affect *you*."

"All right then," she said, standing up. "If you won't let go of this toxin, I can't be around you. When you've purged it, let me know."

"I'll send you a copy of my article," he said.

She slapped the table. "No!" she shouted.

"What?" he demanded.

She colored instantly — something she never did. "You *didn't* write an article," she taunted.

"Of course I did," he said with deliberate innocence.

She crossed her arms like a strict school-marm and peered down at him. "I presume it's not ready for publication," she said.

"I don't remember asking for your opinion," he said. Without kids or complicated careers or finances, they had little need of each other's opinion. This was one of the secrets of a long and happy relationship, Ted thought. They hadn't had a formal marriage ceremony, although Harmony had worn an antique lace gown and he'd donned a navy blazer like Stone's and gray wool slacks with a white shirt but no tie and in front of the entire Peace & Joy community — Mark, David and Dylan now the only remaining members — they'd taken a spontaneous pledge to always be honest and kind to one another. They both espoused honesty and kindness toward all, so their simple "vow" was an easy substitute for the outdated "love, honor and obey." Love was fleeting and ephemeral, Harmony said, a life-long pledge nearly impossible to keep, although Ted felt a fierce loyalty to her that he could not imagine ever fading. Honor — meaning respect — was dependent on whether the spouse did honorable things. How people might change over a lifetime seemed to Harmony random, but to Ted directional and evolutionary, which would bring them ever closer together. "Honest and kind" didn't begin to sum up all the love, passion and occasional frustration they felt for each other or their intention to remain together as a couple, but their vow was at the time the best agreement they could come to regarding their present intentions. It was itself deeply honest and unsparingly kind.

Through the years, several corollaries had proven useful in situations where honesty wasn't kind and kindness wasn't honest. First, kindness above all. Second, never ask the other's opinion — what should I do? — unless you were unconditionally willing to follow the advice offered. In this respect, Harmony was much easier for Ted to deal with than other women. Sydney, for instance, like the lawyer she became, would kick the tires relentlessly, challenging every nuance of any given advice and ultimately doing whatever she'd originally intended, either by a circuitous logic that came to the suggested conclusion or a leap of faith in the opposite direction. Ted couldn't remember Harmony ever asking for an opinion. Of course, the only thing he ever asked her was whether a piece was ready for publication.

"An exposé doesn't have to be perfect, just passionate," he said, meeting her stare head-on. His article wasn't particularly dramatic or emotional; it was a thought piece, not an overloaded rant. It wouldn't expose Harmony to national ridicule, but her closest associates would connect mining in northern Wisconsin with her Potato River property. While most local citizens would no doubt take her side — more jobs and increased tax revenue had major appeal to their economic self-interest — the residents of Peace & Joy would be appalled. Still, she wouldn't want her dispute with Ted to be a public one. She certainly wouldn't want the Peace & Joy artists to know the magnitude of the compromise she was willing to make to augment her lifestyle.

"You'd do more harm than good to your cause if the piece itself isn't good," she said, turning as if to leave him alone at the table.

"Of course it's good," he said. "Or do you have that low an opinion of my ability as a writer?"

"Perhaps it's your opinion of yourself that's inflated," she said spinning back in his direction.

Incensed by her haughtiness, he fought back, not bound by kindness. He rested his elbows on the table and folded his hands. "Inflated? If it were inflated, would I be listening to you? When's the last time *you* were published or got a laudatory review? Won an award? Hell, when's the last time you even sent something out for consideration?"

Her mouth fell open. He felt something shift in him. While the tone of their argument was pure lovers' quarrel, he was now questioning his deference to her as editor.

"It's not about my opinion of myself," he continued, shaking his head slowly back and forth. "It's about the writing. I'm happy to have you read my piece, but I'm going to be the one to decide whether and when to send it out."

"If," she said. She drew herself up, challenging him. Her jaw was set and her lips drawn into thin lines.

He stood up then, stretching to his full height, a head taller than Harmony. "*If. And* when. *And* to whom. It's *my* piece." He felt as he imagined Stone would feel, confident that he was in the right. If he decided to show her the article, she would almost certainly say it wasn't ready for publication, but her opinion would be driven by her personal agenda for mining the property. It felt like a revelation to him. For so long, he'd deferred to her, asking "should I?" When she'd said no, he'd folded. He didn't feel like folding now. Why should he?

Neither Stone nor Sydney would have ceded their personal authority so easily. Perhaps he had acquiesced to Harmony because her assessments of his work seemed so certain, so open and shut. Maybe he'd been secretly relieved. He wouldn't have to face the criticism, the expectations, the jealousy of peers. He wouldn't have to go on book tours. He wouldn't have to be away from Peace & Joy. He wouldn't have to leave Harmony. Immediately he saw that the two — relationship and publication — had become intertwined.

"Why are we behaving this way?" he finally said, holding out his arms. She hesitated, and for a moment he felt panic. If forced to choose, would it be his writing or his lover? Despite his bravado, he felt helpless to decide. She stood motionless while visions of public success dueled in his head with the prospect of private loneliness. He closed his eyes, hoping, but for what he couldn't say.

Then she fell into his arms, her head on his shoulder, sobbing. "I don't want to lose you," she whispered. "Please don't leave me."

"I wasn't planning on it," he said. "Haven't ever thought of it," he said.

"Just a few weeks ago you ..."

"For a day. I said I was sorry. And I came back."

She sat down, and he did too, moving his chair closer to hers. "I know," she said. "But I've seen how you are with Stone, and how easy it was for you to abandon that relationship."

"That's a big word, 'abandon,'" he said. Just because they were brothers didn't mean they had to be best friends. How many brothers were, especially when they were so close in age?

"You wouldn't have seen him this year if I hadn't piqued his interest," she said. "You never talk on the phone. You hardly ever visit one another."

"I'm not a big talker, you know that," he said. "Neither is he. It's a two-way street. You shouldn't worry about us. We're fine."

"You owe him an apology," she said.

"I suppose I do," he said.

"Then do it. Prove to me you are willing to fight for a relationship." As soon as she said it, her eyes wide and alive, he knew she was talking about them.

"I will," he said.

"And let's get to know them," she said. "You can't have a relationship based solely on history. You need some current shared experiences."

He felt his right-hand knuckles tingle. "You don't think a fist fight counts?" he asked, holding up his palm in surrender.

She clasped her hands and held her arms out in a circle, meditation style. "Ummmmm," she chanted, "noooooo."

18

"Why did you send me a story about manatees?"

Stone was lying back in his recliner in his study, reading a book about what the author called the "new economics." He recognized the voice but hadn't read the backside of the clipping he'd sent Ted. "Why did you send me a cracked pot?"

There was silence on the other end. Then, "I didn't send you anything."

"I got a cracked pot — two, actually — from an Upson P.O. box. The cracked one was mended with clay."

"You mean *Kintsugi*?" Ted asked. Stone wasn't surprised Ted knew the term. "It's supposed to be done with gold, so that after it's repaired, it will be even more precious for having been broken."

"Yeah, well, mine didn't get the gold treatment," Stone said.

"They were from Harmony," Ted said. "She's on a mission."

"To get my money," Stone scoffed.

"I think you've made it clear …," Ted said.

Now Stone was irritated. He *hadn't* made it clear. He hadn't responded to her letter and she'd never made a direct ask in person, so he'd never actually said "no." It occurred to him that Ted might now make the ask himself, which would put him in a difficult position. With his finger, he drew a zero on the table.

"I haven't," he said.

"Well, that's between you and her. I told you I didn't know about the letter. And I didn't know about the bowls, either."

"Rather presumptuous of her, if you ask me," Stone said.

"I *didn't*," Ted said.

"Of course you didn't," Stone said, his annoyance tinging his voice. "You're living under that woman's thumb." It was good they were on the phone — Ted might well have punched him again for suggesting that Harmony was his meal ticket.

"Geez, Stone," Ted said. "Get a grip. What do you care about my relationship with Harmony?"

"You're right. I don't care," Stone said.

"You should," Ted said, his voice rising as if to suggest a punchline was coming. "She wants me to apologize."

"For hitting me?" Stone asked.

"I told her that's how brothers settle things," Ted said.

"When they're *adolescents*," Stone said.

"She also happens to believe that my editorial, while justified, was unnecessarily vitriolic." Stone swore under his breath. *Vitriolic.* Of course Harmony would choose a word more highbrow than its everyday synonyms: spiteful, venomous, malicious, vicious. "It was the ad hominem she objected to. Frankly, I didn't think you'd mind the publicity. You know what they say, any press is good press."

"Just like any publication is good publication," Stone said. It was an unnecessary dig, but Ted deserved it.

"Let's not go there," Ted said. "I'm the one who called, right?"

"And the sucker punching? Does Peace & Joy endorse duking it out?" He grinned.

Ted laughed. "She was none too happy with that either," Ted said. "I'm sorry, bro," he said, but Stone thought he didn't sound repentant enough. "You know, dad would've approved."

"I'm sure," he said. "So that's it?" He braced himself, his breath short. Ted wouldn't have the nerve, would he? Unless Harmony was standing over him, hands on her hips, mouthing "Ask him. Ask him." He had come to hate her.

"That's it," Ted said.

There was an awkward silence during which the full measure of Stone's resentment festered unspoken. Ted's genius, his lack of ambition, his irresponsibility, his lack of human empathy. Why was he like that? The fact that they were brothers must be a genetic coincidence.

"Okay, then," Stone said. "Appreciate the call." It was how he usually closed a negotiation that had started out well for his side but ended in a draw.

"We're good, yes?" Ted asked, his inflection evoking Harmony rather than Lou. The hairs on Stone's arms stood up. How could someone as smart as Ted be in the clutches of such a charlatan? "Say," Ted hurried, as if he didn't want to end the conversation in limbo.

"How about we try again? You and Sydney come here for Thanksgiving — yes, we'll have a turkey, fresh and antibiotic-free — and we can give it another whirl. I'd like you to get to know Harmony. She's really very special."

Stone scoffed at "special" and stalled for time as he considered trying again. "Not sure whether the girls will be coming home," Stone said.

"Bring them along," Ted said. "My favorite nieces."

"Your only," Stone began, but stopped. "Well, thanks," Stone said. "I'll talk to Sydney and let you know for sure."

• • •

"Did you tell him we'd bring the turkey?" Sydney asked when he announced Ted's invitation. She'd come into his study to see if there was anything worthwhile on TV.

"*He* invited *us*," Stone said. "Why would I?"

"It's customary to offer to bring something," Sydney said. "We can afford it better than they." She picked up the remote.

"It's a turkey," Stone said, agitated. "She's the one who drives …"

She cut him off. "The Mercedes. I know. I was thinking of it as a peace offering."

Stone scoffed. "*He's the one*," he started.

"We can't go up there if you're going to continue to hold a grudge," Sydney said. She put the remote down, signaling her desire to talk.

"You forget he hit me," Stone said.

"You forget you deserved it," she said.

He was furious. He kicked his legs to tilt his recliner upright, but it didn't budge. He reached down to find the lever that would pop him upright so he could respond forcefully to Sydney's impending lecture, but she turned and left the room.

"You've changed your mind?" he called after her. Just the other day, she'd criticized Ted by agreeing that he shouldn't have punched Stone. Now she was taking Ted's side again. She was *his* wife. She was supposed to be loyal to *him* — "for better or worse." Now it was as if she wanted her cake and tofu, too. Well, fine. Stone had thought they'd done a remarkably good job over the years of maturing into slightly different people while growing together, closer. Until this thing with Ted. Which, of course, had started with Harmony. Because before the letter, Ted and Stone had gotten along fine. Once a year or so was fine. Everything had been fine. He felt on edge.

"Let it go," she said gently, handing him a warm amber snifter of Courvoisier, for a special toast to each other, one usually reserved for anniversaries and birthdays and other celebratory or trying occasions. She sat on the leather loveseat that matched his recliner.

He dipped his nose into the snifter, breathing in the rich aroma of dried apricots and took a sip, letting the flavor explode in his mouth.

"The Wampanoag brought venison," she said. He almost choked on a guffaw.

"Well let's go shoot us a deer," he said.

"Turkey's not authentic at all," she said. "At the first Thanksgiving they also had duck."

"So that's the idea of that turducken thing?" he asked. Last year, they'd been invited to Lou's for leftovers on the day after, and that had been Stone's first encounter with the dish.

"Typical American excess," Sydney said. "Harmony wouldn't approve." She lifted her glass in a toast.

"How do you know the tribe's name?" he asked. "You making that up?"

"My fourth-grade teacher Mr. Trinley was politically correct long before it was in fashion," she said. "He wouldn't say 'Indians,' he always used the proper tribal name. He liked debunking the myths. Our principal thought he was a subversive." Sydney moved to the recliner next to his, facing the blank TV, and levered herself part way back.

"Do you really think I deserved it?" he asked.

"Ted thought you did. What does it matter what I think?" she said.

"It matters if you're taking his side," he said weakly.

"You think I'm still holding a candle for Ted?" she laughed. "Whatever happened to that cock-sure rock star I married?"

"I was never cock-sure," he said.

"Who else puts a clean shirt and underwear in their backpack for a second date?" she asked.

He blushed. "I was very sure about that. You didn't seem to mind."

"At least you made an honest woman out of me," she chuckled.

"If I'd had any inkling you two still had a thing for each other, I never would've made a move," Stone said.

"Aw, c'mon," she said. "You mean you wouldn't have taken just a *teensy* bit of pleasure in winning me away?" When he didn't respond, she went on, "You know, Ted was college." She mimicked a college boy asking for a date: "'Hi, wanna go out Saturday night?' — 'That would be fun.' — 'What do you want to do?' — 'Oh, I'd like to fly the Concorde to Paris for dinner.'" She leaned toward him. "And then there was Stone Hunnicutt, soon-to-be-Esquire, with an index card in his pocket and Plans A, B and C. All cheap eats and no-cover-no-minimum music venues to be explored. And art exhibitions, sporting events, street fairs. Which one would you have wanted to date? The 'man with a plan' or the kid looking for mommy to tell him what to do?"

"Harmony, not mommy," Stone said.

"You know what I mean. The point is you had all the confidence then. What's all this insecurity now? Why not just go buy the red Corvette?" He was surprised she'd allude to such a hackneyed stereotype of mid-life crisis. But she wasn't wrong. Why not now, indeed?

"I don't know," Stone said. Deep down, he knew Sydney was telling the truth. "Harmony's asking for money, making me feel guilty for having it, and resenting me for not giving it. Like it's my duty — what my father would expect me to do. Because I have it and Ted doesn't. But he doesn't have it *not* because he's so devoted to his art, but because he doesn't work for it. As if *I* didn't work — and work hard — for my financial success." She frowned at him with pursed lips. "As if *we* didn't work for it," he corrected himself. "As if money just appeared on our doorstep. But the truth is, he's the one with all the brains, who was supposed to have this bright future...."

"And he's the one your father liked best," she said.

He groaned and nodded a final toast before finishing his drink. It did feel juvenile to still harbor hard feelings about Ted being their dead father's favorite.

"That's another thing you've got to let go," she added.

"It's how I was raised," he said. He took the remote from the table between them. He wanted to take refuge in a binge of *Law & Order* reruns.

"Don't put that on yet. Let's decide what to take to them."

He hesitated, the remote still in his hands. He remembered that Ted favored Detective Lennie Briscoe and his offsides humor, but Stone was drawn to the brooding District Attorney, Adam Shiff, who seemed perpetually caught between the porous rock of hard evidence and the uncertain truths of practicalities and politics. "Anything you think is right," he said, looking at the blank TV screen.

"I suppose wine and chocolates would be safe."

"Harmony would prefer cash," Stone said.

Sydney blew out a loud, exasperated breath. "You are obsessed," she declared.

"I'm not," he said. He gave up on the TV and put the remote on the table between them.

"Oh? Not obsessed, then. You just want to steal her away, too."

He looked at her, a rosy blush rising in her cheeks. "Nonsense," he said, oddly satisfied that she sounded just a bit jealous.

"Then what's the fuss? She's not asking for a lot. She's hardly asking for anything."

He studied the ceiling. In a way, it was a backhanded compliment: she thought ten grand was nothing to them. Still, he thought it was significant. The last time he'd given ten grand from his own pocket, was for his twenty-fifth Class Gift at Harvard, and even then he'd spread it over two years. "It's not the amount."

"Of course it isn't. Gordon & Newman has often given more when the managing partner asked," she said.

"It's the dishonesty," he said, unable to keep himself from sounding self-righteous.

"How do you know it's dishonest?" she challenged.

"It's gotta be. Is the house of any real significance? Are any of the antiques valuable? If they are, why can't they sell them to finance the restoration? Does Harmony or her rag tag tribe of artists even have the wherewithal to complete the project? What's the actual plan?"

"It's a legitimate 501(c)(3), isn't it?" she asked, sounding officious.

"I assume," he said, "but ..."

She popped up and took his iPad from his desk. She typed for a minute and with her backside to the desk, read him the basic facts: "Peace & Joy's in good standing as a Wisconsin not-for-profit. IRS 990 from two years ago shows $34,000 in donations and $41,000 total income. Doesn't ID any single big donors. No foundation or state grants. Harmony is CEO; salary and benefits, thirty-four. Other Board members not compensated. Seems honest enough to me."

"$34,000?" Stone said, sitting up in his chair.

"She could spend it all on shoes and a prosecutor wouldn't care," Sydney said.

"The Justice Department doesn't know a con when they see one," he said in disgust.

"But you are certain *you* do?" she said. "You're telling me you know her better than the Feds?"

"I think I do," he said but he remembered a famous line from DA Adam Schiff: "Always think you have a smoking gun, 'til the smoke blows in your face." She slammed the iPad onto the desk.

"Something *more* you want to tell me? Just how well ...?" She stood with her hands on her hips, looking down at him.

"Stop," he said quietly, and they locked eyes. There had never been a question of infidelity in their marriage. Her pique surprised him.

"*Me*, stop? I'm not the one obsessed with another woman."

"I've told you, I'm not obsessed. I just want to know who she is. She has all this power over Ted."

"How do people get such power? Your father, I can kind of understand. But Harmony? I didn't think she was that hot."

"She's not," he said, although the image of the Aquarian diamond pin at Harmony's ample bosom flitted across his mind.

Sydney turned toward the desk and snapped down the cover of the iPad. She sat down on the edge of her recliner, not looking at him. "You bet I'd also like to know who this woman is who has bamboozled not one genius brother, but two."

"Oh, Sydney," he started, but the genius word gnawed at him.

"If you're so desperate to know who she is, why don't you do what obsessed lovers do: Have her investigated."

"That's not what lovers ..." he started. He was going to say that that's what jealous husbands did, but he stopped. He liked the idea. "I know just the man," he said.

"You wouldn't," she whispered, leaning toward him in a conspiratorial huddle.

"You just said I should," he said, exasperation adding a bit too much volume to his voice. "Well, I ..." She sounded flustered. She should be.

"He'd better be discreet," she concluded.

"He's so nondescript, he doesn't have a choice. He's the ultimate in discreet," Stone said.

"He'd better be, because if Ted finds out, you'll need crutches," Sydney said.

"But you'd take care of me, wouldn't you?" he asked, coaxing her.

"For better or worse," she sighed, and blew him a conciliatory kiss.

• • •

Ollie was more than happy to receive a new assignment from a Gordon & Newman partner so soon. "I'll get right on it," he said when Stone called from his office the next morning. "Are we looking at a potential situation?" he asked. At first Stone didn't understand the question. "Divorce? Insurance fraud?" Ollie asked,

"Nothing nefarious," Stone said, which seemed to him to be a good "detective" word.

"Employment?" Ollie said.

"General background," Stone said. "Just due diligence on a potential financial matter."

Stone hung up and stared at the phone. He remembered the man standing in front of his own PowerPoint slides, his charts projected onto his chest. What an odd way to make a living, ferreting out the secrets of others.

The afternoon mail delivery brought a small cardboard box that had been delivered by messenger. He thanked the young clerk and glanced at the return address. He assumed the box was from the company for whom the firm had recently closed a small deal. The last thing he needed was another acrylic doodad to attest to his experience, but Jackson Wood's name appeared on the handwritten return address. He ripped into the box, furious that Jackson had returned the Pro Bono Award. Just because Stone had settled the case didn't mitigate the wrong he'd done by accepting it in the first place. By not charging Jay, he'd made some form of reparations, but he still felt unworthy.

The icon was wrapped in bubble wrap and there was a handwritten note.

Dear Stone:

I understand and appreciate the sentiment underlying your return of the Pro Bono Award, but frankly, it's our Award to give, and you can't "un-win" it. In my opinion and that of many others, you deserved it. Your commitment to the law and to your clients' interests has always been exemplary.

Best,

Jackson

PS: This is an executive decision. Only you and I know about this.

He understood Jackson's logic. Stone could have declined the Award, but at the time he'd deserved it. He'd been, as Sydney'd said, next in line. When Gordon & Newman filed suit, the Bar hadn't commented on the suit, hadn't demanded the Award back, hadn't officially censured him. There'd been no reason to do any of that. It was a legal case for a client. There'd been a "colorable claim," a reasonable chance of success.

He was grateful that, despite Ted's op-ed piece, there'd been no public spectacle. Still, he felt queasy about displaying the Award at Gordon & Newman, where he'd made such a fuss. Then he heard Sydney's voice exclaiming, "Don't hold a grudge." He put the Award on his desk, facing him rather than his clients. The past was the past. He couldn't undo it. He could only soldier on.

19

"Nothing?" Stone leaned back in his office chair, arms crossed. Dressed again in his olive suit, this time with a mustard, plum and light green-checkered shirt and gold tie, Ollie perched on the edge of his seat, eager to please. "That's a good thing, right?" he said with a little bounce. "For the most part Ms. Miller has a clean record — a couple of tickets in rural speed traps, but that's it. If she has any aliases, they're so deep and rock-solid I didn't come across so much as much as a nickname."

Stone struggled to conceal his disappointment.

"Something else I should look at Mr. Hunnicutt?"

Right then, Ollie didn't look like someone Stone would normally trust to help him make an important investment decision, but what choice did he have? He couldn't think of any new angles for Ollie to follow, and if the man was Lou's go-to investigator, he had to be the best in the business. "I just don't get how she supports herself and that house," Stone mused.

Referring to one of the papers in his file, Ollie said, "Title was passed to her free and clear from the estate of a single woman I believe to be her aunt on her mother's side. Taxes up there are minimal — it's unincorporated, no services to speak of. As you know, there's the farmers' market and the pumpkin sales. According to the local paper, a couple of times movies have paid for the right to shoot the exterior and the grounds. Looks like they have an annual yard sale and donations from the occasional open house. She also has a property on the Potato River, in joint tenancy with your brother."

"You mean a house?" Stone asked. Ted could go live there, away from Harmony. Live on fish and berries instead of zucchini and pumpkin.

"No, sir," Ollie said. "Nothing on it."

"So, it's an acre or so?" Stone asked.

"More like two hundred, sir, as I recall," Ollie said.

"Two hundred?" The size of it astounded him. "So it could be developed," he said. A big sign, "POTATO RIVER PLANTATIONS by SHORE HOMES" flashed in front of his eyes.

"I don't know, sir," Ollie said.

How hard could it be, Stone thought, to put in some sewers or mounds and throw up some A-frames or log cabins or even mini-mansions — whatever the city folk were buying this year. If not Jay, certainly some other real estate "visionary" could "discover" the North Woods. Both Ted and Harmony could enjoy financial freedom. Maybe even trade in the trailer and the historic ruins for a McManse of their own.

"Before I go sir, I thought you might like to see these." Ollie flipped through his files and handed Stone a copy of the newspaper article from the time when Harmony's aunt died, some twenty years ago now. The black-and-white headshot of Harmony Miller showed her thick hair cut medium length and evenly trimmed. Her smile was inviting and her eyes sparkled. Ollie handed Stone the copy. "A real looker, eh?" Ollie said.

Stone gave it a quick glance. In her thirties, obviously wearing make-up and posed perfectly, Harmony was indeed beautiful. Glamorous. She looked, he thought, like a woman of substance. Like Sydney. Professional. Rich. Used to being in charge. The kind of woman who would drive a Mercedes and live in a grand house. She didn't look to Stone like the free spirit hippie Harmony now purported to be. Not the kind of woman who would be romantically involved with a guy who lived in a trailer.

But the caption caught his attention. "Founder, WILIGTS Literary Journal." "What about this literary journal?" Stone asked.

"They filed for bankruptcy five or so years ago. She lost a lot of money on it, although she seems to have satisfied her creditors. Her trust took a bit of a bath." He handed Stone a file with the bankruptcy papers. "I shoulda mentioned that, but it was a long time ago, and a separate corporation." So, she'd lost a lot of cash trying to publish literary fiction. No wonder she was wary of Ted's publication. From her perspective, it was unlikely there was any money in it — probably not enough to recoup her losses — and she was acutely aware of the potential for financial disaster and heartache.

An embarrassed half-grin strained across Ollie's face. "I don't know how far back you want to go with this," Ollie said, and Stone perked up.

"Everything, Ollie. It goes to character," he said.

"Well, when she was nineteen or twenty, something like that, she was a belly dancer." Stone gritted his teeth. He wanted to ask if there was a picture, but that would sound lascivious. "I only know this because I was having a beer at the Full Moon Saloon there on the main street and I got to shooting the breeze with an old-timer." So much, Stone thought, for being discreet, as if word would flash through a small town that some inquisitive outsider — "not from these parts" — was asking about the hippie in the commune on the edge of town. "They had all these like kids' drawings on the walls. Finger paintings, they looked like. And this fellow tells me that at the County Fair, they used to raise money for the Fourth of July fireworks celebration with a booth where the girls would dress up in different costumes, like cowgirls and Whistler's Mother and cats and like that and that you could have your picture taken with them for a donation. Well, he said that one year Harmony Miller dressed as a belly dancer and she wouldn't let them take her picture, but she'd do a little belly dance and while she did, she painted drawings on her belly." Stone laughed out loud. "No, no," Ollie said. "Then she took a piece of paper, plastered it across her stomach and peeled it off. There'd be a picture of Einstein on it!"

Stone leaned back in his chair, flabbergasted. The idea of Harmony belly dancing. Being able to paint herself while dancing. And a portrait of Einstein? He squeezed his eyes shut: there had been a painting of Einstein in the house. Hanging next to Harmony's portrait. Mocking art or mocking sex? He was speechless.

"Einstein!" Ollie repeated. He rummaged through his files. "The paper ran a photo of the picture," he said. Ollie handed a photocopy to Stone. "In color, his hair his red, yellow and blue and the eyes and mustache are black." Stone felt a short pang of disappointment that it wasn't a photo of Harmony's belly. The story said that at auction, an Einstein would fetch a $25 donation. A fortune in the North Woods.

"Interesting," Stone said.

"But not nefarious," Ollie said.

• • •

Caroline, the drama student at NYU, confirmed at the last minute that she wasn't coming home for Thanksgiving, and would wait until Christmas. She'd been invited to a costume party re-creation of the first Thanksgiving at a friend's house on Long Island while the parents were in St. Lucia, and she was going to go dressed as an Indian. "A Wampanoag," Sydney'd corrected her, delivering the lecture on the holiday she'd already given Stone. Meredith, still completing her medical training, couldn't take the time off.

"I miss not planning the dinner," Sydney said as they packed their car the morning before Thanksgiving. Not that they had much: overnight bags, a two-pound gold-foil box of truffles and a case of wine. "I really miss having my own stuffing." She'd been known to eat it cold the next day. "I hate it when people get all exotic about it, oysters and all that extra stuff. For me, just the basics: butter, celery, onions, real breadcrumbs; salt and pepper."

"You're making me drool," Stone agreed, then hoisted the box of wine to the back seat.

"If we drink all of it, there could be a brawl," Sydney went on.

"Then why did you buy so much?" Stone asked.

"I couldn't decide how many bottles — two wasn't enough, four seemed like a lot — so I decided just to get the case — it was cheaper — and they can keep what's left over. It's too much isn't it?"

"Yes," Stone said. "But I doubt they'll send it back."

"I just don't want to be showy," Sydney said.

Stone shrugged. "In some strange way, a single neat carton seems less showy than two or three shopping bags of clanging bottles."

"Yes. That makes me feel so much better." He looked to see if she was serious. She was.

"And if Harmony acts up," Stone said, "I'll finish the case myself."

"Let's not anticipate the worst," she said.

"Be prepared, I say," Stone replied. He reminded her to fasten her seat belt, and then pulled out of their driveway.

"What are you expecting?" she asked.

"Not much," he said. "You know Ted. He'll be just like he always is. Like nothing's wrong."

"Nothing *is*, right?"

"Right." The light had changed at the turn for the highway and Stone beeped needlessly at the car in front of him. Nothing was wrong. And everything was. Having a small family, their Thanksgiving dinners typically included just the four of them. Full of love and celebration, not the brawls of holiday lore. The newspapers had been filled with advice on how to "keep the peace" at the Thanksgiving table, and despite his habit of skipping over such "fluff," Stone had taken a peek. He'd read enough to know that a case of wine likely violated the first rule. While he wouldn't be challenged by having to sit next to a political Neanderthal, he would have to make peace with his own brother, who, the last time they were face-to-face, had slugged him. And only because he thought Ted should live up to his potential. Stone blew out a long breath.

"He apologized," Sydney said. "He invited us up. There's not much else he can do, is there?" She was making an effort to be upbeat, which meant she was worried.

"He could sell the damn Potato River property and the whole money issue would go away," he said.

"Solves the money problem," Sydney said. She made a little circular motion with her chin.

"That *is* the problem," Stone said,

"If you say so," Sydney said.

He wasn't in the mood for her amateur analysis of Ted's problems.

"But you can't admit you know about that without admitting that you spied on him — again," she said. There was both a warning and a tease in her voice.

"Spying was your idea!" he protested.

"You spied first," she said.

"Hogwash," Stone said. He felt aggravated. He wished his girls were coming home and he could pretend that they were in high school again and needed him and weren't off being independent and successful and exceeding his expectations in every way. He'd not expected to miss them so much. "Don't worry, I'll try to be very civil."

"Civil is a start," she said. "I thought we might be working toward brotherly love."

Stone accelerated on the ramp to the highway, heading north out of Madison. The traffic was moderate, building toward the early afternoon pre-holiday rush. After several hours, they were on two-lane roads through towns so small they didn't have stop signs, although most had at least one roadhouse with a pack of Harleys parked out front. In one nameless town north of Tomahawk, Sydney spotted a faded billboard for "Lingerie Lunch" featuring "Girls, Girls, Girls." "I can't imagine that still plays," she said. "All the way up here."

"There's always been money in it," Stone said, brushing away the image of Einstein painted on Harmony's belly. "You know, that's what's really going to happen. She's going to ask me for money. Or maybe she'll ask you, and when we say no, that'll start something."

"How did we get from lingerie to Harmony?" Sydney asked dryly.

Stone blanched. "Just different routes to the same goal," he said. Twenty-five dollars was a lot of money back then, even for Einstein.

"Maybe she won't ask," Sydney said.

"She will," he said.

"She didn't last time."

"There was an altercation that may have derailed her plans," he said. He checked his rearview. Despite the holiday, the only traffic behind him was a gray pickup, some ways back. *He* wasn't the one who'd hit — hit! — his own brother. *He* wasn't the one Sydney should worry about.

"No grudges," she said. When he didn't agree, she said, "We should just give it to her and put all this behind us," Sydney said.

"All what?" His hands tightened on the steering wheel.

"All of this preoccupation with your brother's lover."

"You mean my brother's keeper."

"Whoever she is, she has you under her spell, too. And he's still your brother."

"Then *he* should ask," Stone said. He was feeling stubborn. Already the weekend was starting out poorly, wobbling on the edge of civility.

"I agree," she said, and he relaxed a bit. "But it's not like the two of you have a great track record on communication."

"Usually you can count on family," she added.

"Where is it writ?" he asked, ignoring the fact that Harmony wasn't family. "Who said that just because you were born to the same parents you are expected — no, *required* — to support every harebrained idea they have?"

"I didn't say that," Sydney said.

"But you think it's my brotherly duty," Stone said.

"Duty?" she asked. "Like carrying on the family name, inheriting the farm, becoming the patriarch?"

"Don't mock me," he said, irritated.

"I'm not," she said. "You have to remember that I didn't have a brother or a sister." She smiled — coyly, he thought.

If she'd had a sibling, she'd remember all the annoyances: sharing an HO train table, which of course made practical sense, but didn't give either brother complete freedom to design the model plastic village each envisioned. Ted and he had had to compromise: one part of town old-fashioned and historic to suit Ted; one part sleek and modern to please Stone. "You romanticize the notion of brotherhood," he said.

"Doesn't everyone? I desperately wanted an older brother when I was young."

"What for?"

"So he'd bring home friends," she said. "Boyfriends. And he'd pave the way. Get the first driver's license."

"The first one paves the way. The parents don't know the risks. Then, with the second ..." Stone started. The second was treated with kid gloves. Could do no wrong. Had to be protected. Wasn't even encouraged to share. Ted's first computer was a laptop while Stone had to make do with the old desktop, because he was "familiar" with it.

"They either know what to worry about or give up worrying all together," she said, finishing his thought. "In your case, the old man worried even more."

"Well, sure. To protect the genius."

"All the worse for the poor guy. All of the problems of the older one, with none of the bennies of being the younger." He thought

Sydney was again showing excessive sympathy for Ted, but then she added, "Making it worse, he had *you* to live up to."

Stone slowed as they approached another one-stop-sign town. He'd not thought of it Sydney's way before. Sydney's take on things almost made him feel a new-found sympathy for Ted. She was clever that way, but he wouldn't be fooled. "So what's a brother's duty?" he asked.

He felt her eyes on him as he fixed his gaze on the road ahead. Two lanes. Rolling hills. A teenager's joyride. Danger around every curve. "I'm not telling him how to run his life," he said. "He's letting Harmony do that." He glanced over. She seemed to be holding her breath. "Of course he'd be better off without Harmony in the picture," he said.

"*Of course?*" she said.

He tapped the steering wheel. "I knew you'd agree," he said.

"It was a question," she said.

"It's pretty simple," he said. "Maybe he could support himself if he published his books. If she weren't standing in the way."

"He's not starving. He's not complaining. And, for that matter, he's not the one asking for money. I'd say the man is pretty happy as he is."

"But he's not living up to his potential," Stone said. He turned into the driveway to Harmony's Peace & Joy. In the gray November day, the damp stone of the house looked battered and worn down, old and tired and decidedly not historic.

"Perhaps we should lower our expectations," Sydney said.

Stone stole a glance at her. She obviously didn't understand much about the Hunnicutts. Well, she didn't have to. *He* was the older brother. *He* knew what was expected.

"All I want is to free him from that woman," he said. In his opinion, Harmony Miller exerted an unhealthy degree of control over his brother. Stone understood that love almost always involved a transfer of power. The power he ceded to Sydney — her happiness being the thing that made him happy — was, in his view, well placed. Unlike Harmony, Sydney was not the kind of person who would misuse that power. It wasn't even clear to him that Sydney knew she had anything over him, which meant that they had achieved a good balance, each concerned primarily with the other's well-being. But Harmony held exceptional power over Ted and Stone wasn't sure she could be trusted.

"And I would like to free you," she said. "Both of you," she added. "Can't we take a deep breath? Please, just try to stay open-minded, OK?"

Stone drove around the back of the big house and parked in front of Ted's trailer. They got out and knocked on the door. No one answered. Sydney checked her watch. "It's one. Probably up at the house?" she asked and pointed. As they came up the stairs to the back door, Ted and Harmony opened the door together to greet them.

"Hey! Great to see you both! Thanks for coming," Ted said.

"Welcome," Harmony said. "Come in, come in." Inside, the kitchen was full of activity — the Girls at the sink, rinsing vegetables, Mark supervising Dylan, who was elbow-deep in bread dough. Richard was silently buttering and tearing bread for stuffing. David had his back to them, doing something on the counter. When he turned to greet them, he had a boning knife in hand.

"Just in time," Mark said. "We could use another professional," he gushed, smiling at Sydney.

"At your service," Sydney said. She joined him at the counter, where three slabs of poultry — turkey, duck and chicken — were flayed out. "You boned them yourself?" she asked, turning to Stone to register her surprise.

"It makes stuffing one inside the other so much easier," Mark laughed. Stone smiled to himself. Until last year at Lou's, they'd both assumed that the turducken was akin to Jonah in the belly of the whale, the turkey swallowing the duck which had swallowed the chicken.

"Let her have some tea before putting her to work," Harmony said. She uncovered a plate of thick brown bread and a crock of butter and jam and pointed them to the long benches lining the kitchen table at the window. Sydney and Stone sat opposite each other and Ted sat next to Stone.

"Looks like you're creating quite the feast," Stone said.

"It's a tradition," Ted said. "It's the one day of the year we go all-out."

"I like the idea of a day devoted to gratitude," Harmony said.

"And we have a lot to be grateful for," Ted agreed.

"We brought some wine," she said. "It's in the car."

"We can chill it overnight," Harmony said.

"Probably should serve it at forty-five degrees," Stone said, as Sydney shot him an exasperated look. "That's what it says on the bottle," he said, attempting to apologize.

"Mark's doing his famous turducken," Ted said.

"Have you ever had one?" Harmony asked.

"Last year, at my partner's," Stone said. "Sydney thought it was excessive." Sydney gave him a soft kick under the table. Quickly, he tried to deflect attention from this comment. "*Wonderfully* excessive. Lou's the lead litigator at the firm." Harmony didn't flinch.

"I know who Lou is," Ted said. "I think I called him a henchman."

Stone was surprised Ted would bring up such a sore subject, and absently rubbed his nose. Sydney pressed Stone's foot under the table. "I think you did," he said. "If Lou's a henchman, that makes me, in the original sense of the word, a horse's ..."

"Ass," Ted laughed.

There was an awkward moment and another kick under the table. "I was going to say groom," Stone said. "At least until the nineteenth century."

"At least," Ted said.

"Boys," Sydney said.

"Wordplay," Ted grinned.

"One-upsmanship is still one-upsmanship," Harmony sighed.

"She doesn't quite get us," Ted said.

"Most normal people wouldn't," Sydney said.

"We aren't most people," Ted and Stone said in unison. They turned to each other, apparently surprised, but not. How many times had their father answered their teenage objections to his latest rule or scheme with just that sneer, "*We are not most people.*"

Ted broke into a belly-laugh. "Remember, Sydney, when you came home that first time, ready to wow the man with your grapefruit?"

Stone inhaled deeply, trying to figure out where Ted was going with his story, and hoping it wouldn't lead to a flare-up of some petty jealousy. At the time, Stone, though innocent, had been worried that the old man would take it out on Sydney for dumping Ted.

"Did he call me stupid?" Sydney asked. "I don't remember."

"No, he didn't call you stupid," Stone said, straightening up. "I wouldn't let him do that."

"Like you could stop him," Ted said with a shrug. "What I remember is that Sydney called *him* an idiot."

"I didn't!" Sydney protested, shaking her head at Harmony. "Where do they get this stuff?" she asked.

"They're brothers," Harmony said.

"Oh, I loved you that day," Ted said. Stone flinched, but Ted continued, oblivious. "He thought you were agreeing with him, not slicing him open. I think your exact words — and someday I'm going to use the whole scene in a novel — were, 'You're right, sir; any idiot could do that.'"

"So, you see, we aren't most people," Stone said, bringing the conversation back to where they'd started. "Pick a group, any group — marines, Packer-backers, math nerds — all the same. Whatever *they* are, *we* aren't."

"Terminal uniqueness," Harmony said.

Stone took a deep breath.

"That was Thaddeus Newton," Ted said, without spite.

In the moment of considered silence that followed, Mark called to Harmony, "Can you help me with this engastration?"

Harmony leaned across the table to Sydney. "It's contagious," she said confidentially, but loud enough for Stone to hear.

"Harmless enough," Sydney said. "Doesn't hurt anyone."

Harmony slid off the bench to help Mark. "Nothing like a good portmanteau," Stone said, grinning.

"That's what Pop always said," Ted agreed.

"Ha!" They both laughed loudly.

"I thought that was luggage," Sydney said, her hands on her hips.

"Also a word made up of part of another word, carrying other words, as it were," Ted said. "Like those designer dog names. Cockapoo and Peekapoo and Labradoodle."

"Not that we believe in interfering with nature like that," Harmony said, mildly chastising him. She shared a knowing look with Sydney.

As if amused, Ted said, "Or *not* interfering. Letting the beasts breed as they will, they'd naturally make a few Labradoodles." He blew a kiss to Harmony at the counter. She tossed her curls as if she were a young girl and blushed.

When the Thanksgiving engastration — the turducken — was laced together and stored in the refrigerator, Stone offered to take Ted and Harmony into town for dinner, but Harmony declined. The tradition at Peace & Joy was a soup-and-bread supper the night before the next day's feast. Imagining a thin vegetarian broth, Stone worried that he would be forced to fast. He was relieved when Mark produced a hefty potato-leek soup with toppings of green onions, cheese and crumbled bacon, as well as several loaves of hearty wheat bread.

After supper, Harmony asked Sydney if she'd like to join her in the East Parlor, the one, Stone remembered, with the Magritte imitation. As if on cue, Ted said, "Stone and I will clean up."

"Good night, dear," Harmony said to Ted. "Peace and joy," she added, sounding more like a spiritual guru than a lover. That afternoon, around the kitchen table, Harmony and Ted had seemed like a loving couple, comfortable with themselves and each other in the trusting way of people who easily fall asleep in each other's arms. Harmony had even seemed quite ordinary, gentle in her spiritual guidance and somewhat understanding of the Hunnicutt ego. If she'd been angry with Ted about Stone's first disastrous visit, she seemed now to be almost fawning over him.

"Sweetest dreams," Ted said, a bemused smile crossing his face. Stone wondered if everything was as copacetic between them as Harmony obviously wanted it to appear.

The Girls, Mark and David began clearing the dining room table. Stone watched Harmony and Sydney disappear down the hall.

"So, a little role reversal," Ted said.

"They're going for cigars?" Stone joked.

"Harmony doesn't have a lot of women up here who are her equal," Ted said.

"What about you?" Stone said.

"She's my teacher," Ted said. "By any measure, I am not her equal."

"I meant, are there any men up here who are, well, not on your level, but at all close?" As he spoke, Stone felt the familiar stab of inferiority. "Someone like Andrew, maybe?"

Ted picked up three glasses in each hand and backed through the door to the kitchen. Stone followed with the last of the dishware. "Thanks, guys," Ted said to the clean-up crew. "Now, scoot. My brother and I will take it from here." Stone looked at the stack of colorful stoneware bowls and bread plates and said, "I'll dry."

"If you mean for friendship," Ted said, surprising Stone that he would pick up on his question. "Yes, of course. Mark and David are serious artists and Dylan, when not cowering, is quite an interesting person if you can get him to talk. Richard, the painter, is a real genius, actually."

Stone hated the "genius" word; it was bantered about too often. "Couldn't prove it by me," he said.

"He's not into proving anything," Ted said.

"How do you know he's even an artist?" Stone asked. "I thought he didn't share his work. For all anyone might know, he spends his days painting walls."

Ted said, "He's not painting to anyone's expectations but his own." Stone thought Ted's voice stiffened on "expectations."

"Aren't we supposed to expect art from artists, poetry from poets?" What was wrong, Stone wondered, about expecting people to be who they professed to be, to do the things expected of the role they'd adopted? Demand excellent work from young attorneys. Expect them to be ambitious, work nights, weekends. Make the law not just a jealous mistress, but the love of their life. Let go those who don't measure up.

"So then, see art, not graffiti; hear poetry, not gibberish," Ted said.

"In the eyes of the beholder?" Stone scoffed. "Much too philistine for me."

"See for yourself," Ted said. "Every year, after Thanksgiving dinner, Richard unveils a piece."

"I still believe in generally accepted notions of excellence," Stone said.

"Of course you do," Ted said. "You win all those accolades."

"You've won some, too," Stone said. "Don't tell me they didn't matter to you."

"At the time," Ted said. He abruptly turned his attention to the soup pot, which had been scraped nearly clean by the last few diners.

"But not now?" Stone asked.

"Not so much," Ted said. "I think I've outgrown all that stuff." It sounded like something Harmony would make him say. Perhaps, Stone thought, Ted secretly found awards and honors satisfying.

"You stopped competing," Stone said matter-of-factly. Ted reached for a fresh scouring pad. "You gotta play to win," Stone added, mimicking a radio commercial for the state lottery.

"I was fired," Ted said. He rinsed the pot rigorously with the water nozzle. Stone thought perhaps Ted was intentionally drowning himself out.

"When you didn't get tenure? I thought you were relieved," Stone said.

"Yes, and no. It was a cushy job. Teaching was OK. It gave me a lot of free time." He held the pot bottom-side-up and shook it. "But really it took a lot out of me. Constantly disappointing those young writers."

A couple of classes a week? A handful of pages to read? How could that take "a lot" out of a person? At work, Stone often read one hundred pages of legal documents a day and stayed late when there were more. "Disappointing?" Stone asked.

"The promising ones were deflated, and the others wrongly buoyed by the critiques." Ted turned his attention to the sink, sprinkling scouring powder over the stainless surface and rubbing back and forth with a green scratch pad.

"You can't help that," Stone said. "But what about your own writing. Your readers?"

"Right. I was in constant fear of not living up to their expectations of me, or even to my expectations of myself. The thought of publishing, of going back on a tour of university bookstores and backwater colleges, facing all those eager faces — *if* anyone showed up. Sometimes there would be six people in the audience — and there I was, the supposedly big deal prize-winner and half of the six were shooting poison darts at me and questioning my talent: 'why you?' and I had no answer. *Why me?* I don't know." He handed the pot to Stone. "No need to dry," he said.

Stone put the pot on a towel. Ted picked it up and put it back on the stove — ready to go again in the morning for oatmeal or later, for soup or stew. "Why do you care so much?" Ted asked. "You're worse than the old man."

"What does that mean?" Stone demanded.

"Really? You don't think you're driven to all those lawyer awards on the tide of his expectations?" Ted asked. Borderline condescending, Stone thought.

Stone stared at the plaque he'd noticed on his first trip, when he was chopping purslane. The words blurred. He'd needed reading glasses for years, but now his distance was going as well? What had it said? Something about living well and eating well, by Virginia Woolf, who everyone knew had filled her pockets with rocks and walked into a river. "My awards aren't for merit. They're purely subjective. Hooks for fundraising."

Ted shrugged.

"Besides," Stone continued. "I was talking about *you*."

"You were channeling the old man," Ted said.

"Hardly," Stone said. "I'm the last person …" Is that what he was doing, holding on to his father's expectations of the genius in order to justify his own lock-step adherence to his father's definition of success? Had he ever allowed himself to step off the path? How had Ted felt entitled to chart his own journey?

"The point is," Ted said, "I'm not good at playing that role. I'm not good at meet-and-greet, you know that. I hated it. I actually broke out in hives before a reading in New Haven."

Stone chuckled. It was hard for him to imagine his brother being intimidated, even at Yale.

"They're all the same," Ted said.

"Slam dunk for you," Stone said.

"No," Ted said. "I'm not good at managing other people's expectations."

"Dad's outlandish expectations," Stone said quietly. He felt his cheeks flush. If you were going to be a lawyer, you ought to be Chief Justice. If you were as good as a Hunnicutt was expected to be. "Lawyer of the Year" in a midwestern state didn't cut it.

After a beat, Stone added, "Sydney says it's a miracle either one of us turned out to be even close to normal." He dried the last bowl and added it to the nearest pile.

"You have no idea what it was like," Ted said.

"I was there, remember?" Stone glanced at the freshly dried bowls. He'd stacked them, he realized, by color, like Harmony's library: yellow, blue, green and red.

"Yeah, but you got the A for effort. For some reason, *I* had to be perfect. And then pretend that it was easy for me."

"It *was* easy for you. And believe me, I didn't get any credit from the old man for effort. Effort was the proof that I was stupid."

"No," Ted said in genuine disagreement. "Dad would always say 'the kid's got gumption.'"

"Gumption?" Stone felt a surge of adrenaline. "As in 'how dare that untalented piece of crap try?'"

"Gumption, as in 'he cares, he's unstoppable, he'll outrun us all.'"

Gumption. Stone felt his eyes begin to water. Watching his genius brother scrubbing the sink, for a moment Stone thought, yes! He had outrun them all, hadn't he? Even if he'd never gotten "credit" for his success. He and Ted were silent, acknowledging the revelation that their father had indeed played them against each other.

Ted pointed to the kitchen table. While Stone slid onto the bench, Ted reached into the top shelf of the pantry, moved a giant clear container of brown rice and produced a bottle of Courvoisier. He poured shots into each of two ceramic mugs. "Camouflage," he said, handing Stone a mug. "Remember the relay?" he asked.

"At Janesville?" At a high school track meet, he and Ted had run the 440 relay together and Stone had dropped the baton. "Thanks for bringing up one of my most inept and embarrassing moments."

"*You?* Why do you think *you* dropped it?" Ted asked.

"Because the baton landed on the ground?" Stone said, trying to take the sting out of a childhood memory that still haunted him. "The announcer called it. It didn't end up in your hands, did it?"

"No, not in my hands," Ted said. "Which is the point, isn't it? The announcer — some yahoo's father — announced that 'Hunnicutt dropped the baton.'"

"Like I said."

"I thought *I* dropped it," Ted said, as if Stone needed the obvious spelled out for him. "You were all so apologetic and took responsibility and I guess I was a kid and thought you wouldn't say you dropped it unless you had. But I was pretty sure I was the one."

Stone shrugged. He'd been the oldest. He'd wanted to be *the* "Hunnicutt," long before the announcer called him out.

Ted said, "The politically correct statement is, '*it was dropped*.'" He laughed at the absurd exculpatory of the passive voice. "Truth is, *we* dropped it. Two ends of the baton. Two hands."

Stone felt something shift in him. Ted had looked up to him! He'd been the older brother, relied upon to shoulder the responsibility like a man so that Ted could remain the untarnished childhood star.

Maybe it hadn't been so easy for Ted after all. Maybe that had been Stone's imagination, not Ted's reality. "To us," Stone said. Ted raised his glass and nodded.

20

The brothers finished the last of their brandies as Harmony and Sydney strolled in, Harmony holding Sydney's elbow in that possessive way of hers. Stone raised a skeptical eyebrow in their direction, but Sydney appeared to be as much in Harmony's thrall as Ted was. Maybe she was enchanted; perhaps merely amused. Stone felt oddly betrayed by that, as if the three of them were ganging up on him. Could Harmony have recruited Sydney so quickly? He had to admit that he'd thought Harmony was a force to contend with — he, too, had been somewhat intimidated by her, especially during the tour of her color-coded library. But Sydney was not the type to be intimidated.

Stone looked again at the two women. Sydney, standing tall in black slacks and a champagne cashmere turtleneck, seemed to dwarf Harmony, although she was only an inch or two taller. Harmony's round shoulders made the red and brown elephants lumbering across her caftan seem docile and ornamental rather than solid and sturdy.

In comparison, what a remarkable woman Sydney was: grounded, authentic, unflappable — the real thing, not a financially strapped heiress costumed as a spiritual guru. He was lucky Sydney had chosen him, but if she didn't shake that charlatan's clutch right that second, he might say something he'd regret.

As if reading his mind, Sydney broke free of Harmony and came over to the kitchen table, putting her hands on Stone's shoulders and massaging them. "A lot of fun things to see," she said. He scooted over and she sat down. Harmony joined Ted, glanced at the mug and said, "Sydney, would you like to join the boys in a glass of brandy?" Having been found out, Ted smirked at Stone, tilting his palms up in surrender. "She's a sensitive and hyper-observant soul," he said, putting his arm around Harmony.

Sydney, not used to being the last to catch on, hesitated a moment and declined the offered drink. "Saving up for tomorrow," she said. Stone hoped she meant she was saving up to have one with him later.

"Did you know Harmony's father was a famous artist?" Sydney asked. Stone shook his head. He seriously doubted it.

"Famous in Upson," Harmony corrected, her hands clasped not-so-humbly at her chest. "He taught at Northland College, over in Ashland."

"That's how Harmony collected many of her most interesting pieces," Sydney said.

Ted jumped in. "Professor Miller gave his first-year students exercises in imitation, to familiarize them with various artists and techniques. The most talented of his students understood they were to observe the stylistic details of the artist, then imitate it in their own personal way. The more plebeian students made slavish imitations."

"So they got As?" Stone asked cynically. He remembered vividly the look on Ted's face when that Pia woman won the Midwest Prize and confessed to her conscious imitation of *Little Women*. "Was the assignment to imitate or to personalize?"

"Lawyers!" Ted laughed, then looked at him sadly. "Who knows? Many went on to successful careers in art — teaching, running galleries, selling pottery, writing criticism, designing domestic interiors."

"Few became working artists," Harmony said seriously. "Very, very few." Stone almost agreed, "few artists *work*," but with a glance at Sydney, held his tongue.

"And those are the ones who later sent back their first imitations to Professor Miller as thank you gifts," Sydney said. "Isn't that cool?" She'd totally missed the oxymoron, "working artist," but then again, she wasn't as critical of others as Stone.

"Some were indeed so good — like a slice of cake — that it would take an expert to testify that it wasn't a real Magritte," Harmony said.

"So what does that tell us?" Ted said, his chin lifted with an air of disdain. "That as a society we value the artist's name more than his or her art?"

"It's the originality of the concept, isn't it?" Stone offered. "Magritte's idea was novel."

"Perhaps Magritte stole it from the student at the easel next to his," Ted said. "But ol' René got credit for it." There was a trace of resentment in Ted's voice.

"Everyone's a bit of a plagiarist," Stone said. "The point is that he did it, did it well, and got paid for his labor."

"Some do, some don't," Ted said. Like that nanny in Chicago who died and left boxes of negatives, never printed. For her, apparently it was about taking the pictures, not developing them or selling them."

"Or not having the means to print them," Sydney said. She was a poverty lawyer through and through. "Photography was more expensive in those days, and a much more difficult process."

"She didn't take the pictures for the purpose of making money," Harmony said.

Stone realized he'd opened the door to a conversation about money and he braced himself. "Probably not," Stone conceded. "But she did support herself. She worked."

"Ted works," Harmony said, defensively. "Are you insisting he make money from his art?"

If Ted had money, he wouldn't be beholden to a woman who asked his brother for money behind his back. Stone gathered himself. "Why not?" he asked, holding Harmony's gaze. "That *is* what people do. You might call it bourgeois. I call it taking responsibility for one's life and his talent," Stone said. Sydney's foot pressured his, but he ignored her. "It's his gift. Why not use it?"

Harmony kept her voice even. "He's written four novels," she said.

"Five," Stone said. There had been four boxes and one published novel. He felt a pinch on his thigh.

"Five," Harmony said flatly.

"Yes, and the nanny, Vivian Maier, took thousands of pictures, but it wasn't art, in my view, until someone printed them, cropped them, selected them, arranged them, and titled them. It was then that they became art. It was her eye, her subjects. But someone else's choices — of selection and interpretation — that ultimately rendered them art, made an artistic statement. Not random happenstance. Not a traffic camera or dashboard video. Volitional." Stone took a breath, impressed — and surprised — by his own eloquence in this matter. "That's what a published book is: Art."

"Maybe *not* being published is art," Ted said. "Ever hear of the Future Library Project?"

"No," Stone said abruptly. He detested any logic that attempted to prove that nothing was something, as if silence was music, or a blank page a poem.

"I thought the future of libraries was an online database. No book ever out-of-print or culled from the shelves," Sydney said. Of course she was willing to engage Ted's flight of fancy.

Ted shook his head. "There's an artist in Europe who planted one thousand trees in Norway in 2014, to be used to make paper in 2115, on which to print the first editions of one hundred books she is commissioning — one a year until 2114. Margaret Atwood was the first, and no one will read her book until it is printed, on paper from that forest, in 2115." Ted sat back.

"Then you don't really know if she wrote anything, do you?" Stone said.

"She gave them a manuscript, counselor," Ted said.

"She gave them a box, weighted to feel like a manuscript," Stone corrected him.

"Atwood's an honest woman," Ted said.

"She writes *fiction*," Stone said, palms up. "Maybe she put an old first draft in a box and called it a day. Like the preacher who owed a guy $5000 and repaid it when the guy died by writing a check and slipping it into his coffin."

Ted smiled. "I think the preacher was a lawyer," he said.

"Of course you do," Stone insisted. "The point is, you have *unpublished* novels. Put one in a damn time capsule if you want, but meanwhile, you've got three other publishable novels *and* you've got a publisher begging for them." Under the table, he felt Sydney's foot on his.

Stone glanced at Harmony. She lowered her chin, a bull before its charge. He clenched his fists, resolved that this would not end as their last visit had. Harmony's voice was surprisingly sympathetic. "It's kind of you to care so much about your brother," she said. "But if I may say so, you seem to care disproportionately about his worldly success."

He hated the way she said, "worldly."

Sydney — ever the mediator — said, "Of course they love each other, Harmony. They just want the best for each other."

Harmony turned to Sydney and asked, in what sounded rhetorical in nature, "Do you have siblings?"

"I have two daughters," Sydney retorted. "You?"

"All right, ladies," Ted intervened. "We're all tired," he said. "Why don't we call it a night?"

Sydney stood up, a strained smile on her face.

Harmony also rose. "So, will you join us for morning meditation?" Stone hated the exaggerated cordiality of the invitation. No. Meditation wasn't his thing, and his meditating wasn't going to bring Ted to his senses.

Before he could formulate a polite refusal, he heard Sydney gush, "We'd love to."

"Well, then," Ted said, slapping Stone's back a bit too hard. "Come by my trailer at 6:15."

Still stinging from the slap, Stone said, "That's my running time." He looked at Sydney, daring her to contradict him. She stared back, implacable.

"We'll see you all in the morning," Harmony said, as if what he'd said was of no consequence. "Do wear comfortable clothes."

"I don't have comfortable clothes," Stone complained to Sydney as he got in the car.

"Wear your running clothes," she said, a wicked smile on her face. Despite himself, he chuckled. "When's the last time you went running at 6:15?" she asked.

"I think about it a lot," he said, with a sly lilt of defensiveness.

"Seriously," Sydney said, amused. "What you've got on will do." He was wearing chinos, a blue button-down shirt and a navy blazer. "Lose the blazer and the belt. Wear the shirt out and roll up your sleeves."

"I call that sloppy, not comfortable," he said.

"I think the idea is to avoid distraction. Whatever makes you comfortable in your own skin. For you, of course, that might require a suit and tie!"

She was mocking him, but it wasn't far from the truth. He liked the feeling of being buttoned-down and buttoned-up. "I've never meditated before. Have you?" he asked.

"A few times, at mandatory stress-management training sessions at work. Kind of like watching TV and not paying attention."

He laughed.

"Without sleeping, I mean," she winked.

• • •

He didn't sleep well, the motel mattress lumpier than he recalled. He woke about four, which didn't auger well for meditation. These days, whenever he woke up earlier than his normal 6:45, he felt exhausted all day. If he closed his eyes to meditate, he'd be a goner.

Sydney was right, of course. Ten thousand was not a burden, so why did the whole situation feel so serious, so burdensome? What was wrong with him that his brother's life felt so much like a weight upon his own?

"Sydney?" he whispered, hoping she was awake. She wasn't. He started counting back from one hundred by sevens, but that required too much attention to induce sleep, so he rolled over and tried to think of nothing at all. The next thing he knew, an alarm was buzzing on someone's phone and the old-fashioned clock radio was blaring country music, the bass throbbing and the fiddle scratching.

"Helluva wake-up call," he grumbled. "Puts me in a perfect mood for meditation."

"Good morning to you, too," she said. She offered him a Styrofoam cup of coffee. "It's not bad," she said, nodding toward the small cof-feemaker on the credenza.

"Is caffeine permitted before meditation?" he asked. He assumed there were rules, and even if he didn't know what exactly he was doing, he didn't want to seem like a novice.

"Probably OK for an amateur," Sydney said.

"Amateur?" She might as well have said "stupid."

"The point of meditation is to become 'awake,'" she said. "Aware." She held out the Styrofoam cup. "You need your coffee in the morn-ing," she said, "just like you would for your run." She smiled a wicked smile. "Be careful, it's hot," she said, just as he took a sip.

His tongue slightly singed, Stone put the cup down to cool. He went to brush his teeth, came back and sat on the edge of the bed, the flavor of peppermint quickly washed away by the coffee.

When she turned down the radio, the room felt quiet. The motel wasn't far off the road, but there was little traffic early on a holiday morning.

"How long does this meditation last?" he asked.

"Forty-five minutes or so, I think," Sydney said.

"What am I supposed to think about for a billable hour?" he asked. What a waste. At least a million bucks worth of time a year. It would drive him crazy if he thought about Ted the whole time.

"I think you're not supposed to think about anything," Sydney said.

"Thinking is what I do for a living," Stone protested.

Sydney sighed. "This isn't work. It's more like relaxation," she said. "When we did this at work, they said the idea was to empty out. To just observe your 'monkey mind.' If a thought comes up — and it certainly will — don't dwell on it. Just notice it and gently dismiss it."

He was relieved at the way she said "gently dismiss it" — there was just enough mimicry of Harmony in her breathy explanation to suggest that she possibly shared his cynicism. "Who'll know?" he asked.

She looked at him as if not sure of his meaning.

"Who'll know what prurient thoughts I might be entertaining rather than gently dismissing them?" he asked, and rubbed his hands together, imitating, in his own mind, a cartoon of the "big bad wolf."

She was sitting on the other side of the bed, putting on khakis and a sweatshirt.

"Your left ear twitches," she said.

"It does not," he said, and swung his legs over the bed to grab her around the waist. "Is it twitching now?" he asked, nibbling at her lower back.

"Better not be," she giggled, "we're late." She twisted around, kissed the top of his head, and said, "We gotta go. We don't want to be late to the doing of nothing."

Ted was standing next to his trailer dressed in gray sweatpants and a gray-and-red "UW Athletic Department" sweatshirt. It occurred to Stone that if Ted could do this, so could he. Of course, Ted had been doing nothing for years, while Stone had been racking up the billable hours. But he knew how to relax, too: he'd been to the Caribbean. He could relax with the best of them.

Sydney and Stone followed Ted to the house and up the grand staircase to a large room that was painted off-white. It was topped by ornately carved crown molding and had a gleaming light oak floor. The shades were open. The sun wouldn't rise for another half hour. Most of the residents were already sitting cross-legged in a circle; the Girls stretching their torsos over their legs like hairpins. Harmony entered the room in a gold-embroidered white caftan, smiled benignly at her charges and sat down in what was obviously her customary place. With her back to the window, she was enshrouded in a hazy halo of pre-dawn light. There was a burnished gong by her side. Stone and Sydney found places in the circle and lowered themselves to the floor.

Harmony sounded the gong, and while the tone reverberated further and further away, she held her arms in front of her, and repeated, "Hello. Let go. Hello. Let go. Hello. Let go." Her voice was hypnotic. Stone breathed in and out.

This isn't hard. What's the big deal? Oh, that's a thought. Goodbye, thought. Well, that's a thought, isn't it? Dear God, how much longer? Breathe.

He took a deep breath, noticing the raspy sound of it, and cleared his throat. The sound reverberated as loud as thunder in the silent room. He looked around to see if anyone had noticed. *Don't do that again.* He took another breath, and a third.

How long was that?

He stole a glance at Sydney, her eyes half-closed, her body — always full of energy — now subdued. As he turned again to face the middle of the circle, he realized that his motion had stirred the air, possibly disturbing the others. *Should I say I'm sorry? Then they'll know I had a thought. It's not natural to think nothing. It should count that I'm not thinking about work, or anything specific, shouldn't it? Gunning for an A, are you? Where did that come from?* His stomach felt heavy, but his shoulders soon relaxed. He noticed the first before the second. Perhaps a minute more passed. Then an image presented itself: a manuscript box in a vault. *No one will read her book for a hundred years. I'll be dead. Like this? Doing nothing. Thinking nothing.*

He felt his heart thumping — slowly, dependably. That meant he was alive. *What is a book if not read? It will be read, just not now. Who will know if it's been read or not? What's the difference between that book and Ted's? Don't think about that. Breathe.*

Gosh, I'm bad at this. Ted was sitting across from him, radiating comfort, peace, perhaps joy. *Such bull. If you don't put it out there, if you just retreat from the world, it can't hurt you. You can't lose if you don't play. If you don't play, you won't win. But Ted's not starving. Not killing himself working. Seems happy. Like the laborer in that gospel story who gets work at the last minute and gets the same wage as the guy who worked all day. How fair was that? Breathe. So what if Ted's not living up to his potential.*

His palms felt cold and his back hurt. He'd been slumping, so now he straightened up. *Goodbye thoughts. Hello. Let go. Hello. Let go.*

Let go of what? Potential? Expectations? The ravings of an old man, long gone. Outlandish. Why shouldn't Ted be free of their father's demands? Just because you did everything the old man wanted, Stone. What you did was what you did. What would the old man say? Why do I still care?

Goodbye thoughts. For a few seconds or minutes — he didn't know which — he was free of them. Then another thought intruded. *What could you have done differently?*

Goodbye, thought. He didn't want to think about that; he didn't even know *how* to think about that. In the stillness, he could see that there was some value in dismissing his thoughts.

From nowhere, the gong sounded again. Stone opened his eyes. Around him the others bowed "Namaste" to the center, then stretched their arms over their heads, arched their backs, bent forward to put their noses almost to the ground. Sydney yawned and took a deep, deep breath, then raised her eyebrows and nodded at him. He smiled solemnly and nodded back. *Piece of cake.*

Ted stood and offered Harmony his hand, helping her to her feet. Sydney offered her hand to Stone. Stone looked over at Ted, wondering if Ted knew how badly he'd failed at meditation. But Ted had already turned to Harmony, apparently not at all curious about Stone's meditative experiences.

"Breakfast?" Harmony asked the group and, hand-in-hand with

Ted, led the way out of the room. Sydney and Stone lingered.

"You OK?" she asked.

"Survived," he smiled. It was the first word that came to his mind, but it was woefully inadequate.

"Refreshing," she said.

He wanted to say "disturbing," but he didn't feel like discussing how he'd failed to achieve serenity.

"Nirvana?" he said. He realized how little he understood the concept.

"I don't really know what that means," she said. He was grateful for her honesty. Then she added, "At least in this context, I don't know," which confused him, suggesting that she *did* know in some contexts. He *really* didn't know.

"Was this the same as it was before?" he asked.

"Maybe easier?" she said. "Before, we were all beginners. You could almost feel the anxiety. You know, a bunch of competitive lawyers all trying to ace a test for the first time." She gave him a sidelong glance.

"I can see how that would ruin it," he said, hoping to avoid self-incrimination.

"This was much calmer," she said. "For the most part, there wasn't that fear in the room."

"What fear?" he asked, wiping his palms on his chinos.

"All kinds," she said. "Fear of nothingness, non-existence, loss of ego, fear of self." She sounded more knowledgeable than she'd let on. "It was a half-day course," she said. "They gave us professional responsibility credit for it." Those were the continuing legal education credits most difficult to come by, usually for ethics and professional courtesy. Not usually awarded for doing nothing.

"You guys coming?" Ted stuck his head in the doorway.

"Just debriefing," Sydney said. "Say, did I see the whole house? Is there more to see?"

Ted shook his head. "Not sure what all you saw," Ted said. "We can ask Harmony later. It's not mine to show."

"You could sell your trailer and buy half the house," Stone said. He shouldn't have blurted that out, but the thought had just occurred to him.

"One, I couldn't afford it, and two, the Foundation technically owns the house," Ted said, apparently not taking any offense.

"Oh," Stone said. A dozen legal issues regarding the Foundation's tax-exempt status and Harmony's private use of the place came to mind, but he dared not raise any of them. Ted arched his eyebrows and smiled, perhaps appreciating Stone's new-found restraint.

• • •

After a leisurely breakfast of grapefruit and homemade bread and jam, Ted, Stone and Sydney left for a walk around the perimeter of the property. They started toward the east, along a sparse wood leading to a field of unharvested browned-out corn.

"Shouldn't this be in by now?" Sydney asked.

"We rent these twenty acres to a local guy. He watches the market pretty closely, tries to time his harvest just right to avoid storage costs. I guess at this point, the weather doesn't hurt the corn. I'm not much of a farmer."

"Then how did you end up here?" Sydney asked. "All these years, I never pictured this place being so … so remote," she said.

"What did you imagine?" Ted asked.

"I thought it would be like a small liberal arts college campus," she said, laughing. "Don't ask me why," she added.

"Wishful thinking?" Ted laughed.

She shrugged. "So how …?"

"While I was traveling, I heard about the place. I was low on cash and it seemed like a good place to start over." Sydney seemed to accept that answer at face value and stopped to take a picture with her cellphone of a bright yellow shriveled ear of corn.

They walked on, leaving Sydney behind. "What about the money from dad?" Stone asked. Ten years ago, their father had died and left half of his modest estate to a scholarship fund and a quarter to each of his sons.

"It was a good trip," Ted smiled. "I didn't have that much left. I bought a second-hand trailer, put a little in stocks for a rainy day and gave the rest to Harmony." Stone wanted to ask about Potato

River but didn't.

"So living in a trailer saved you from the streets?" Stone asked. "I would've given you a room, you know, if you'd asked."

"I know. You probably would have. But you had Sydney and the girls …"

"We have a guest room," Stone said, just as Ted said, "And anyway I didn't want to be a fifth wheel."

"To bunk at your place would've made me feel like a failure. Like that's what I should've done: married, become a doctor or lawyer or nuclear physicist or whatever the old man thought I should be."

"You could've. You know that," Stone said. "You could have done anything." Ted smiled sadly as Stone squelched a rising anger. Ted could've done anything, but he hadn't. Didn't have to. Stone continued, "You've already done something most people can't do. And you've done it five times."

"Harmony helped me see that what I do is inherently selfish," Ted said. "She says the world doesn't need my books, but I need to write them."

"I get that," Stone said. "You'd be the first to admit the world doesn't need another damn lawyer. But it's what I do and once in a great while, it's useful to someone."

Sydney jogged up behind them in time to hear Ted say, "I'm not sure a novel is ever that useful." She noticed a skinny red tractor that had been left to rust in a half-cut field.

"You don't believe in entertainment?" Sydney said. "Don't tell me your workaholic brother has converted you that quickly." She turned to take a picture of the abandoned tractor.

"I'm not a workaholic," Stone said. Yes, he worked hard. But he enjoyed what he did.

"Only because I won't allow it," Sydney said. She knelt to get a different angle on her picture.

He resented her comment. She made it sound like he had to work too hard at being a lawyer. All he did was serve his clients as best he could, and they determined when and where and how hard he worked.

Ted breezed over "workaholic." "I was taught a novel should do more than entertain," he said.

"Like what? Inform? Inspire?" Sydney stretched her hands over her head, as if she'd just finished a 5K run. "Some people refuse to be informed or inspired. The person most likely to be informed or inspired is yourself."

They continued walking. The day was light gray, but crisp. "That's basically what I was telling Stone," Ted said. "It's rather selfish but writing entertains me."

"And I'm just saying" — Stone wished he could stop using that phrase — "that publishing might feed you so that you could be entertained some more."

"Crass commercialism," Ted scoffed. "Great literature should have a noble purpose."

"There he is again," Sydney said, throwing up her arms. "The ghost of Thaddeus Newton. When will you boys ever learn to lower your standards from grandeur to something much more human?" She turned to Ted, "How about publishing being the completion of the creative process?"

"To feed the ego of the writer," Ted said stubbornly.

"To end the writer's isolation," Sydney said. "To invite readers to end theirs."

Ted stopped. After a few steps, Sydney and Stone turned around. Ted appeared lost in thought. Sydney waved to Ted and he hurried to join them.

They'd come full circle and were a hundred yards from the house. From a distance, Stone could appreciate that it looked historic. Three stories, turreted, a little ginger-bready for modern tastes, but perhaps worth saving.

"Last one home is a green pig," Sydney said in a child's voice.

Ted and Stone looked at each other. "I've been called worse," Stone said, shaking his head. He wasn't in the mood to run.

"*Citius!*" Ted said and took off.

Stone quickly realized that with a late start, he couldn't possibly win, but it wasn't like him not to try. "Wait for me!" he cried, but of course they didn't. When he got to the steps of the house, panting from his sprint, Ted and Sydney together cried, "Green pig!"

"Cheaters!" he cried. Ted put his arm around Stone's shoulders and Stone shrugged him off. He shouldn't gloat about winning an unfair race. How condescending. Had it been a fair start, he was sure he would've kept up.

Ted shook his head, as if amused. Then he turned to Sydney, a serious look in his eye. "Would you mind if I borrowed Stone for a minute?"

"That's fine. I wanted to see if I could help inside," she said, and disappeared through the kitchen door. Stone watched her go, annoyed to be left alone with Ted in the aftermath of his defeat.

"What's up?" Stone asked reluctantly. Something important, from the look on Ted's face — his brows hovered low over his eyes. Ted pointed toward the fountain and the Airstream.

Stone tensed, ready for the starting gun. Of course Ted would now ask him, brother-to-brother, for his financial help. Despite all his rantings about how Ted should work, he knew, deep down, that he would give Ted whatever he needed, or claimed to need, and that Sydney, Harmony and his dead father would all be satisfied that he'd done the "right thing," the thing expected of him. There would be some satisfaction in that, but he resented it in a way difficult to explain. Slowly, he was beginning to understand: Ted had always been free to do whatever he wanted, to be whoever he wanted to be, and still be "my son." Stone had felt he had to earn that love, to prove himself worthy of the title.

"It's about Harmony and me," Ted said.

"Harmony?" Stone asked. Not the money? "You two seem to get along pretty well."

Ted sat on the edge of the drained fountain, where Stone joined him, the chill of the cement sending a shiver up his spine. "We do. Usually," Ted said. "But something's come up. She's feeling financially insecure. Not that she really is, mind you, but mid-life and all that. She's tired of the simple life, of making sacrifices to support this mangy group. She'd like a few more creature comforts, perhaps some travel."

"Rules out selling the Mercedes, I guess," Stone said casually, trying to temper his sarcasm.

"We own some property on the Potato River," Ted said. Stone feigned surprise, letting his jaw fall. "Crazy name, isn't it? In joint tenancy. Half mine."

"I know what joint tenancy is," Stone smiled. He got up and shuddered from the cold. Ted nodded his agreement and pointed to his trailer. It reminded Stone of a silver ice bucket they once had, but he assumed it would be at least slightly warmer. They could turn on the stove if need be.

Ted continued, "Of course you do. And that's my question. Can she force me to sell it? Or lease it?"

"I'm not totally familiar with all the technicalities of joint tenancy," Stone said, his usual gambit when he thought there could be exceptions to a legal concept he didn't work with every day, "but I think she can only transfer the rights *she* has — an undivided half interest in the property." In which case, Stone thought, Ted should go along with her, sell the property, and solve their money issues.

Ted opened the door to the Airstream, which didn't feel perceptibly warmer. Ted took off his jacket and gestured to the table; Stone left his jacket on and sat down. Ted sighed. "Some outfit wants to lease the property and dig a copper and manganese open-pit mine — ten years, total reclamation, guaranteed compliance with all federal and state laws."

"Could be lucrative," Stone said tentatively. "The answer ..."

"A disaster!" Ted exclaimed, his fist pounding the table.

"Jeez!" Stone winced, remembering both Ted's punches and his own boxing fiasco at the gym.

"The point is, I feel like it's driving us apart. I'm not going to sign the lease."

"But it could solve ...," Stone tried again.

Ted interrupted, "It would be a rape of the environment."

"Oh, I see," Stone said. "I'm surprised that Harmony would even consider it. Usually environmentalists are knee-jerk opposed to such things," he said.

"She's never knee-jerk about anything," Ted said, "but it's a total turn-around. A side of her I've never seen before."

"The money's for the house, right? Her artistic mission?" Stone asked. He rubbed the spot where Ted's fist had landed. The table felt almost as cold as the cement outside.

"That's what she says, but there are other ways, if that's her goal,"

Ted said. He put his elbows on the table and folded his hands together, then rested his cheek against one hand. "I think this is more personal. The aunt and uncle who raised her stole some money from her. Left her some, too, but maybe, at a certain point in life, you don't know when enough is enough."

Stone sat still, annoyed at himself that his mind felt so empty. Usually he'd have a dozen solutions by now, a bunch of ideas for clients seeking his business advice. He couldn't remember Ted ever asking for his advice as an adult about anything, especially love or relationships. Maybe it was the morning meditation, but he felt now like a blank slate.

"Anyway, I wanted you to know," Ted said, standing up. "About us. And my rights. And, again, that I didn't know that she'd asked you for money. You know I wouldn't do that myself."

"You could, you know, on your own account," Stone said. Sheepishly, he added, "But for Harmony, it didn't feel right." He also stood, hoping they would go up to the big house, where it might be warmer.

"Thanks, bro," Ted said. "Thanks for listening." He hung his arm around Stone's shoulder, and even though Stone didn't shrug him off this time, Ted quickly removed it, as if afraid he'd crossed a line.

"I wish I could do more than listen," Stone said.

"Nah. It's my relationship," Ted said. "Not much anyone can do." He took a deep breath, then nodded to Stone.

Emboldened by Ted's need for him, Stone said, "You forgot you're looking at the Best Business Lawyer in Wisconsin. What I'm really, really good at," he said, "is solving problems with creative solutions." He unzipped his jacket, as if to get down to work, and sat back down.

"Pro bono publico?" Ted asked, joining him at the table.

"And occasionally for friends or family," Stone said. An idea was beginning to form.

"The only way out I see," Ted said, "is to welch on my principles and sign the damn lease. Like it's a duty of loyalty that I owe my life partner."

"The mine won't pay off for a few years, will it?" Stone asked, but he knew the answer. "Usually there's an advance, like a down payment, and then a percentage of gross or net profit or some other accounting fiction, and an annual guarantee. Am I right?"

"Probably," Ted said. "But no guarantee that I remember, and very little up front."

"So that's it," Stone said. "I'll buy out Harmony, and then you and I will own the property together. Maybe put a cottage on it for our retirement. Harmony won't have to wait for her cash."

"What's a Hunnicutt cottage? A McMansion by Jay Shore? She'd be in an uproar over a development like that. Not just rape, but an eyesore to boot!"

"Sydney detests Jay's style of home," Stone said. "Besides there's not enough of a market up here."

"Not today, but someday. You know: 'If you build it, they will come.' Isn't that what Jay Shore does — sell people more than they need before they need it?"

"Ever try to sell Sydney on something she doesn't want?" Stone smiled, and the amusement of some private memory flashed across Ted's face.

"I'm pretty sure Sydney wouldn't consider property on the Potato River a good investment," Ted took a new tack. "It's money she could be donating to the poor."

"We give plenty to the poor," Stone said. "Besides," he started.

"We're not poor," Ted said, suddenly defensive.

"I didn't say you were," Stone said, holding Ted's stare so that he wouldn't look around at the trailer, which would, of course, be misinterpreted as an accusation. He thought he should rezip his jacket, but that might give offense. "It's not a hand-out. It's an investment in the land. Investing in the land will appeal to Sydney. And, since I have no interest in mining or in Jay Shore's development, your conscience will be clear."

Ted stared at his hands, folded in front of him on the table. Then he opened them, reminding Stone of his meditation pose, and asked quietly, "Will it be OK with Sydney?"

"Of course. She wanted to just give Harmony the money today."

"This would be more than ten thousand," Ted cautioned.

Stone tried not to smile at the irony. Sydney had been right. Ten thousand had been the easy way out; he'd just had to talk Ted into taking more! "She'll get a kick out of having title to some land on the prestigious Potato River," Stone said gamely. "The real question is," Stone said, "will Harmony go for it?"

"She should," Ted said. "It's a brilliant solution."

Stone beamed with pride, pleased that Ted hadn't used that awful word, "genius."

"She's been biding her time, assuming I'd come around like I usually do, but it's been the elephant in our bed ever since she received the offer. When she got all involved in trying to get you and me back together, I took that to mean her conscience was torn about the lease."

"Ask her for a fair price," Stone said. "Better yet, get an appraisal. You don't need to tell her I'm the buyer. She thinks I'm made of gold, but I'm not."

"A pretty good imitation," Ted said.

21

When they arrived back at their motel to get ready for the feast, Sydney was first out of the car. She fumbled with the old-fashioned key on its green plastic fob, and the door finally creaked open.

"Green pig?" Stone remembered to ask.

"Don't you remember? A duck and a monkey race," she said. "They each get help. Hitch a ride with a girl on a bicycle, a horse, a taxi, an airplane — that sort of thing. Kind of like cheating, but they're each doing it, trying to win, like that TV program, that *Amazing Race* thing."

"And the loser is a green pig? Isn't that disparaging of green pigs?" Stone asked.

"The green pig lobby is up in arms," she said. "What I remember is something about winning and losing graciously. I doubt your father read it to you."

"I'm a good winner," he said. Hadn't he been gracious at the Bar Association dinner?

"You are," she said. "Really, you are."

"And I'm a good loser, too," he said.

"I wouldn't know," she said. "I don't remember seeing you lose."

He studied her face, hardly a wrinkle. Despite the run back to the house, her hair was smoothly in place, just the slightest curl under her chin. She was as pretty as the day they'd met back at Harvard; it was hard to believe their daughters were now almost as old as they were that day in Langdell Hall. The significance of her words sunk in. "That's very kind of you," he said, surprised and flattered. In fact, he couldn't remember any major losses, at least not in his legal career. Running wasn't his field of expertise. The baton thing no longer counted.

"It's your brother who doesn't know how to win," she said.

"Ted's won plenty," he said reflexively. Proportional to his lack of effort, Ted had won more than his fair share.

"But he doesn't enjoy it like you do. Not that you gloat, just that winning makes you happy. You were great at the pro bono dinner. Very gracious."

"I was?" He opened the motel door and waved it back and forth to air out the ubiquitous pine cleaner smell.

"*After* I talked you down from your pedestal of false guilt," she said. "But Ted — I don't know if he'll ever get over himself enough to win or lose, especially when the game is subjective: winners always have their detractors and losers their promoters. You have to be pretty secure with yourself and, if you ask me, your father made that just about impossible."

"Funny," Stone said. "I was thinking Ted was the one who'd escaped the old man's expectations."

"Only on the surface," she said. "You're the one who played through them."

He flopped on the bed, smiling at the ceiling. Ordinary acoustic tile. An odd water mark spread over several tiles, suggesting an exploding champagne bottle. More than any meditation, Sydney's words assured him, comforted him, made him feel whole in a way that had eluded him for so long. It occurred to him that he hadn't had to fight Ted or anyone else to marry her. For whatever reason, they had chosen each other as if no other choice were possible. She was *his* Harmony. His peace and joy.

She paused, studying him as he sat on the bed. "It's like a Sunday afternoon," she said, her lips curling at the corners. With almost adolescent excitement, he stretched his arms up and open toward her, welcoming her as she lowered herself on top of him, her weight comforting. They kissed deeply, and then she raised herself to her knees and started unbuttoning his shirt. Almost overwhelmed by the tenderness he felt for her, he stroked her cheek, and then they settled into their familiar but — remarkably — still exciting lovemaking, disrobing each other slowly, teasing each other in anticipation. He sucked her breasts. She nibbled at his ears. They rubbed and touched familiar places as if for the first time. She gave a little shout and he released himself. "I love you, babe," he said.

"You're the best," she said. "Really. You are my best."

They dozed, and when they awoke, he realized he hadn't told her about his conversation with Ted. He reached over and took her hand.

"So here's the deal," he said. "I hope you're OK with it." He told her how they could soon be the owners of their own piece of the North Woods.

"I normally would advise friends not to go into joint ownership unless they have a clear written agreement," she said, stroking the still damp brown hair on his chest.

"We're not friends," he said, which came out wrong.

"It's a little like hiding money in a mattress," she continued tugging at his damp hair. "But I suppose at least one of you can afford it." He put one hand under his pillow, hoping for a first strike, but she hopped from the bed, using her pillow like a fig leaf. "Besides," she laughed, "you're brothers. I'm sure everything will work out fine." Then she whipped her pillow at him and turned for the shower. He retaliated, but his pillow barely reached her behind. She had a second, smaller pillow, and let it rip. "I win," she gloated. "First prize, my own potato patch in paradise." Even at her age, she had a lovely butt, small and firm. He closed his eyes and yawned contentedly. He was a lucky man, indeed.

When the shower stopped, she came out wrapped as best she could in one of the motel's thin towels. "Do you think there will be hors d'oeuvres before dinner?" she asked, seemingly oblivious to its inadequacy.

"I was just wondering that myself," he said.

"Usually after," she said suggestively.

"I was thinking about dinner parties. At home, we don't usually have a snack before, do we?"

"Usually just nuts," she said.

"I hope they don't do a lot of speechifying before the meal," he said.

"You mean praying?" she asked. "Like at Lou's?" Last year, at Lou's day after celebration, one of Lou's brothers launched into a tirade of gratitude that lasted so long the gravy congealed in the bowl like scalded milk. During the ordeal, Sydney had kicked off her shoes while the group held hands and Lou's dog had picked one up and run off with it. When it was time to go home, they found the dog in the breezeway dining on black patent leather.

"They weren't very comfortable anyway," Sydney had said.

"Sorry about that," Lou had said. "We all expected him to become a preacher, not a dentist. When my brother gets going," he said, "he doesn't know how to stop."

They laughed in the shared memory and Stone added, "Prayers, gratitude lists, anything that comes between me and a turkey leg."

"Turducken," she corrected.

"Ted says they grill a turkey, too," he said.

"Makes sense," she agreed. "They have a lot of mouths to feed. Better hold back on the turkey leg to make sure no one else wants it."

He scowled, then studied his face in the mirror above the sink, considering whether he needed a quick shave.

"Yes," she said from the bed, although he'd not asked her opinion. When he returned, she put her fingers around her ears. Obediently, he trotted back to the bathroom to wipe the last of the tell-tale shaving cream.

Sydney dressed in black slacks and a rust and gold Indian print satin blouse. She wore a gold choker of hefty links. He held the motel door open for her.

"Today's statement?" he asked.

"Grateful for everything I have," she said. "Especially for a husband with excellent taste in jewelry."

"As am I," he said, "grateful to have such a beautiful wife to buy jewelry for."

"Enough," she said. "Let's hope our gratitude gets us through dinner with the wackos."

"I don't think they're wackos," he said. "Except for Harmony. "I meant the Hunnicutt brothers," she laughed. "Any conflict between the others would be so civil as to be boring. The brothers — they're more likely to engage."

"Not today," he promised.

They met Ted and Mark huddled over the Weber kettle at the back of the house. A large turkey was smoking on the grill. Ted, in charge of the side dishes, walked inside with them, leaving Mark in charge of the bird. A couple of people were working at the stove.

"Where's Harmony?" Sydney asked. She thought it odd that

someone who put herself at the center of a community like this wasn't also playing mother hen, and a brooding, cooking one at that.

"Being in charge isn't her thing," Ted said. Stone opened his mouth to object. Sydney caught Stone's eye. He kept his comment to himself.

"Well, it all seems to run quite smoothly," she said.

"Cooperatively," Ted said.

The Girls were at the kitchen table, admiring their pies — two pumpkin and two apple. "There they go," Heather moaned. Small cracks were emerging on top of the pumpkins.

"That always happens," Ted said. "Only the store-boughts don't."

"I've tried everything," Sydney offered. "Lowering the temperature, cooling them in the oven, taking them out early …"

"They'll be perfect just as they are," Ted said.

Mark kicked at the door and Ted jumped to open it, then stood aside so that Mark could bring a deep, black-and-white speckled metal roasting pan containing a perfectly bronzed bird. The small crowd in the kitchen applauded. "It needs to rest for fifteen and then we'll be ready," he said.

The recycling artists, Alan and Alexis and then Richard straggled in, and lastly, Harmony. Her long hair had been gathered on top of her head in a mass of curls, with exotic beaded pins holding some in place. In her gold-threaded tunic from the morning and a pair of gold-hoop earrings, she looked the part of queen bee. If not, strictly speaking, "in charge," she was, at the very least, the one everyone wanted to please. Heather and Sunshine got up from the table to offer their seats; Mark offered her a first taste off the tip of his carving knife. Ted touched his ear and gave her a broad smile.

Harmony surveyed the scene, her fingers moving against her side. "Minus two?" she asked no one in particular.

"Dylan" — who Stone remembered as the paranoid one — "isn't having a very good day. I'll take him something later," Mark said. "And Cody went to see his folks."

David's partner, Mark, began the march to the dining room, carrying a covered pot, and the others followed. All the dishes were arranged on the sideboard in the dining room.

Harmony gestured for everyone to sit. She remained standing, lifting up her palms, like a TV evangelist. Stone resigned himself to a long homily as his stomach growled. Sydney rolled her lips but didn't look at him, as if to help preserve his innocence.

In a breathy, but authoritative voice, Harmony intoned:

> Great Spirit
> We thank you today
> We thank you for Mother Earth
> We thank you for Grandmother Moon
> We thank you for Grandfather Sun
> We thank you for the four directions:
> the east
> the south
> the west
> the north
> We thank you for all our relations:
> the winged nation
> creeping and crawling nation
> the four-legged nation
> the green and growing nation
> and all things living in the water
> Honoring the clans:
> the deer …

Harmony paused and took Ted's hand, then continued:
> the *white* deer

Stone noticed that at the insertion of "white deer," Ted touched his eye with his free hand and smiled an almost holy smile, reminding Stone of Ted's early days as an altar boy, before their mother died. He didn't know why white deer should be singled out, but assumed it was just more spiritual mumbo-jumbo he didn't understand. Apparently, it meant something to Harmony and Ted. She went on:

> the bear
> the wolf

the turtle
the snipe
Great Spirit
We thank you today

Feeling in the spirit of things and reluctantly impressed by Harmony's choice of prayers, Stone added "Amen!" assuming that was the expected response. He felt embarrassed when he was the only one to echo his thanks in the traditional way. Wisely, Sydney had paused and as a result had had time to hear the others add their own, more personal, affirmations: *Namaste. Right on! Blessed be. Verily. For real. Peace. Let it be.* Sydney squeezed his hand and whispered in his ear, "whatever." Thinking she was correcting him, he repeated, "whatever," and the Girls giggled. He wasn't sure who else heard him; Ted and Harmony were kissing a little longer than their usual public peck; Mark and David were hugging. "Lovely prayer, Harmony," Stone recovered. "Thank you."

"I've never heard of a white deer," Sunshine said. "What a beautiful image," she gushed.

"Oh, it was all beautiful," Heather said. "Like Harmony, for whom all of us are very grateful. Thank you, Harmony!"

"The white deer is a sacred symbol of our connection to the land," Harmony said, her voice awash with humility.

"There's a herd of them over near Rhinelander," Mark said. "They're actually a protected species in Wisconsin."

"I think the prayer says we should all be protected," Sydney said. She smiled at Ted and Ted nodded shyly, then gave a thumbs-up to Stone. At first Stone thought he was approving Sydney's remark, but then realized that Ted had sold Harmony on their deal.

Mark pointed to the buffet. "Sydney and Stone, as our guests, will you please go first?"

"Guests?" Ted cried. "They're family! Family holds back!" Everyone laughed, all apparently familiar with the holiday rule.

"Rules are meant to be broken," Stone said.

There was a murmur of agreement from the group. "Nice talk coming from a lawyer," Ted challenged.

Stone urged Sydney toward the buffet. "Let's not keep them waiting," he said. "As I understand Harmony's prayer, we're all relations. Someone in the family has to go first."

"Did she mention the scum nation?" Ted chuckled.

"What's all this animosity toward lawyers?" Sydney asked, pretending to be indignant.

"Yeah, you used to like lawyers as I recall," Stone said, raising his eyebrows toward Sydney.

"Just brotherly banter," Ted said. "Besides, did I say anything about lawyers?"

"Sounded like snipe nation to me," Sydney said.

"One of the few times my brother got the better of me," Ted said. Stone shot him an inquisitive glance; he didn't remember ever getting the best of Ted. He took a second spoon of sweet potatoes and half a spoon of green beans amandine.

"Don't you remember?" Ted asked. "My first time at the local baseball diamond, you told me to ask the coach for the keys to the batter's box."

"Oldest snipe hunt in the world," Mark laughed.

Stone blushed. He didn't want these aging hippies to think he'd been a mean older brother. In truth, he only vaguely remembered that incident with Ted; what he remembered more clearly was the public humiliation when his father had played the joke on *him*. It was one of those teams where everybody got to play, regardless of skill, and Stone, wearing a new uniform at least one size too large, had felt particularly small and lacking in skill. Their father hadn't played the prank on Ted, the better athlete, so Stone had. Ted had come back after asking the coach the foolish question looking hurt and perplexed. What Stone remembered now was that first taste of power — a power that came with knowledge, but at another person's expense.

The tradition at Harmony's Peace & Joy was that after the big meal, but before the pies, each member shared one of their creative efforts. Harmony said this was how artists expressed gratitude. "Our creativity is our breath," she said, standing up from her seat at the table to emcee the ceremonies. Stone prepared for the worst. If Ted's novels weren't ready to be shared — and Ted was a genius — why would Harmony spoil dinner by foisting on them the inferior creative output of this bunch of misfits?

"Freely given to us so that we can freely return our art to the universe," Harmony said, her tone rising with enthusiasm. It occurred to Stone that Harmony must lower her exceptional standards for this one day when effort alone could be applauded. How arrogant. Stone rubbed his stomach; in any event, a break before pie would be welcome.

"David?" Harmony said. "You always have something fun for us." Fun? Not spiritually uplifting or deadly serious? That was hopeful.

David stood up. He was wearing a tweed jacket with his blue jeans, his version of "dressed up." The jacket had brown suede patches at the elbows, and his reading glasses were pushed up on his head. To Stone, he looked like an Ivy League poet.

"What I have today is a kind of cento, an ode of sorts to community, to mutual inspiration and encouragement and to you, my friends." He waved several yellow lined sheets covered in a neat blue ink. He flipped his reading glasses down and cleared his throat. "This is called 'Hand-in-Hand, a Runcible Rap.'" He read:

> They dined on mince and slices of quince,
> which they ate with a runcible spoon,

[here, his audience, recognizing *The Owl and the Pussycat*, howled, but Stone was puzzled]

> while I nodded, nearly napping. Suddenly there came a tapping
> as of someone gently rapping, rapping:
> The time has come, the Walrus said, to talk of many things —
> things fall apart, the center cannot hold.

David looked up from his pages and smiled to see if they were getting it. What was he supposed to get? Plagiarism as an art form? Or a literary IQ test?

I saw the best minds of my generation destroyed by madness;
though they go mad they shall be sane; all that is gold does
not glitter,
not all those who wander are lost.
Hope is the thing with feathers, for the caged bird sings
of freedom;
then the bird said nevermore, and that has made all the
difference.

Stone looked at Sydney. He recognized lines from poetry he'd
learned in high school as well as Maya Angelou, and was that Gins-
berg? Sydney nodded her agreement ever so slightly. David's voice
rose triumphantly:

My noon, my midnight, my talk, my song. Sing Heavenly
Muse!
I celebrate myself, and sing myself, a piece of the continent,
a part of the main.
Let us go then you and I, hand-in-hand, on the edge of
the sand.
And dance by the light of the moon.
Old age should burn and rave at close of day; gather ye
rosebuds while ye may.

Ted and Harmony smiled broadly and the Girls giggled. Stone
had to admit he was fascinated. Stone was getting the most obvious
references, but some were obscure. Still, the poem, or the plagiarism,
stirred something in him. He felt a new respect and admiration for
the artists of Peace & Joy. David's ode required both knowledge and
creativity.

I am the master of my fate, I am the captain of my soul.
And I have promises to keep.
Grow old along with me, the best is yet to be.

He bowed, Japanese-style and sat down. The group sat stunned. Then Ted stood up and applauded. "Bravo!"

"Masterful," Harmony said. "Let's hear it again."

"It's amazing how it sounds as though it means something," Stone said.

"No need to parse it, Stone," Mark said. "It's about the feeling."

"You're right, Stone," David said. "I'm not sure it parses all that logically, but it conveys a certain hope and joy, doesn't it?"

"Indeed," Stone said, eager to disengage. In fact, he had enjoyed the poem. He should've kept quiet.

"Logic analyzes problems and mistakes," Harmony said, as if ready to deliver a sermon. "In happiness and joy, we find solutions."

Stone thought she was reprimanding him and felt the hairs on his arms tingle. Was she ungrateful? Then Ted put his arm around Harmony, which Stone thought was intended to quiet her. "I'd love to hear it again," Stone said.

"Wait a minute," Mark said. He disappeared into the hall and came back with a stand-up bass. He plucked a few strings in a folksy-blues rhythm. "Ready when you are."

David read his poem a second time, with Mark's improvised bass line adding dramatic effect. The result reminded Stone of a documentary he'd once seen about the beat poets of the 1950s. Mark, Alan, Alexis, the Girls, Harmony and Ted all joined in the last line, "The best is yet to be." They all clapped and in the short silence that followed Sydney asked, "Does anybody know what a runcible spoon actually is?"

"It's a spoon with," Ted started to answer, but Alan stopped him.

"Speaking of inspiration, for some reason Alexis and I just finished a series of spoon art. This, my friends, is a runcible spoon." Alan held up a fork curved like a spoon, with three broad prongs, one of which had a sharp outer edge. The handle was covered in faux fur and feathers. "And this is 'Elliott's Coffee spoon.'" He held up a tarnished silver spoon encrusted with small brown beads from a broken brooch he'd found at a garage sale.

"For measuring out life," David said. Stone began to feel not so illiterate after all; he'd thought the reference to "The Love Song of J.

Alfred Prufrock" had been obvious. But the idea was wildly creative. How did these people come up with these things?

Alan passed the two spoons around and said, "Our last share today is 'Lovin' Spoonful.'" The spoon's handle was wrapped in yellow and orange red yarn and the bowl was filled with miniature jellybeans.

Richard, the artist Ted had termed a genius, unveiled an abstract oil painting on a traditional canvas, several feet square. Four smaller squares were painted in green and brown circles. Stone thought the piece too simple to be "genius." "Reminds me of an aerial view of fields," Sydney ventured.

"Wonderful!" Richard said. "From the mountains in Costa Rica, looking down the valley." He beamed. "But when you have a chance, look closely at the brush strokes. You might just see some creatures hiding in the fields!"

Stone let his jaw drop. "Seriously?"

Richard nodded that it was possible. Obviously, that was part of his intent.

"Amazing," Stone said, resolving that he would look closer later. It was hard to imagine that level of detail. If he saw any creatures, how could he sure they were deliberately put there by the artist? Luckily, it occurred to him that might be Richard's point, which saved him from revealing his ignorance of modern visual art.

The Girls explained that their creative contribution would be the pies. They all agreed that Mark's bass-playing and his turducken were works of art. That meant that only Harmony and Ted had not contributed.

Stone wondered whether Ted would "share," whether he would be deemed "ready" to share. Surely there must be a few paragraphs from one of the novels that met whatever impossible standards Harmony imposed. Stone felt a pang of regret — he would've liked to hear Ted's work brought to life by Ted's voice. Looking around the table, he sensed the group's fondness for Ted. He couldn't help but think that left to his own devices, Ted would've shared something. At least, the boy he was in grade school and high school would gladly have made something up on the spot. And it would've been wonderful.

"You, first," Ted said to Harmony. Stone gazed skeptically at Sydney, who put her hand on his knee. He dropped his chin slightly, to let her know he wasn't intending to misbehave. They were here to "kiss and make up" with Ted, not to pick more fights with Harmony.

Harmony reached under the table and came up with two small bundles, each wrapped in velvet: one purple, one gold. "Dylan wanted me to share this with all of you," she said, untying a gold cord at the top of the purple package and letting the fabric drop, revealing a six-inch high glazed teal blue vase with a rounded belly base and a thin neck.

"Simple, but elegant. And nearly perfect," she said, passing it to her left, away from Stone, to be held in turn by each person at the table. Stone bit his tongue. Why were people like Harmony so stingy in their praise of others? Anything hand-made would have at least the tiniest "irregularities." Ted had called the Girls' pies "perfect," even with a half-inch crack down the middle. So even with the tiniest flaw, Stone thought, the vase could be deemed perfect — *perfectly itself.* Shouldn't someone as supposedly spiritual as Harmony know that?

She might counter that she was just being "honest" — the term "brutally honest" came to mind — but what was the point of that honesty, other than to promote herself? Judgmentalism masquerading as honesty, disguising insecurity.

When the vase came around to him, Stone ran his hand over its silky curves. He looked closely but could find no flaw. The trouble with Harmony was how much she appeared to be like his father. *Citius. Altius ... Criticus.* He smiled and passed the vase to Ted. "Perfect," he said.

"I think so, too," Ted said, apparently not aware that he was in any way disagreeing with Harmony.

"This one is mine," Harmony said. "For Ted and Stone." She handed the gold velvet bundle to Ted. After Stone pulled the ribbon at the top and the velvet fell away, Ted held up a nearly identical teal vase, but this one had been broken and repaired, just like the bowl Stone had received in the mail. It had two vertical cracks and a horizontal one. This time, the repairs were painted gold.

"Kintsugi," Harmony whispered, her tone reverential.

"Wabi-sabi," Stone said, and Harmony looked surprised. Ted lowered the vase.

"Embrace the flawed and imperfect," Stone translated for the others. "Your vase, Harmony, is perfect, just like Dylan's." As he stared at Harmony, he could see Ted's profile turned to him and felt, for at least that moment, that he had gained Ted's complete attention and respect.

"That is so," Harmony said with that air of spiritual authority that drove Stone crazy even as it now amused him. She sounded somewhat shaken. Still, she continued, her voice wavering with emotion. "Like our relationship with the Divine Other, each break in that relationship brings us closer to the Divine Truth. As if there is a string connecting us. Our transgressions against each other cut the string. Then, when we tie it up again, we are that much closer to the Other."

"I understand," Stone said, his tone matter of fact.

"The vase, repaired, is beautiful in its own right!" Sunshine said. "What kind of glue did you use?"

Sydney tried to squelch a laugh, but it came out as a snort. Stone elbowed her. "I'm sorry," she said. "Something caught in my throat."

"You were always a terrible liar," Ted said, as if no one else was in the room.

"I ... I just thought it funny that Sunshine took the metaphor so literally," Sydney said. "I'm sorry."

"I did?" Sunshine asked, innocent. "I thought that was the point, that we accept change, accept fate, don't get attached to things as they are."

"That *is* the point," Ted said gently. "The transition to glue was a little quick." They all chuckled knowingly. "Harmony was trying to teach us something more."

"It is what it is," Harmony sniffed. "I don't teach. I don't know enough to teach. I just am. I show." Sometimes you tell, Stone thought. Sometimes you bully. You tell my brother what he should do. But Stone knew better than to contradict her. He was more interested in Ted's reaction to what Harmony was "showing" with her bowls.

"So what's the teaching, Teddy?" Heather asked. Stone was surprised she had called him Teddy, but her tone was affectionate.

"I think Sunshine said it. Also something about letting go of expectations that others have of us." Ted questioned Stone with raised eyebrows.

"Good luck with that," David said. "Why do you think I had to crib my poem?"

"I loved that you shared it with us," Sydney said.

"It was a great poem," Stone added. "Very entertaining."

Ted paused, nodded in Stone's direction and then went on as if there had been no interruptions. "You know, sometimes the problem between brothers and sisters is that it's hard to escape them. No one can ever know us like they do. We know what it was like in our childhood homes; we know what values we were taught and what our parents expected of us." Ted had donned an old tan leather sportscoat for dinner, and Stone focused on a scratch on the left lapel. "I think sometimes we hang on to our parents' expectations for our brothers and sisters long after our parents are gone, even if we've overcome them ourselves, but more so if we've failed to overcome them."

For a moment, Stone sat stunned, Ted's words sinking into the pit of his stomach. Then he released a silent breath.

"My father is bat-shit that I'm up here trying to write a novel," Sunshine said. "But as long as I'm supporting myself, I don't think he has a say, do you?"

"Hell, no," Heather said. "It's your life, not his. Who is he to tell you what to do?"

"It takes a certain maturity to buck your parents, Sunshine, but sometimes it's not that easy," Sydney said. "It's different for different people. Stone and Ted's father, for instance, was quite an imposing character."

"A legend in his own time," Ted said.

"In his own mind," Sydney added. In my mind, too, Stone thought. He could let go of the old man's dizzying dreams and expectations, both for Ted and for himself. He could stop channeling their father.

"It's like this, Sunshine," Mark said. "I have a nephew who was a piano prodigy. His parents wanted him to go to Juilliard. He also wanted to go to Juilliard. For some reason, he wasn't accepted. So he dropped piano altogether. Hasn't played a note since. Spends his time selling men's suits at Brooks Brothers and trading commodities on the side. That's a case of expectations totally destroying persons, destroying their creative spirit. He could've studied someplace else and excelled just the same. Like Michael Jordan not making his high school varsity team the first time." Stone didn't know whether the kid should've aspired to Juilliard or not, but he knew what a shame it would have been if Jordan hadn't persisted.

David added, "Who you become has a lot to do with what other people want from you and what they reward you for. It's hard to become the person you were meant to be all by yourself."

"How do you know who that is?" Heather asked.

"Think about the face you had before you were born," Sydney said.

Startled by Sydney's koan-like aphorism, Stone inadvertently mouthed, "What?"

"What?" Sydney said. "I've done some reading."

Ted reached over and put his hand on top of Stone's.

"*Citius, altius,*" Stone said. They each had tears in their eyes.

Harmony looked around the room. "So, we're ready for the pies, Girls. We have a lot to be thankful for."

"Just a minute, dear," Ted said, standing up. "I think I have something to share."

Harmony's eyebrows shot up. "We didn't plan ..."

"In honor of my brother, I'd like to read the first few pages of my latest novel, which I expect will be published soon by White Pelican Press." Stone flinched; he wasn't sure he'd heard right.

The Girls squealed in excitement and Mark and David applauded. Richard, Alan and Alexis all joined in. Only Harmony looked dumbfounded. Sydney was grinning from ear to ear. Stone broke into an elated smile. Ted winked at Stone. "And I am dedicating the next book to the love of my life, to Harmony, for all of her artistic support and inspiration over the years." Blushing, Harmony watched Ted closely, holding her breath as if he were on a high wire and not yet safely across.

"How exciting!" Sydney said. "It's finally ready?"

As if Sydney had asked her a question, Harmony said, "I never said that they weren't ready." She sounded testy but not angry. "I said *Ted* wasn't ready."

Stone saw Ted suck in a breath. "Yes, dear, you *have* said they weren't ready," Ted said.

"Sometimes a person hears what they want to hear," Harmony said flatly. "An artist must detach himself from the work. A novel is a novel. It isn't you. As Stone said about the vases, both you and the novel have imperfections." Stone was shocked she'd mention him and wondered if that was her apology.

"So 'ready' isn't perfect?" Ted asked.

"Of course not," Harmony said. Stone furrowed his brow. He thought he was beginning to understand her point of view.

"Then what does 'ready' mean?" Ted asked, raising his palms.

"When the artist is ready to let both accolades and criticism bounce off him like scattered thoughts in meditation." She let her wisdom sink in. "Only the artist can decide if a work is ready. The work was freely given to the artist, to be given freely to the community. When the artist is free."

"You let me believe …" Ted said, pointing his index finger somewhat angrily at her.

"What you wanted to believe. You don't need to publish to earn my love. And you won't lose it if you do."

Ted withdrew his accusing finger and dropped his hand to his side.

Stone reached for Sydney's hand. He remembered the day he made partner at Gordon & Newman. Sydney had been happy for him of course, but not elated. Other spouses — Lou's first, for instance — had taken their husbands to fabulous dinners or opened expensive bottles of champagne in anticipation of their new-found wealth. He remembered that he and Sydney had made grilled cheese sandwiches and opened an ordinary bottle of red wine. "You don't seem very excited," he'd said as they were clearing the dishes. "Aren't you happy for me? For us?"

"Of course I am," she'd said. "But I would've loved you anyway."

What Stone heard now was Harmony's profession of unconditional love for Ted. A respite from a dead father's expectations. A yoke lifted from his shoulders. He hoped Ted felt the same. A renewal of their brotherly love.

"*Absolutus amor*," Stone said, remembering the title of Ted's second book.

Taking a few white sheets from his pocket, Ted corrected him, "Actually, despite the title, I think unconditional love is more correctly '*amor sine condicionibus*.'"

BOOK CLUB QUESTIONS

1. Do you think sibling rivalry is common? If so, do people outgrow it?
2. Do you think that parents have favorite children? Who is most affected, the favored or the unfavored? In what ways?
3. Was Stone wrong to copy Ted's files and share them with Ted's publisher? What was his motivation?
4. When Stone felt guilty about reading Ted's private papers, he thought that "no harm, no foul" justified his action. Do you agree? *Was* there actual harm to Ted?
5. Do you trust consumer review sites? Which categories (e.g., products, restaurants, movies, travel)? If a review site has one extremely negative review and several good ones, how much credence do you give the negative one? How should companies handle negative reviews?
6. Sydney and Harmony have different partnering styles. How would you describe them? Which would you say is healthier?
7. Have you ever received a sign, like the white deer, that helped you make a major decision or solve a problem?
8. What words would you use to describe Ted and Stone's relationship?
9. How does the Master Tailor Noge Katsu influence the narrative?
10. If you could give Harmony some personal advice, what would it be?
11. Does being a lawyer sound like fun? Rewarding?

ABOUT THE AUTHOR

Mary Hutchings Reed is a retired lawyer whose novels and short stories often feature strong women characters facing contemporary social issues.

She is extremely proud of her Irish twin sister, Donna Steele, actress, director and founder of a successful professional theater, whose brilliance and creativity have always inspired Mary to strive to be her best self.

Donna adapted a stage play based on Mary's third novel, *Saluting the Sun*, and Donna's daughter, musical actress Amy Wolski, wrote and directed the music for its November 2023 premiere in Chicago. Donna also produced and directed the premiere of Mary's musical, *Fairways* (music by Curt Powell) in 2006. We are grateful for our successes, support each other in our failures, and are blessed with unconditional love and respect.

Mary is happily married to Dr. William R. Reed, with whom she enjoys sailing, golfing, gardening, entertaining, competitive bridge and exploring the world on cruise ships. After more than forty years in Chicago, Mary and Bill now live in Walworth in southeast Wisconsin.

PHOTO: BARBARA NITKE

Courting Kathleen Hannigan
(Ampersand, Inc., Chicago 2007)

Courting Kathleen Hannigan will be of special interest to women lawyers and law students, professional women, and women everywhere who are curious about the social history of women in law and the professions, law firm cultures, and the sexual politics of law firms. This is an insider's view of how large law firms work, and what it was like to be among the first big wave of women in law firms — before maternity leaves, diversity programs, alternative work schedules, and before the discovery of glass ceilings.

Warming Up
(She Writes Press, Berkeley 2013)

Approaching forty, unemployed but well-off, talented but unknown, functional but depressed, former musical actress Cecilia Morrison reluctantly seeks therapy, but it takes a runaway teenager to change her life when he cons her out of sixty bucks. Although she once won leading roles, Cecilia now can't bring herself to audition for parts, and her therapist, an amateur sculptor, can't take the first swing at a hunk of marble his wife gave him before she died.

Whether at the apex of one's success or just starting out, *Warming Up* speaks to everyone who's ever wondered, "what's it all about?" or who finds themselves doing something they never thought they'd do, whether it's singing in a subway to earn some "dough-re-me" or running out of an important audition, chased by a ghost. Reed offers a unique perspective on a homeless teen using his innate abilities as a con man to help his sister and her baby escape their damaged childhoods, and sympathizes with a perfectionist's struggle to express himself creatively in a medium in which he is a mere amateur.

Illinois Library Association, Soon to be Famous Author Project (Top Three Finalist); Top 10, Writers Digest Self-Published Book Awards, Mainstream Fiction; Top 15 Finalist, Book of the Year Awards (INDIES), Foreword Reviews; Top 10 Finalist, Eric Hoffer Book Awards, Mainstream Fiction; Short List Finalist, William Wisdom-William Faulkner Prize for an Unpublished Novel, 2011

Saluting the Sun
(Ampersand, Inc., Chicago 2015)

Who is safer, a twenty-three-year-old woman who plays the glass harmonica on the streets of New Orleans and lives in a commune-style house with other free spirits, con artists, and petty thieves like herself, or a rising television weathercaster who resides in a luxury high rise in Chicago with her emotionally volatile husband? When Nevaeh Thera gives up her street life to live with her cousin, star meteorologist Dawn Ann McKnight and her photographer husband, Derek Baldwin, a life-threatening truth is exposed and both women learn that you can't start over, but you can start again.

Long List, William Wisdom-William Faulkner Prize for an Unpublished Novel, 2011; Top 10 Finalist, Book of the Year Awards (INDIES), Foreword Reviews

One for the Ark
(Ampersand, Inc., Chicago 2016)

For a small-town conservative mayor and his liberal activist wife, politics, principles, and personalities collide when the Blessed Virgin Mary appears on an underpass, a farmer wants to build an "exact replica" of Noah's Ark across from the State Forest, and their daughter makes a startling, life-altering decision.

Third Place, (Bronze Medal), Book of the Year Awards (INDIES), Foreword Reviews; Top 5 Finalist, International Book Awards; Third Place, Colorado Independent Press Association's EVVY Award for Best Cover, 2017 (David Robson, Robson Design)

Kind Eyes
(Ampersand Inc., New Orleans, 2020)

The award-winning stories in *Kind Eyes: Gentle Reading for Troubled Times* draw the reader into relationship with the ordinary people in our lives—lovers and strangers, friends and families. In these pages, we meet memorable characters:

- A charming, homeless teenage con
- A couple who divide their lawn into left and right at election times
- An actress with Alzheimer's
- An insecure "Lawyer of the Year"
- A dog with a taste for rum cake.

Top 15 Quarterfinalist, BookLife Prize

Free Spirits
(Ampersand Inc., New Orleans, 2023)

In 1865 in New York City, wives were the property of their husbands, prostitutes were rich, and famous men were often frauds. Escaping an abusive marriage in Illinois, Daniella Maysfield finds herself at the Mission for the Rescue of Fallen Women, where a savvy prostitute becomes her best friend. Inspired by real events — the speeches of Victoria Woodhull in her efforts to amend the Marriage Laws, the trial of spirit photographer William H. Mumler, and P. T. Barnum's American Museum — *Free Spirits* is the story of a woman's struggle for independence.

Finalist, 2021 Tuscarora Prize from Hidden River Arts for an Historical Novel; Finalist, 2023 Pacific Northwest Writers Association Prize for an Historical Novel; 2024 Independent Press Award, Distinguished Favorite: Historical Fiction; 2024 Independent Press Award, Distinguished Favorite: Book Cover Design (David Robson, Robson Design, Inc.)